# HOSTAGES

# HOSTAGES

## DRAMATIC ACCOUNTS
## OF REAL-LIFE EVENTS

PHIL CLARKE
and
GORDON KERR

**Futura**

A *Futura* Book

First published by Futura in 2009

ISBN: 978-0-7088-0171-0

Produced by Omnipress Limited, UK

Printed in Great Britain

Futura
An imprint of
Little, Brown Book Group
100 Victoria Embankment
London EC4Y 0DY

An Hachette UK Company

Photo credits:
Front cover: Corbis
Inside pages: Corbis

# CONTENTS

Introduction................................................. 8

**PART ONE: ALIEN INTERVENTION**

The Abduction of Barney and Betty Hill ............ 16

Betty Andreasson ......................................... 24

The Buff Ledge Camp Abduction .................... 31

The Schirmer Abduction................................. 39

The Pascagoula Abduction ............................. 46

Travis Walton ............................................. 54

**PART TWO: POLITICAL PAWNS**

The Dawson's Field Hijackings ........................ 64

The October Crisis of 1970 ............................. 75

The Munich Olympic Hostage Crisis ................. 87

Patty Hearst ............................................... 99

Tiede Herrema ............................................ 111

The Dutch Train Hostage Crisis ...................... 122

The Hijacking of Air France 139 ..................... 132

Aldo Moro ................................................. 143

The Iranian Embassy Siege ........................... 155

The Iranian Hostage Crisis 1979-1981 ............. 167

William Buckley .......................................... 179

Terry Anderson ..................................................... 187

Terry Waite ......................................................... 198

Air France Flight 8969 .......................................... 208

United Airlines Flight 93 ....................................... 218

Ingrid Betancourt ................................................. 226

The Nord-Ost Theatre Siege ................................... 235

The Beslan Hostage Crisis ..................................... 246

Margaret Hassan ................................................. 255

Kenneth Bigley .................................................... 261

Alan Johnston ..................................................... 267

## PART THREE: A QUESTION OF INSANITY

Leon Bearden: Continental Flight 54 .................... 278

Colleen Stan ...................................................... 286

Gary Heidnik ...................................................... 297

The Incarceration of Elisabeth Fritzl ................... 306

The Alta View Hospital Incident ......................... 314

Stephanie Slater ................................................. 325

David Koresh and the Siege at Waco ................... 336

Marc Dutroux ..................................................... 345

Natascha Kampusch ............................................ 353

Joseph Palczynski ............................................... 364

The Abduction of Elizabeth Smart ...................... 374

The Abduction of Katelyn Kampf ....................... 382

The West Nickel Mines Amish School Shooting . 388

The Johnson Space Center Shooting ............... 396
Lisa Nowak ............................................. 405

## PART FOUR: FOR FINANCIAL GAIN
Charles Ross ........................................... 414
Edward Cudahy Junior ............................. 422
The Lindbergh Baby Kidnapping ................... 432
Frank Sinatra Junior ................................. 443
Barbara Mackle ....................................... 452
The D. B. Cooper Hijacking ........................ 462
The Chowchilla Bus Hijacking ..................... 470
The Miracle of Cokeville............................. 480
Gladbeck Hostage Crisis ............................ 485
Holly Sheldon – Express Kidnapping................ 494
Shannon Matthews ................................... 505

# INTRODUCTION

Hostage-taking has become very fashionable in recent years although, of course, it has always been around, a handy tactic to be used by anyone trying to gain advantage or leverage of some kind. From time immemorial, hostages have been taken whether in sieges, when entire cities could be held hostage for months or even years until everyone starved to death or the besieging army got bored, or to ensure good behaviour. Vlad the Impaler was taken hostage as a child by the Ottoman Turks in the fifteenth century in order to ensure the good behaviour towards the Turks of his country, the principality of Wallachia. Threatened with invasion, Vlad's father, also called Vlad, promised to become a vassal – servant – of the Sultan and both his younger sons were handed over to the Turks to ensure that the promise was kept. Vlad never forgot or forgave his treatment at the hands of the Turks and tens of thousands of them died horrendously as a result.

Recent hostage-taking seems mainly to have been a preoccupation of minority groups attempting to gain political leverage of some kind. Islamists, Chechens and others have become past masters of the art of kidnapping and of using the hostage over a period of time to gain global media coverage for their cause or to try to persuade governments to release their comrades. Results are often negligible and a disturbing number of deaths have recently ensued as governments steadfastly refuse to bend to the will of the abductors, the thinking being, of course, that if they give in to one, it will serve only as encouragement for the others, leading to a spate of kidnappings.

There have been some dramatic losses of life, of course, in recent hostage situations. The Beslan Hostage Crisis in which a group of armed terrorists took 1,100 hostages in a school in the town of Beslan in the Russian republic of North Ossetia, ended horrifically in the deaths of at least 334 people, 186 of them children. The Moscow Theatre hostage crisis, known also as the Nord-Ost Siege, was staged by Chechen terrorists. On that occasion 850 hostages were taken and at least 129 of them died horrifically when a toxic substance was pumped into the auditorium.

Political hostage-taking can be very dangerous not just for hostages, however. In these situations, the actions of governments are carefully scrutinised and they often become a measure of how effective a government or a ruler is. The 1979 storming of the American Embassy in Teheran by militant students loyal to the Muslim leader Ayatollah Khomeini, in which sixty-five Americans were taken hostage, sparked an international crisis lasting more than a year that tested the United States President Jimmy Carter to the limit. As the world watched, Carter failed in a disastrous mission to free the hostages; helicopters were downed by mechanical failure and Carter was humiliated. His humiliation was complete when the hostages were freed just hours after Ronald Reagan, who had beaten him in the November 1980 presidential election, took the Presidential Oath of Office on 20 January 1981.

The Middle East is where kidnapping has become a daily threat for any westerner or non-Muslim living or working there. In war-torn Lebanon extremist Shiite groups began kidnapping people in 1982 to advance their cause and obtain the release of Islamic activists from Israeli prisons. During this time a number of British hostages were taken and held for extraordinarily long times. Terry Waite, an envoy of the Archbishop of Canterbury, seeking the release of other hostages in Lebanon, including the British journalist, John McCarthy, was held for almost five years, the first four of which were spent entirely in solitary confinement, an exacting ordeal. American journalist, Terry Anderson, was a captive of the Shiite Hezbollah organisation for an extraordinary six years and nine months.

Those early hostages were often released. In recent and more extreme times, however, hostages taken in Iraq and Afghanistan face the very real danger of horrific death at the hands of Islamic extremists often with links to Osama bin Laden's al-Qaeda. Engineer Ken Bigley and much-loved care humanitarian relief worker Margaret, are just two of the victims of the new, brutal form of hostage-taking, their deaths being broadcast on the internet. Others, such as BBC journalist, Alan Johnston, kidnapped in Gaza and freed after four months and a global media campaign, have been more fortunate.

Hostage-taking or abduction comes in many different forms. There are countless instances of criminal abduction. One of the most recent examples has also become probably one of the most notorious cases in criminal history of holding a person against their will. The world was stunned by the news that the Austrian Josef Fritzl had been holding his daughter prisoner for twenty-four years in the basement of the house he shared with his wife and other children. She had seven children by him and was raped by him thousands of times. Another Austrian girl, Natascha

Kampusch was held for more than eight years by her abductor, Wolfgang Priklopil until her escape in August 2006.

Horrific though those stories are, the girls kept prisoner by the Belgian paedophile, Marc Dutroux, suffered an even worse fate. Kept in the basements of several of the houses he owned, the girls were subject to torture and sexual abuse. Four of them died, two of them starving to death in their dungeon, when the man he had delegated to feed them failed to do so.

One can question the sanity of men such as Dutroux, Fritzl, Priklopil or self-styled messiah, David Koresh, who led his religious cult, the Branch Davidians, in the siege that took place at Waco in Texas that ended in the deaths of many of his followers. Some hostage situations have been instigated by people who have either been clearly psychotic or undergoing a psychological crisis themselves. The case of Gary M. Heidnik who kidnapped, tortured and raped six women in Philadelphia in 1986 and 1987, shows clear evidence of psychotic behaviour. Heidnik aimed to capture ten women and have children with them, in a kind of perverse search for love that only provided horror and terror for his victims. He even went as far as feeding the flesh of one of his victims to the others, after grinding it up in a food processor.

12

# PART ONE

# ALIEN INTERVENTION

# THE BETTY AND BARNEY HILL ABDUCTION

Betty and Barney Hill were an American married couple who had an extraordinary experience in 1961 that would become one of the most famous and most talked about cases of alien abduction in the history of ufology – the study of the phenomenon of UFOs. Many have doubted the veracity of what the Hills said they experienced that night; as a mixed race couple – he was African-American and she was Caucasian – they were undoubtedly under a considerable amount of stress; marriage between blacks and whites was not as readily accepted as it is today, especially in a United States mired in racial unrest. It was also a time when the Cold War hung like a dark cloud over the world; there was a fear of nuclear holocaust and at the same time man was focusing attention on conquering space. For the Hills, space may just have come to them that fateful night.

## HEADING DOWN THE HIGHWAY

It was the night of 19–20 September 1961, and they were driving back home in their 1957 Chevrolet Bel Air to Portsmouth, New Hampshire, from a holiday in Canada, escaping the bad weather that had been threatened for their holiday. The highway was empty as they headed south through northern New Hampshire. Just south of Groveton on Route 3 they both noticed a bright light in the sky. At first they thought it might be a shooting star, but its movements were not those of a shooting star. It stopped completely next to the moon.

Betty told Barney to stop the car so that they could get a better look. It would also give them the chance to walk their dog, Delsey. He went to the boot of the car and took out a pistol he kept there just to be on the safe side. He was worried that there might be bears in the area and the pistol would come in useful if there was one in the vicinity. Betty took a pair of binoculars from the car and directed them towards the bright object in the sky. She could now see that it had flashing multi-coloured lights. When Barney said that it must be a plane, Betty remained unconvinced. Its movements were all wrong for an airliner or a jet.

They got back in the car and set off once more, still peering at the object which every now and then would disappear behind the mountains and then return, seeming to move towards them before pulling away again. At one point it even seemed to land on top of one of the mountains.

A little later, the craft seemed to descend rapidly towards their car and Barney slammed on his breaks coming to a halt in the middle of the road. It hovered about a hundred feet above the road as the terrified couple looked on. Barney got out and edged carefully towards the craft which moved slowly across the road and hovered above a field on the eastern side. He put the binoculars to his eyes and was astonished to see figures peering at him from the windows of the spaceship. Suddenly they all jumped to an instrument panel that he could see inside, leaving one figure at the window who seemed to communicate with him telepathically, telling him to stay where he was and continue looking. Red lights appeared out of the craft's sides and a structure appeared underneath it. The craft moved closer, to about fifty feet from the car and hovering fifty to eighty feet above them.

Barney was, of course, terrified. He turned and ran back to the vehicle, screaming to Betty, 'They're going to capture us!' He jumped back into the car and floored the pedal to get away. Betty meanwhile continued to look for the object which seemed to have vanished, although Barney feared that it was actually directly overhead, above the car.

There were loud noises from the rear of the car and the body was vibrating. Meanwhile, the Hills felt exhausted and had a tingling sensation running through their bodies. The noise from the rear stopped but returned a little later and Barney swerved the car from side to side to try to get rid of it. Eventually, when the noise had disappeared, Betty turned to Barney, saying, 'Now do you believe in flying saucers?' He replied, 'Don't be ridiculous!'

They arrived home in Portsmouth around dawn, not realising at the time that the journey that should have taken around four hours had actually taken them seven. Betty refused to let Barney bring their cases into the house as she was concerned they might have radiation on them. Barney noticed that the leather strap on his binoculars was torn and had no memory of how that had happened. He had a bizarre compulsion to examine his genitals in the bathroom, but found nothing unusual when he did. Each had a long shower – they felt extremely dirty for some reason – and then independently they did drawings of what they had seen. Their drawings were almost the same as each other, suggesting they had each seen exactly the same thing.

## VIVID DREAMS

Strangely, they could not remember much and what they did recall seemed fractured and difficult to place chronologically. Barney remembered exclaiming the words, 'Oh no, not again!' but was unable to recall the context. There were other strange things. Betty's dress was torn and was covered in a pink powder and some pink stains.

The next day, Betty, worried more that they might have been contaminated in some way, rather than wanting to tell her story, telephoned Pease Air Force Base to inform them of what had happened. She was interviewed on the phone for about half an hour and told not to worry about it.

Soon she began having nightmares about the experience which eventually became so bad that she decided to get help. In the dream she found herself walking in a forest with two small men beside her. Barney was also there but appeared to be in a trance. The little men were about five feet tall, wore uniforms and caps and had no hair on their bulbous heads. They all walked up a ramp and into the spacecraft before Barney was taken off to be examined separately. This was explained to her in English by the creature who appeared to be the leader.

Another man arrived who told her he would examine her. He sat her down on a chair and shone a bright light at her. He cut off a piece of her hair and looked at her eyes, ears, mouth and hands. He scraped some of her skin onto a glass slide. Removing her dress, he told her to lie on a table. He then proceeded to inject a long hypodermic-type needle into her abdomen causing her considerable pain. However, he merely rubbed her forehead with his hand and the pain subsided.

When the exam was complete, another creature came running into the room and started examining her mouth, pulling at her teeth. They had been amazed to find Barney's dentures and wondered if her teeth also came out. She tried to explain that humans tended to lose their teeth as they grew older, but the aliens could not understand the concept of aging or even the idea of a year.

Before she left the craft, Betty asked for a keepsake and was given a book filled with symbols. It was taken back, however, after an argument had broken out between the creatures. She also asked the leader where they had come from. He pulled down a star map but told her she would not understand.

In her dream, the couple were escorted back to their car and then watched the spacecraft disappear into the sky.

## UNDER HYPNOSIS

After several interviews and the appearance of a ring of warts around Barney's genitals, the Hills decided to undergo hypnosis to learn the truth of what had actually happened to them. They elected to ask Dr Benjamin Simon, a Boston psychiatrist to carry it out. Barney had undoubtedly been terrified by his experience and it showed during his sessions with Dr.Simon. It was so traumatic for him that the doctor ensured that he forgot everything again when he awoke. The creatures he described were not too dissimilar to what Betty had described in her dream. They had large, almost wraparound eyes, a slit for a mouth and small noses. Their faces tapered down to a small chin.

Barney recalled a cup-like object being placed over his genitals, perhaps explaining his later warts. It has been suggested that they were obtaining a sperm sample although he was adamant that he did not experience an orgasm. They inserted a tube in his anus, he recalled and examined the rest of his body carefully. He thought someone counted his vertebrae.

Betty's sessions came up with more or less the same information that she had remembered from her dream although she did succeed in recalling and describing the star map which would become the subject of a great deal of speculation.

The Hills carried on with their lives, making little effort to court publicity, apart from allowing a book to be published detailing their experiences on the night of 19 September.

## FURTHER SIGHTINGS

Barney Hill died in 1969, but Betty lived to the age of eighty-five, dying in 2004.

She had many further sightings of UFOs over the years but vividly recalled one incident. A few months after their terrifying ordeal she came home to find a pile of leaves on the kitchen table. Puzzled, she started to clean up the mess. There she found the blue earrings she had been wearing when they had been abducted. She had lost them that night and now they had been returned.

They knew where she lived!

# BETTY ANDREASSON

Since the first reported case of alien abduction in the 1950s there have been many similar cases, some more believable than others. One case stands out from the crowd, that of the abduction of a woman from South Ashburnham, Massachusetts on the night of 25 January 1967. The case of the abduction of Betty Andreasson has become one of the most celebrated of all such tales of encounters with beings not of our planet or dimension, and has stood up to detailed scrutiny and many years of ridicule for Betty and her family. It fascinates many; cyberspace is awash with articles and message boards still discussing it more than forty years after its occurrence and no fewer than five books have examined it.

## STRANGE LIGHTS AND BEINGS

That fateful night Betty was working in the kitchen of her home in South Ashburnham. In the living room were her mother and father and her seven children. It was just after 6.30 in the evening and the lights in the house had been switched on to lessen the gloom of the winter's evening. Suddenly, the house lights noticeably blinked, switching off momentarily before coming on again. Everyone was surprised and the children were frightened by the sudden darkness. Betty ran into the living room to calm them down but at the same time, her father passed her, making for the kitchen. He had noticed a strange red light shining into the house through the window. It splashed on the walls on the other side of the room and he was anxious to find out where it was coming from.

Through the window, he was confronted by the bizarre sight of five small figures hopping towards the house. To begin with, he thought they must be neighbourhood children dressed up but there was something strangely otherworldly about them. This fact was confirmed when they came through the wooden door at the back of the house and appeared in the kitchen.

The five – Betty would later call them 'Beings' – were small, between three and five feet tall, with one, the tallest, seemingly the leader. They had large oval or pear-shaped heads with large almond shaped eyes; their noses and ears were no more than tiny holes in their grey skin and there mouths were slits. They had arms, legs and hands with only three fingers while covering their bodies were tight-fitting blue uniforms, a belt at the waist and a body strap across their chests. On the upper sleeves of their uniforms was a gold eagle insignia.

Betty immediately sensed that they were not there to do her or her family harm; she felt a sense of peace. She has described them as giving off a feeling of love and since that evening, she has compared them to angels. They communicated with her, speaking not through their mouths but using a form of mental telepathy, the words forming somehow inside her head.

To begin with, she found it difficult to understand what the Beings were saying. Thinking that they were asking for burnt meat, she tried to fry them some. As smoke rose from the pan, however, they became alarmed and jumped back. They tried again and it transpired that what they were actually asking for was 'knowledge tried by fire'.

Betty thought for a moment before deciding that they could only mean the Bible whose knowledge had been criticised and argued about for hundreds of years – 'tried by fire'.

Meanwhile, the rest of the family had been placed into what seemed to be a state of suspended animation. Betty became concerned about them and her daughter was wakened from her trance in order, presumably, to show that no harm had come to her. She was then returned to her trance-like state.

They led Betty from the house out into the garden where she was astonished to see their spacecraft standing there on four legs. It was silver and saucer-shaped with orange and red lights pulsing from it and three or four other similar but smaller machines in a circle underneath it.

## ENTERING AN ALIEN WORLD

Entering the craft which she has described as huge inside, she was taken to an upper room before being brought down in an elevator. She was ordered to put on a white robe that they had ready for her. She was then examined by several of them before being allowed to put on her own clothing again. She was next taken into a room like a hut with chairs along either side. She sat on one of the chairs and was briefly submerged in some kind of liquid.

When the liquid had drained, she was escorted by two Beings who had donned black hoods, through a tunnel and into a room with a red atmosphere. There she was startled to see bizarre creatures with eyes on the end of long stalks. She was certain at this point that she had been transferred to another place, perhaps to a mother ship.

One of the Beings, whom she identified as Quazgaa, told her that he was locking secrets in her mind that would only be released when the time was right. He warned her that it would be a long time before her own race would believe her when she described this incident. They seem to have put some kind of block on her memory before letting her go and it would only be later, under extensive regressive hypnosis that these extraordinary events would return to her.

## TIME TO TELL HER STORY

When she returned home, four hours after the Beings had first arrived in the kitchen, her family had also been made to forget everything. No one ever mentioned the incident and the only evidence that something odd had happened was a dream that Betty's daughter, Becky, had about little clay men, a memory, no doubt, from when she was awakened to confirm to her mother that no harm had befallen her. Betty, on the other hand, recalled everything up until the moment that the Beings had turned up in the kitchen.

Betty put it all behind her, as things began to go wrong for her family. Her father died, her two sons were killed in a car crash and her husband walked out on her never to be seen again. But eight years after that night, she saw an advertisement in a local newspaper placed by Dr J. Allen Hynek, a renowned UFO researcher, looking for people who had experienced an encounter with aliens. She wrote everything down and posted it in a letter to Hynek. She heard nothing, however; her story was considered too weird to be taken seriously. But two years later, when another study was being undertaken, her letter was uncovered and she found herself in front of an investigative panel made up of an electronics engineer, an aerospace engineer, a telecommunications specialist, a solar physicist, and a UFO investigator.

The investigation of her remarkable claims was exhaustive. She underwent character analysis, polygraph – lie detector – examinations, a psychiatric review and an exhausting fourteen hours of regressive hypnosis. Her daughter, Becky, was also subjected to the tests and the two did not differ one iota in their version of events that night. However, the hypnosis also uncovered other instances of abduction in Betty's life that had been expunged from her memory. She recalled an instance in 1950 when she looked at what she thought was the moon, but soon realised could not be as it was increasing in size as it came towards her. She described being taken to the World of Light to see the creature she called 'the One'. Something was planted in her head, a tracking device, she believes. This same object was removed from her through her nose when she was being examined on the spacecraft in 1967. She believes there were actually two more encounters in 1944 when she was a child, although she does not believe she was taken anywhere during those incidents.

The conclusion of the panel was that Betty and Becky were sane individuals who believed absolutely what they were telling investigators.

After keeping her experience secret for years, Betty became famous when she wrote a successful book about her abduction. She also re-married, to one person who understood what she had gone through. Her new husband, Bob Luca, had also been abducted by aliens.

# THE BUFF LEDGE CAMP ABDUCTION

The strange happenings at Buff Ledge Camp took place on 7 August 1968. The Buff Ledge Camp was a private girl's summer camp situated on Lake Champlain, north of Burlington in Vermont, positioned in a grassy clearing in the middle of woodland. A fifteen feet-high bank, fringed with trees, overlooked a stretch of beach nearby and jutting out from the beach was an L-shaped dock that reached out more than a hundred feet into the lake.

Michael Lapp, who was sixteen at the time, was employed at the camp as a maintenance man and to ferry water-skiers out from the dock to a ramp in the lake. Nineteen-year-old Janet Cornell was a water-skiing instructor. On that August day, all was quiet. The camp swimming team had gone to Burlington to take part in a swimming gala and the other campers had gone away on overnight visits away from Buff Ledge. The camp was deserted.

## THREE GLOWING OBJECTS

Michael and Janet took advantage of the downtime to relax in their swimming costumes at the end of the dock. Late in the afternoon, however, their relaxing afternoon turned into an experience that they would remember for the rest of their lives; once they had undergone regression hypnosis, that is.

As they watched the sun begin to go down over the waters of the lake, a bright light suddenly appeared in the sky. Michael thought that it must be the planet Venus putting on an early evening show for them. That was soon proved to be incorrect when the light suddenly swooped downwards in a long slow arc, forming into a cigar shape that seemed to glow. It came to a halt and three smaller white lights emerged, one at a time, from close to its right end and from underneath it. The large object then retraced its flight path and disappeared in seconds.

The three glowing objects began to fly over the lake, performing complex manoeuvres, executing loops and zigzags before descending together from the sky. They would stop and then just as suddenly start moving again. Throughout these actions, which lasted about five minutes, they were coming ever closer to the couple on the dock. Suddenly they formed a triangle and two of them sped off in different directions, leaving the third object alone. As they moved they made a sound that Michael later described as being 'like a thousand tuning forks.' The remaining object, which, he noted, was shaped like a domed disc, flew over their heads and stopped, allowing them to notice that it had a band of coloured light rotating around its edge that seemed to pulse in time with a complex array of sounds – varied tones and pitches. The thing then shot straight up into the sky and vanished for a moment. Just as quickly, it reappeared, tilted onto its side and plunged vertically into the waters of the lake. A small tsunami of waves occurred and the pair noticed a wind begin to buffet the dock.

A few minutes passed before it dramatically re-emerged from the water, gliding rapidly towards the dock before stopping about sixty feet from them, hovering about twenty feet above the water. They could now see that it was about forty or fifty feet across and as tall as a house. The glow that the craft had emitted had faded somewhat and they could now make out two figures inside a transparent dome, figures that they later described as 'childlike'. They could clearly see that the beings had large, hairless heads, big almond-shaped eyes beneath which were two openings for a nose and a tiny mouth. Their bodies were short and they were wearing skin-tight silver or grey uniforms.

## A FORM OF COMMUNICATION

Michael sensed that they were communicating telepathically with him. When he experimentally slapped his knee, one of the beings also slapped his. He heard them say to him that he would not be harmed, that they had come from a distant planet, that their race had already visited Earth a number of times and had come back after the first nuclear explosions.

The craft manoeuvred to within ten feet of the dock and then as it moved overhead, Michael jumped up to touch the bottom of it as it hovered above him, but failed to reach it. At that moment, however, a beam of searing white light was emitted from the spaceship. Michael and Janet fell to the dock and felt themselves losing consciousness. Michael recalled later that he felt as if he was floating up and that he had sensed 'soft lights in a dark place'. Both of them later described the light as having an almost liquid feel, that it made them feel as if they were floating freely in the air. Michael said it was so bright that he could see the bones in his hand like in an x-ray.

He suddenly became worried that they might be kidnapped and taken away. He screamed, 'We don't want to go!' but the next thing he knew was that he was lying on the dock looking up at the object, Janet lying beside him, drowsy and disorientated. It was now dark and he could hear the voices of the swimmers returning from Burlington. There was laughter and the sound of car doors slamming. Most of them went straight into their cabins, but two girls had spotted the strange glow coming from the direction of the dock. As they ran towards the beach, the UFO's beam was suddenly extinguished and it rose a little, directing a sequence of flashes across the camp. It then tilted up over the lake and sped off, vanishing in seconds.

He and the two girls helped the dazed Janet to her cabin. Both she and Michael were unaccountably exhausted.

## RECOLLECTION UNDER HYPNOSIS

No one really believed what Michael told them they had seen. Even Michael's own family disbelieved him when he told them about his close encounter and he tried to account for the time that seemed to have been lost that night between the white beam of light and the time that they had reawakened in total darkness.

Michael and Janet did not discuss the encounter – indeed Janet did not remember much at all apart from some lights in the sky – and after summer camp was over, they went their separate ways. As the years passed, however, Michael began to have disturbing dreams in which he was kidnapped, taken against his will and sat in front of humanoid beings talking to them. Ten years after he had sat at the end of that dock, he contacted the Center for UFO Studies. Janet was contacted and both she and Michael agreed to undergo hypnosis to uncover what really occurred that August afternoon.

Under hypnosis Michael recalled being whisked upwards and then standing next to one of the aliens inside the craft. There were screens and consoles on the dimly lit deck and he could see out of the transparent dome. He saw two of the creatures examining Janet who lay on a table. They seemed to be monitoring what they were finding on a rectangular panel on the wall. The creatures he now saw had three-fingered hands and in the middle of their large eyes were black pupils. Their skin was greenish-blue.

Michael conversed with one of the beings who expressed surprise that he was alert enough to ask questions. Michael said he felt warmth towards this creature and no fear.

They descended to the deck where Janet was being examined and he watched as they scraped skin from her arm with an instrument that resembled a pencil. A triangular contraption then descended from the ceiling and began to suck fluids from Janet's body orifices. The creature told Michael, when he became concerned, that they were merely 'spawning consciousness' – possibly removing eggs from her for reproductive purposes.

When it was Michael's turn to be examined, he suddenly passed out but was conscious that the small craft was approaching the larger craft they had seen earlier. Waking up, he realised that they were now inside the mother ship. A beam of light seemed to grab him and his alien friend and pull them across the room they were in and through the wall. An elevator took them upwards and they moved along a long corridor before entering a large domed room.

This room was filled with aliens. Michael was seated on a chair and a helmet was placed on his head. Suddenly, as they looked at a screen behind him, they all applauded and seemed pleased with what they were seeing. Next, he was taken to another room where the alien touched his hands and they were suddenly in a landscape of trees, grass, fountains and a purple sky. Humans strolled about as if in a daze. Janet appeared next to him and Michael says he just fell asleep. The next thing he knew, he was lying on the dock with Janet beside him. He received a final message from his friend, telling him not to worry, that they were his friends and cared about him. He then heard a voice say, 'Goodbye, Michael.'

## EXTRAORDINARY SIMILARITIES

What made this encounter so extraordinary was that Janet's testimony under hypnosis was remarkably similar to Michael's, confirming much of the detail he had given, right down to the aliens' skin colour and garments. This was even more extraordinary because they had not spoken to each other in ten years and had not corroborated their stories after the incident or since. Even more amazing was the fact that Janet had no recall whatsoever about the incident, apart from what she called a few bright lights in the sky.

Events at Buff Ledge Camp that afternoon can never be fully explained but as alien abduction stories go, it provides some of the most compelling evidence that there may be other beings out there in space and they might be taking a close interest in our progress – or lack of it – down here on Earth.

# THE SCHIRMER ABDUCTION

The first indication that twenty-two-year-old Police Sergeant Herb Schirmer had that anything was wrong was when a bull in a corral at the edge of town began to act strangely. It was restless and banging its head against the fence, making Schirmer worry that it might break out. It was after midnight on 3 December 1967, and he was making his customary nightly rounds in the town of Ashland in Nebraska.

## LIFE-CHANGING EXPERIENCE

At around 2.30, he was out on Highway 63, at the point where it intersected with Highway 6. All had been quiet up until then; no one was out and about at this time of night. Suddenly, however, Sergeant Schirmer's life was irrevocably changed by the sight of some red lights that seemed to be hovering above the road.

At first he thought it was a truck in the distance but as he drove closer, he switched on the powerful lights on his patrol car and found himself looking at a saucer-shaped object hovering about eight feet off the ground. It had a row of seven oval-shaped portholes, measuring about two feet across and under the portholes ran a catwalk that encircled the craft. The object's surface seemed to be made of aluminium, or a similar material that shone brightly in the light thrown by his vehicle's beams.

As he watched, legs appeared from beneath the object and it settled on the ground. A white blurred object approached his car and he believed it to be something that was alive. His first thought was to pull out his gun; he felt threatened. But something prevented him from doing so. The being seemed to be holding something and from it came a greenish gas that enveloped Schirmer and his car. The creature now pulled something from a holster and aimed it at him. He became paralysed and passed out.

The police officer next started walking towards the spacecraft beneath which a hatch opened and a ladder appeared. The ladder was cold to the touch, as was the inside of the craft, he later recalled.

The aliens inside were smaller than the average human being, about four and a half to five feet in height. They wore tight-fitting silver uniforms with a winged serpent on the chest and boots and gloves. Their uniforms came right up over their heads, like a diving suit and on the left side was a tiny headphone with an aerial-type projection coming from it.

They were a grey-white colour with long, thin heads and unblinking almond-shaped eyes that seemed almost oriental. Their noses were flat and their mouths were no more than slits towards the bottom of their faces. It was the body form of the 'grey', the classic extra-terrestrial being most often seen by humans.

He was taken on a tour of the ship by the creature who appeared to be the leader. He told Schirmer that they had a number of bases on Earth, several in the United States and off the coast of Florida. Another was located in the Polar region, while there were a few more off the Argentinean coast of South America. He told Schirmer that their ships could not withstand radar and it could knock them out of the sky. However, there was never any wreckage as the mother ship always destroyed them before they hit the ground.

Schirmer was escorted from the ship and the two crew members that had been waiting outside climbed back in. He went back to his patrol car and turned round to see flames emerge from beneath the craft. The entire ship seemed to brighten before his eyes, tilted upwards and then shot off at great speed, making a siren-like sound.

Sergeant Schirmer climbed back into his patrol car

and drove back to the police station where he arrived feeling very odd. He felt sick and nervous and his body was weak as if he had exerted a lot of energy. He was surprised, however, at the time. It was 3 o'clock. He had only been in the aliens' presence for ten minutes, according to his log, but it felt to him as if he had been with them a lot longer. In the log at the station he wrote, 'Saw a flying saucer at the junction of Highways 6 and 63. Believe it or not.'

A few hours later, after the sun had come up, Police Chief Bill Wlaskin visited the site of Schirmer's alleged encounter with alien beings to see for himself. He looked around the area described to him by his sergeant and came upon a small metallic object. It was later analysed to be made of iron and silicon and dismissed by investigators as no more than 'ordinary corroded earthly waste'.

## UFO RESEARCH

It was shortly before Herb Schirmer's 'abduction' that UFO researchers began to record a new category of sighting. It had started in Brazil when a farmer had claimed to have been abducted by aliens. Antonio Villa-Boas described how he had been forced into having sex on board the craft onto which he was taken. He explained it away as a type of interplanetary breeding experiment that the aliens were carrying out.

Then in 1961, Betty and Barney Hill recalled under hypnosis being abducted by aliens. Again Betty Hill believed their abduction to be part of a breeding experiment. The United States Air Force became so worried about the increasing number of UFO sightings and instances of alien abduction that it enlisted the help of Colorado University in investigating them. The Condon Committee was established, beginning its work in 1967. This body pounced on Herb Schirmer's account of his abduction just eight days after it took place, inviting the policeman to Boulder where he underwent hypnosis by Dr Leo Sprinkle of the University of Wyoming in February 1968, just a few months after the incident. He described the events of that night, adding that the spacecraft drew its energy from power lines and the aliens had bases on Venus.

Although Dr Sprinkle was convinced that Schirmer did actually believe what he was telling them, the Condon Committee reported that 'evaluation of psychological assessment tests, the lack of any evidence, and interviews with the patrolman, left project staff with no confidence that the trooper's reported UFO experience was physically real.'

## NASTY AFTER-EFFECTS

Sergeant Schirmer had begun to experience some ill

effects after his ordeal. He suffered from recurring headaches, felt ill and discovered a red welt on his neck approximately two inches long and half an inch wide located on the nerve cord just below one of his ears. He often experienced a buzzing in his ears before going to sleep.

There were psychological scars, too. He believed he had been having precognitive dreams and had felt 'concern and hurt' since the sighting. More worryingly, his sleep had become very disturbed and he had once woken up to find his hands around his wife's neck, choking her. On another occasion he awoke to find himself trying to handcuff her. She began to hide his gun at night, fearing what he would do next.

Not long after Herb Schirmer reported back for duty at Ashland, Police Chief Wlaskin resigned and his former sergeant replaced him as Chief. He found it difficult to be taken seriously by the locals, however, who constantly reminded him about his alien abduction and poked fun at him because of it. He lasted only two months in the job before resigning. By that time his wife had decided enough was enough and had walked out on him.

Dr Sprinkle described how on one occasion while under hypnosis, Herb Schirmer had suddenly seemed to be slipping away. He began to speak as if he was one of the aliens on the spacecraft, as if the voice was being channeled through him. The voice announced ominously that they would be returning from time to time to keep an eye on Herb. It has not been reported whether they did or not.

# THE PASCAGOULA ABDUCTION

It had started out as a quiet evening's fishing. On 11 October 1973, forty-two-year-old Charles Hickson and nineteen-year-old Calvin Parker, who worked together at a local shipyard, had settled down on a pier on the west bank of the Pascagoula River in Mississippi.

On this particular night, Hickson and Parker saw something move towards them in the sky and from it emanated a blue light. The object was long and emitted a buzzing sound. The two men were terrified and the younger man, Parker, became instantly hysterical. It hovered above them for a short time before an opening appeared in one end and three figures came floating out, moving very fast towards the two men. They had pincer-like appendages and two of them used them to grab Hickson's arms. He suddenly felt as if he was paralysed and just before he fainted, he observed Parker being seized by the third creature.

## TREATED LIKE SPECIMENS

The two men were floated upwards and into the craft, where they entered a brightly-illuminated chamber. Still, Hickson later claimed, he could not move although he was by now conscious.

Still floating, he was put into a reclining position and they began to examine him using a large eye-like instrument that appeared from the wall and scanned back and forwards across his body. Under hypnosis, he would later recall that other beings were watching this activity from behind what seemed to be a glass screen. He would surmise that the creatures that had brought them on board were, in fact, robots. He also divined this from the buzzing sound they had used to communicate either with each other or with the creatures in the ship.

After turning his body on each side and scanning him thoroughly, they left him floating in the air and left the room, presumably, he thought, to perform the same activity with Calvin Parker. They returned shortly afterwards, dragging his young friend. They then returned Hickson to the riverbank where they had originally found them, carelessly dropping him to the ground. As he lay there, he looked up to see Parker standing motionless beside him, his arms outstretched.

Parker later described falling in and out of consciousness. He recalled being taken on board the craft, hearing a whistling sound and a click. He caught a glimpse of the interior lights as he was floated outside and when they set him down on the river-bank, he was still unable to move. He was crying uncontrollably and was in a state of shock. Hickson heard the noise he had heard at the start of the incident and looked up to the sky just in time to see the craft, blue lights flashing, shoot upwards and disappear at a height of about fifty feet off the ground. He says it vanished in less than a second.

For the next forty-five minutes, the two men sat in their car trying to calm their shattered nerves and make sense of what they had just experienced. Hickson slugged on a bottle of whisky as they wondered what they should do. It seemed like the kind of thing that should be of interest to the military, they reasoned, and decided to call the Keesler Air Force base in Biloxi, about thirty miles away.

## TELLING THEIR STORY

The Air Force, however, once very interested in sightings of UFOs, now had no interest in them and an incredulous sergeant recommended that they take their story to the local sheriff's office. Worried about the welcome they would receive from the local police, however, Parker and Hickson decided it would be best to go to the local newspaper, the *Mississippi*

*Press Register.* They drove across town to find the offices closed. They decided to contact the Sheriff's office after all.

They were not alone that night in seeing strange goings-on in the Pascagoula area. Not long after Hickson and Parker's experience, a local man, a former pilot, called in to inform the Sheriff that he had seen an unidentified flying object near the river. Others, including a city councillor, also made sightings that same evening. They had all seen an odd blue light in the sky at around the same time. A Pascagoula man reported that when he checked his front door before going to bed that night, he saw a large object with red revolving lights hovering about ten feet above a streetlamp. He presumed it was something to do with the local air force base and went to bed.

A couple of days after the sightings, a meteorologist in Columbia reported that he had seen a strange radar echo on 11 October. At first he surmised that it was no more than a plane but it remained stationary for some time before his radar jammed.

Then, a few weeks after the incident, a United States Coast Guard vessel and some fishermen had an unexplained encounter with an unidentified submerged object at the mouth of the Pascagoula River. The object played hide and seek with them for forty minutes before disappearing.

The call by Hickson and Parker was taken by a deputy who was so struck by the distress in the men's voices as they explained what had just happened to them that he had no hesitation in asking them to come in and explain their experience in more detail. They arrived at about 10.30, bringing with them two catfish that they had caught earlier in the evening as if this one small piece of evidence would support their entire story.

Sheriff Fred Diamond listened to their story, believing not far into it that it was a hoax. However, he then left them in a room which, unknown to them, was set up with recording equipment so that every word they said could be listened to afterwards. The results were surprising. The two men spoke to each other about what had happened and were obviously still in some distress.

Hickson: I've never seen nothin' like that before in my life. You can't make people believe . . .

Parker: I don't want to keep sittin' here. I want to see a doctor.

Hickson: They better wake up and start believin'. . . they better start believin'.

Parker: You see how that damn door come right up?

Hickson: I don't know how it opened, son. I don't know.

Parker: It just laid up and just like that those sonsa bitches . . . just like that they come out.

Hickson: I know. You can't believe it. You can't make people believe it . . .

Parker: I paralysed right then. I couldn't move . . .

Hickson: They won't believe it. They gonna believe it one of these days. Might be too late. I knew all along they was people from other worlds up there. I knew all along. I never thought it would happen to me.

When the officers listened back to the tape they started to take Charlie and Calvin a little more seriously. They interrogated them for two more hours but their stories remained unaltered. Furthermore, they both insisted that they wanted to take a lie detector test. Hickson took a test lasting two and a half hours and passed although it was later suggested that the examiner was inexperienced and that the test should have lasted the entire day.

They were taken a few days later to the Air Force base at Keesler where they were found not to have been exposed to radiation and were then interrogated at length by senior officers.

By now the story was well and truly out and Pascagoula was soon swarming with reporters and UFO researchers. Two experts who examined the men came away saying that they believed that they had undergone some kind of experience. They had intended to hypnotise them but Charlie and Calvin were still too fragile after that night to undergo the stress of revisiting it under regression hypnosis.

## A HOAX OR THE TRUTH!

Charles Hickson turned down all offers of money to tell his story in book or movie form, believing that if he accepted money, his story would be thought to be merely a cheap get-rich-quick stunt. However, many still scorned his claims. Renowned journalist and screenwriter, Joe Eszterhas wrote in *Rolling Stone* magazine that the site of the alleged incident was in full view of two twenty-four hour toll booths and that none of the people on duty that night had reported seeing anything unusual. Neither did anything out of the ordinary show up on security cameras at a nearby shipyard, he claimed. He fell down heavily on the side of those who believed the incident to be a hoax.

Charlie Hickson did not help his cause by suggesting, years later, that he was still in touch with alien beings. His son Eddie described a flat, grey object about the size of a coin that warmed up every time he was about to receive a communication from them. Charles became a star turn at UFO conferences in his area and said, 'I know that these things are strange and I do not expect to be believed, but I hope that one day people will believe in it.'

The Pascagoula abduction has become one of the greatest of all the alien abduction incidents. The two men involved passed lie detector tests and seem utterly convinced, in themselves, that what they describe actually happened. As ever, it is, of course, impossible to prove but there were all those other sightings that night to consider. Are there too many to be explained away as the ravings of a couple of deluded individuals? Who knows, but as J. Allen Hynek, who used to investigate UFO sightings for the United States Air Force, said of the Pascagoula case: 'There was definitely something here that was not terrestrial.'

# TRAVIS WALTON

Like the rest of the crew piling into their boss Mike
Rogers' truck for the drive back to Snowflake,
Arizona, Travis Walton was exhausted. They had
been hired to fulfill Rogers' contract with the United
States Forest Service to thin out brush and
undergrowth from a huge area – in excess of 1,200
acres close to Turkey Springs. It was hard work and
when they fell behind schedule, they were forced to
work even longer shifts, from six in the morning until
the sun went down at night.

## LIGHTS AND NOISES

On this particular night, 5 November 1975, the tired
men were startled by a bright light that seemed to be
shining from behind a hill ahead of them. As they
drove nearer the hill they saw a large silver disc that
appeared to be hovering over a clearing. They
estimated it to be about eight feet in height and,
perhaps, twenty feet in diameter.

Rogers slammed his feet on the brakes and the truck came to a halt. Suddenly, however, Travis Walton jumped from the vehicle and started running in the direction of the disc. His shocked colleagues shouted after him to stop, but he paid no attention and continued running. Suddenly, they heard loud noises, somewhat like a turbine starting up, coming from the object. It seemed to wobble from side to side and Walton who had stopped, began to back away from it. At that point, the men in the truck later reported, a blue-green ray of light shot out of the disc, striking Walton who was lifted about a foot into the air and thrown back about ten feet. His body lay sprawled motionless on the ground.

Rogers, snapping out of his stunned trance, was certain that Walton was dead. He put his foot down and sped away along the forest road, everyone meanwhile peering out of the rear of the vehicle terrified that the disc might be following them.

Some four hundred yards along the road, he braked again. The men discussed what they had just witnessed and elected to go back to rescue their colleague. They returned to the place where the beam of light had thrown him, but after half an hour of searching there was still no sign of either him or the silver disc.

It was 7.30 at night by the time law officers in

Heber, near Snowflake, were informed that a member of a logging crew had gone missing. The officer who took the call, Deputy Sheriff Chuck Ellison met the shaken loggers at a shopping centre where they told him what they had witnessed. They were distraught at the loss of their colleague which helped to convince Ellison that their incredible tale might be true. Senior officers arrived to be told the same astonishing story before travelling with some of the men back to the scene of the incident.

As more police and volunteers arrived to join the search, the senior police officers became sceptical about the story. They could find not a shred of physical evidence that their account was true. They also became very concerned about Travis Walton's wellbeing in the harsh cold of a night in the mountains. Dressed only in jeans, a denim jacket and a thin shirt, he was not equipped for the temperatures he would be facing.

By the following morning they had searched a wide area around the place where Travis Walton had disappeared but still there was no sign of him. Their natural suspicion was that there had been an accident or Walton had been murdered by a colleague or by all of them and that the loggers were using the story to cover up a crime. When Mike Rogers and Travis's brother Duane arrived at the scene to find no officers engaged in the search, Duane was furious. He managed to persuade the authorities to re-launch the search with renewed vigour. By the afternoon of the 6 November, helicopters, mounted police and jeeps were scouring the area.

## SUSPICIONS

Of course, it was impossible to keep the story from the media and within a few days it was worldwide news. Journalists and ufologists began to flood into the area. Numerous theories began to be promulgated. One arose out of an interview Mike Rogers gave, in which he said that he had been afraid that his team would not complete their contract on schedule and he hoped that Walton's disappearance might help the Forest Service to look upon them more favourably. People became suspicious that Rogers had concocted Walton's disappearance to buy time. Another interview with Duane Walton revealed that he and his brother had been interested in UFOs and that he had once seen one. People began to wonder if the entire incident was just a prank.

Complicating matters was the Walton brothers' mother, Mary Walton Kennett, who would only answer questions from the police or reporters on her front porch. They began to wonder if she was perhaps hiding someone inside the house.

They made every member of the logging crew take a lie detector test. To questions of whether they had harmed Walton or knew where his body was, they all answered 'no' which the man administering the test said was truthful as was the fact that they had actually seen a UFO. Sheriff Gillespie announced following the conclusive results of the test that he now accepted that the men had indeed, seen an unidentified flying object.

## TRAVIS RETURNS

Travis returned on the night of Monday 10 November, five days after he had disappeared. Grant Neff, his brother-in-law, answered his telephone in Taylor, Arizona to hear a weak, strained voice speaking at the other end. 'This is Travis,' the voice said. 'I'm at a phone booth at the Heber gas station and I need help. Come and get me.' At first Neff was certain the voice was that of another joker – there had been plenty – but as that thought crossed his mind, the man speaking to him became hysterical, screaming down the line, 'It's me, Grant . . . I'm hurt and I need help badly! You come and get me!' Neff called Duane Walton and the two men drove at speed to Heber.

They found Travis, unshaven, dirty and crumpled up in one of the phone booths. He was dressed in the clothes he had been wearing when he had last been seen, seemed to be in a confused state and was very agitated, ranting about beings with terrifying eyes. When they told him he had been gone for five days, he was astonished; to him it had seemed like just a few hours.

Duane made the mistake of keeping Travis's reappearance secret, hoping to allow his brother to get his strength back. This, of course, only persuaded sceptics that the brothers were involved in a massive deception.

They did find out, however, when an employee of the telephone company who had been keeping an eye on phone calls to and from Walton family members, reported that someone had called the Neff household from a payphone in Heber at 2.30 that morning. They took fingerprints from the booths but found no trace of any belonging to Travis. Suspicions grew that Travis had been nowhere near the phone box, but others blamed that on the fact that the officers had dusted for fingerprints in the dark and that was why they could find no evidence that he had made the call.

By the afternoon of 11 November, news had leaked that Travis was back. He became a pawn of the media and of UFO research groups desperate to meet him and get to the bottom of what would undoubtedly be a sensational story. One research group, APRO (the Aerial Phenomena Research Organisation), offered him a medical examination which took place at 3.30 that afternoon. They found him to be in sound health but discovered two abnormalities. Firstly, he had a red spot at the crease of his right elbow that looked as if it might be result of an injection and secondly, an analysis of his urine revealed a lack of acetones. Acetones result from a period of starvation when the body begins to break down its own fat in order to survive. There were also no bruises as a result of his fall when the ray of light lifted him into the air.

The authorities were furious that no one had informed them of his return but when Travis began to tell Sheriff Gillespie what had happened to him during those five days, his anger abated somewhat.

## TRAVIS'S STORY

He said that after he approached the silver disc, he could recall nothing until he woke up on a bed, a bright light above him. He described the atmosphere as heavy and wet. He was having problems breathing, his body ached, his head hurt and he thought he must be in hospital.

He was surrounded by three figures, less than five feet in height with no hair at all on their heads. They had huge, domed, frightening brown eyes and small ears, noses and mouths. He jumped up and grabbed a glasslike object from a shelf, waving it at them threateningly and shouting at them to keep away. They left the room.

He left the room and passed through a hallway into a round room with a high-backed chair in the centre. He sat in the chair and the room lit up. He pushed a short lever on the arm of the chair, setting in motion the numerous lights in the ceiling, somewhat like a planetarium. He stood up and the lights disappeared but turning round saw a large, humanoid figure wearing blue overalls and a clear, glass-like helmet. The man's eyes were large and bright gold. He immediately fired questions at the man who merely smiled and motioned for him to come with him. Following him along a hallway, he came to a steep ramp leading into something like an aircraft hangar. Behind him was a craft like the one in the forest, but it was twice the size of it.

There were other disc-like craft in the hangar and more humanoid beings – two men and a woman. They replied to his questions only with the same grin he had received earlier from the first humanoid. They led him to a small table, laid him down and placed a mask – like an oxygen mask – over his face. He passed out and the next thing he knew, he was outside the petrol station in Heber from where he telephoned Grant Neff.

Under hypnosis, Travis's memory of the incident

was exactly the same as his conscious memory but he could account for only perhaps two hours out of the five days during which he had been missing.

The results of a subsequent polygraph test remain controversial. The man in charge of the test, John J. McCarthy, insisted that Travis had failed it and had even tried to cheat. More charges of conspiracy and fraud followed, but he undertook two more tests, both of which he passed.

Travis Walton remained in Snowflake, eventually becoming foreman at the local lumber mill. He is an occasional guest at UFO conventions.

# PART TWO

# POLITICAL
# PAWNS

# THE DAWSON'S FIELD HIJACKINGS

In the morning of 6 September 1970 three crack teams of militant hijackers boarded three America-bound planes with the aim of focusing the world's attention upon the Middle East. In one of the most daring acts of political blackmail, a trinity of winged targets was forced to land on an abandoned desert airstrip where over three hundred passengers and crew spent seven sweltering days held hostage.

## THE PFLP

Formed in 1967, and consisting of thousands of angry guerrilla fighters, the Popular Front for the Liberation of Palestine or PFLP was a collective response to the years of enforced exile the Palestinians had undergone after the Second World War. With hundreds of thousands living in refugee camps far away from their homeland, militant factions fused together to recover their lost status often by force.

Believing their political plight lacked the necessary worldwide awareness to bring about change, co-founder George Habash led his resistance movement on attention-seeking attacks. The Front had cut its terrorist teeth on numerous highly-publicised acts of aggression including one of the first examples of air piracy; the hijacking of El Al Flight 426 from Rome in July 1968. Now, in 1970, they were ready for a more complicated scenario developed to create maximum disorder and, as a result, kick up a storm of global proportions.

Following a summer ceasefire between Egypt and Jordan – a move opposed by the PFLP – Habash publicly vowed to turn the Middle East into a hell. True to his word he swiftly began plotting the ultimate terrorist act of the time. Wishing to punish the United States for its involvement in the peace proposals along with its ongoing support for Israel, he planned the hijacking of three New York-bound flights on a weekend to ensure a healthy number of returning American holidaymakers were taken. On Sunday 6 September 1970 the skyjack teams were in place to cause a scene and hit the headlines throughout the world.

## DOUBLE TAKE AT DAWSON'S FIELD

At approximately half past twelve, as the Boeing 707 flew over the North Sea on its final leg of a trip to JFK

Airport, the first cell struck commandeering the TWA Flight 741 from Tel Aviv. Managing to gain entry to the cockpit, the armed terrorists forced Captain Wood to alter the plane's course for the Middle East. Meanwhile another hijack unit was working its militant magic having boarded Swissair Flight 100 at Zurich Airport. As the commercial aircraft carried its 155 passengers and crew over France an unknown female voice informed air traffic control the flight had been hijacked. The pilot was then forced to make an about-turn diverting the Douglas DC-8 from its American destination back across Europe.

The world waited with baited breath unsure where in the Middle East these two stolen aircraft were headed. Around six hours after their double seizure the answer came. Using torched oil drums as makeshift landing lights, the two planes were forced to land on a 300,000-foot-long landing strip in the Jordanian desert. This was Dawson's Field, a former RAF training airfield named after Sir Walter Dawson, a British Commander in the Levant, which was now under the control of guerrilla forces. The two planes sat on the hard-packed sand only fifty feet apart with over three hundred hostages inside. The PFLP made no move to issue demands; they were waiting for another arrival at the desert airstrip which they had now rechristened Revolution Airport.

## BAD GUYS BUMPED

The plot to make the world take note of the PFLP cause included the hijacking of a third commercial flight destined for New York. A skyjacking outfit of four extremists boarded El Al Flight 219 at Ben Gurion International Airport in Israel with the intention of rerouting to Dawson's Field. However their hijack plan was hamstrung before it could leave Tel Aviv.

The flight's security chief alerted Captain Uri Bar Lev of a potential threat aboard the plane. Two of the skyjack team sitting in first class had raised the suspicions of Israeli security having shown Senegalese passports with sequential numbers. The captain chose to have the pair removed from the flight halving the hijack squad.

The two extremists left on board were Patrick Arguello, a Sandinista rebel fighter from Nicaragua, and Leila Khaled, a striking Palestinian ex-teacher who were travelling as a married couple under false Honduran passports. Twenty minutes after take-off from their stopover in Amsterdam the duo made their move. At 13.45 hours Khaled removed two hand grenades from her brassiere and, barging her way through first class, showed them at the cockpit spy-hole. As her partner caused chaos back in economy, Khaled threatened to blow up the plane if she was not given entrance.

Captain Uri Bar Lev had a difficult decision to make. At considerable risk to the safety of those on board, the pilot chose not to open the cockpit door to the armed terrorists. Instead he put the plane into a negative G nosedive throwing the two hijackers off-balance. In the ensuing chaos Arguello was shot four times by a sky marshal and Khaled was pinned down by an Israeli security guard as the plane made an emergency landing at Heathrow Airport.

With Arguello mortally wounded and Khaled in custody the hijacking had failed but the terror in the September skies was not over. The two hijackers bumped from the flight had not been discouraged from their duty. With weapons undetected, the two extremists going by the names Diop and Gueye boarded Pan Am Flight 93 to New York and commandeered the Boeing 747 at 15.30 hours.

Captain John Priddy was then ordered to land at Beirut and, while the plane refuelled, the two persistent Popular Front members were joined by nine comrades and enough explosives to turn the jumbo jet into a fireball. While the cockpit and fuselage were wired to blow the flight crew managed to persuade the skyjackers that the Boeing 747 – at two and a half times the size of a Boeing 707 – was too large to land on the desert strip in Jordan. Having been an improvised endeavour with no thought given to its size the terrorists believed this to be true and changed the destination to Cairo. Moments after touching down and with barely enough time to evacuate the passengers and crew, the aircraft exploded. Amazingly all those aboard made it to safety although the hijackers were promptly arrested by Egyptian police.

## THE GREAT DIVIDE

Meanwhile, back at Revolution Airport, the three hundred and nine hostages were settling in for their first night in the desert. The following morning, unable to wake from their shared nightmare, they looked out of the windows to see they were surrounded. Tanks, troops and artillery from the Royal Jordanian Army had arrived during the night to besiege the hijacked planes.

As the oppressive sun rose the world's press descended upon the desert airstrip in the middle of the northeast dust plains. With as many as sixty journalists at the scene, the PFLP decided they would hold a press conference to convey their anger and demands. Paraded before television cameras, the hostages were told to sit on the sand while Bassam Abu Sharif, the group's spokesman, put forward their intentions via loud haler. The terrorists informed reporters the hostages would not be released until a number of their comrades behind bars in both Europe and Israel were liberated. To make matters worse Sharif imposed a seventy-two-hour deadline after which the planes containing the passengers would be destroyed.

The Red Cross were swiftly called in to act as mediator and managed to acquire the release of one hundred and twenty-five women and children who were transferred to the Jordan capital of Amman. There they were placed in three hotels: the Intercontinental, the Philadelphia and the Shepherd. Yet despite this positive step, an ominous atmosphere was developing on the two grounded aircraft. The captives were being divided into groups and details of their religious beliefs were taken along with their passports. The Arab militants then began calling out names.

Six people were selected including two Rabbis and Jewish-American Jerry Berkowitz and were promptly escorted off the plane. The PFLP had decided these chosen few would be held elsewhere in a secret safe house miles away in case the Israeli government decided to mount a rescue attempt.

## THE FIFTH PLANE

By the fourth day of their captivity the hostages were experiencing considerable discomfort. Trapped inside their metal prisons roasting in the hundred degree heat, they had no electricity and the toilets were overflowing. Stocks of food were running low and the warm water they were offered contained chlorine tablets making it unpleasant to drink.

Added to this was the threat of death looming over their heads as the clock ticked towards the PFLP deadline. No formal agreement had yet been reached between the countries involved. While Great Britain, West Germany and Switzerland were prepared to negotiate the militants' release, Israel was against any such discussion with the Palestinian rebels.

To add further pressure for acquiescence to their demands a further plane – BOAC Flight 775 – was hijacked by the PFLP bringing another one hundred and fourteen hostages to Dawson's Field. Once the Vickers VC-10 landed alongside the other confiscated aircraft, the terrorists repeated their directive. Palestinian prisoners including Leila Khaled must be liberated from the prisons of their oppressors before any of the hostages were to be set free.

## EXPLOSIVE FINALE

As the White House moved closer to an all-out strike upon the Palestinian strongholds in Jordan, bringing six destroyers to the Lebanese coast and placing twenty-five Phantom jets on standby, the terrorists at Dawson's Field began to panic. Fearing an imminent attack, the demolition squads began to rig the planes with explosives. On day seven of the sand-based standoff the PFLP extremists began to evacuate all three of the planes. Thinking their nightmare had come to an end, the hostages were relieved to be leaving their winged prisons. As the convoy of vehicles containing the passengers vacated the area the three aircraft suddenly exploded. Thick plumes of black smoke rose from the flaming wreckage adding yet more heat to that of the desert sun.

With over $50 million worth of aircraft burning behind them, the freed hostages made their way to safety. Unfortunately, for some of them, their ordeal was not over. Several vehicles in the line pulled away from the pack. These unlucky few were made up of flight crew and Jewish passengers such as sixteen-year-old Barbara Mensch who was told she was now a political prisoner. They would remain in custody for the duration of the crisis, classified as subjects under interrogation.

## CAPITAL CONFLICT

Meanwhile events away from the airstrip had turned volatile. In what became known as the Black September crisis, clashes between the PFLP and King Hussein's Jordanian army had swept through Amman some thirty miles away. On the brink of civil war, the monarch was attempting to quell the rising revolutionary verve which was sweeping across the northern part of his kingdom in direct response to the hijackings. Caught in the middle of the fighting were the women and children released first from the two planes. Trapped in their hotels with stray mortars rocking the buildings to their foundations the released hostages now found themselves in the middle of a war zone.

As the conflict neared the Syrian border, its Prime Minister sent over tanks to help the PFLP against Hussein who had realised his rule was now seriously under threat. Several more days of fighting continued with the United States and the Soviet Union on the brink of coming to the aid of Jordan and Syria respectively. World War Three was averted, however, when Syrian forces withdrew from Jordan on 25 September suffering heavy losses.

On the same day, the king's forces found sixteen hostages in a Wahdat refugee camp and this was followed by further rescues in and around Amman. With negotiations finally breaking the deadlock the last remaining captives were exchanged for Leila Khaled and six other PFLP prisoners. Flown to freedom, the hostages were met by President Nixon at Leonardo da Vinci Airport in Rome, who vowed measures would be taken to prevent a repeat of this harrowing crisis.

## AN OMINOUS FUTURE

With the signing of a peace treaty in Cairo by King Hussein and Yasser Arafat, leader of the PLO – the umbrella organisation under which the PFLP belonged – the Black September Crisis was brought to an end. For Habash's resistance fighters, the hijackings were seen as successful acts of terrorism. The events at Dawson's Field had resulted in the liberation of seven comrades, the destruction of four planes and considerable worldwide publicity for their crusade.

However by the following summer the problems in Jordan had resurfaced eventually leading to thousands of Palestinians being expelled once more from their settlements. A large number left for Lebanon from where, fuelled by an unchecked hostility towards the West, they plotted once more to attack the United States and its allies. These future plans would reveal a more aggressive and sophisticated PFLP movement prepared to go to great lengths to draw the world's eyes upon their plight.

# The October Crisis of 1970

During the autumn of 1970 in Canada's eastern province of Quebec, a double kidnapping by two separate cells of a revolutionary movement hell-bent on creating an autonomous state forced the government to invoke the War Measures Act. With civil liberties suspended, arrests came as thick and fast as the falling Maple leaves in a frantic attempt to find the hostages and bring their takers to justice.

## THE RISE OF THE FELQUISTES

Canada has endured a complex social history before and after becoming a federal dominion in 1867 with far more to its existence than just maple leaves and Mounties. Split into provinces, an inherently divergent land developed with some intense cultural clashes between the French and English Canadians. These conflicts had persisted ever since the Anglophones migrated north following the American

Revolution during the late 1700s and in no place more so than Quebec.

Halfway through the twentieth century this predominantly francophone area in Canada's east revealed its dissatisfaction at the social status quo. The Quebecois had become frustrated with what they saw as the usurpation and absorption of their heritage by an increasing English-Canadian cultural dominance. To fight against this gradual damage to their identity, pro-active radical groups began to form calling for their beloved Quebec to be granted sovereignty. The most feared of these secessionist movements was the FLQ – the Front de Liberation du Quebec.

Founded in the early 1960s by Georges Schoeters, a Belgian activist and Che Guevara admirer, this separatist faction broke away from an existing group insisting a harder line be taken against their Anglo Canadian enemies. Funded by a wave of bank robberies, a bombing campaign targeting English businesses and key economic landmarks began with nearly one hundred attacks over a seven year period. The Felquistes, as they became known, wanted a revolution and, with their attacks growing more violent as a new decade dawned, it seemed they would go to any lengths to force one.

## WARNING SIGNS

During 1970 two incidents occurred which should have given the authorities concern over a potential new focus for the FLQ. On 26 February 1970 Montreal police stopped two men in a rented panel truck. Inside the vehicle they found a shotgun, a basket large enough to hold a man and a communiqué announcing the kidnapping of Israeli trade consul Moshe Golan.

Despite having foiled an apparent abduction, police only charged the men with illegal possession of a firearm and conspiracy to kidnap. Released on bail, the pair promptly disappeared into the shadowy FLQ underworld. One of the men was Jacques Lanctot who would return in the autumn to try his hand at hostage-taking once again.

Yet another presage of the October abductions came on 21 June when, following an informant tip-off, police raided an FLQ hideout in the Laurentian mountains. Searching the secret Provost cottage, they discovered 140 kilograms of dynamite, assorted firearms and one hundred and fifty copies of a ransom note to be used in the kidnapping of American consul-general Harrison Burgess. The warning signs were there. However the authorities failure to act on them would prove costly and result in one of the most notorious terrorist incidents to befall the Canadian government.

## CROSS KIDNAPPING

The FLQ consisted of a collection of underground cells working independently of each other but all reporting to the movement's leaders. One such subdivision was the Liberation Cell made up of six revolutionaries. These included Marc Carbonneau, Yves Langlois, Nigel Hamer, Jacques Cossette-Trudel and his wife Louise Lanctot. The sixth member was her brother, Jacques Lanctot, who had been arrested back in February for the unsuccessful kidnapping of the Israeli consul.

The selection of a new victim to force the creation of a self-ruled Quebec took place and US Consul John Topping was a considered target for a while. However, it was agreed their actions would have more of an impact among Anglo Canadians if a British envoy was taken hostage. Eventually they settled on James Richard Cross, the forty-nine year old British Trade Commissioner to Canada, and in the early morning of 5 October two members of the Liberation Cell paid a visit to his plush Westmount residence. Dressed as delivery men with a bogus birthday package, the activists pulled out their rifles and snatched the diplomat from his doorstep. Much like their native Mounties, the Felquistes had finally managed to get their man.

## DEADLY DEMANDS

Later that day at around three o'clock authorities received the nationalists' communiqué listing seven clear demands for the release of James Cross. Twenty-three political prisoners were to be released as well as the name of the police informant used during the foiled Burgess plot. The FLQ manifesto was to be broadcast and published throughout Canada, police were to call off the hunt for their hostage and 450 Lapalme postal workers who had been fired because of their support for the secessionist movement were to be reinstated. In order to effect their escape, an aircraft was requested to transport the kidnappers and their lawyers to either Cuba or Algeria. Finally, an FLQ-imposed voluntary tax of $500,000 in gold bullion was to be placed aboard their getaway plane.

The following day Prime Minister Pierre Trudeau spoke for the Quebec and Ottawa governments in declaring the demands unreasonable. This prompted threats of Cross's death if their requests were not met. To prevent these threats and buy authorities more time to find the kidnapped consul, the government agreed to what they saw as the least damaging demand: the printing and broadcasting of the FLQ manifesto.

On Thursday 8 October the rebel mission statement was read out in French on national television. Little was known about the true extent of the pressure group's power and the declamatory tract portrayed an image of a potent revolutionary force, instilling fear into Canadian government. Dubbing Quebec a society of slaves, the manifesto was a call to arms for French Canadian labourers to rise up against their English bosses.

After proof of life had been procured, negotiations for Cross's release began and by the weekend safe passage had been granted to the Liberation cell members to bring an end to the incident. Meanwhile, hidden away in a secret hideout, Cross asked his captors what they planned to do with him. The response was positive; he would be held for a few days before being freed. Sadly, an unforeseen event on Saturday evening would prevent this plan from happening.

## LAPORTE KIDNAPPING

Unbeknown to Jacques Lanctot and his fellow insurrectionists, another separate cell had decided to make their own mark for Quebec autonomy. Led by twenty-six-year-old Paul Rose, a school teacher with strong Marxist leanings, the Chenier Cell – named after a nineteenth century rebel hero – had kidnapped another high-profile politician.

Paul, along with his brother Jacques, had been driving down to Texas on a gunrunning expedition when they heard of the Cross abduction. In an attempt to prove themselves as the most aggressive of the FLQ cells, the brothers hurried back to Montreal to take their own hostage. At 6.18 pm they grabbed Vice Premier and Labour Minister for Quebec, Pierre Laporte, from his Saint-Lambert home while he was playing football with his nephew.

Unlike the Liberation-run abduction, this kidnapping suffered from being executed on a whim. Insufficient funds led to Laporte's wallet being emptied to provide for the delivery of a string of communiqués around town. The next day a letter from captivity by Laporte to Premier of Quebec, Robert Bourassa was broadcast stating despite his predicament he was in perfect health and being treated well. James Cross had also been permitted to write a series of letters which were read out on air, serving to aid the Felquistes' objectives, spreading their message and a sense of their authority.

## FEARS OF INSURRECTION

This single-minded media focus on the exclusive dramatised the efforts of the FLQ which increased public sympathy for their cause. French language schools closed throughout the province as an unsettling rise in support forced authorities to consider military action. A week after the Cross kidnapping Trudeau ordered the first wave of army deployment codenamed Operation Ginger involving up to a thousand troops to keep the peace. Three days later Operation Essay began as Canadian authorities sent a further thousand soldiers into Montreal and Ottawa to ensure the safety of its citizens and public buildings.

As a clear military presence stood watch over these cities, a crowd of over three thousand FLQ supporters attended a protest rally in Montreal's Paul Sauve Arena. Believing this assembly could be a prelude to a nationalist revolt, a statement was issued by the government announcing they were prepared to release on parole five political prisoners. In addition safe conduct was offered to those involved.

As night fell, Premier Bourassa and his cabinet waited for the Felquiste response to their offer. As dawn approached on Friday 16 October they were still waiting. Fearing this lack of a reply denoted an imminent insurrection, the Quebec leader liaised with Prime Minister Trudeau, suggesting emergency powers be granted to the province to quell any potential uprising.

## ACT OF AGGRESSION

With municipal elections due to take place in less than ten days time, Trudeau risked losing considerable support by providing Quebec with the authority to suppress this secessionist threat. However, at 4 am that morning the Prime Minister of Canada announced he was invoking the War Measures Act. A relic from the Great War, this gave far-reaching powers to the Quebec authorities, allowing them to apprehend and detain FLQ members and sympathisers for up to ninety days without trial.

This suspension of civil liberties made Canada the only Western democracy to utilise war powers during peace time. Two hundred and fifty suspects were hauled into custody in the first twelve hours of the act's introduction as further troops were deployed in a show of force against the Felquistes. While some were critical of the act – including future Premier Rene Levesque – the unprecedented military response obtained widespread approval with around ninety-two per cent of Quebecois in favour.

At ten o'clock the following morning yet another communiqué came through from the Liberation cell. This message declared, while they were not prepared to release James Cross until the six remaining demands were met, they would however suspend the death sentence against their hostage. This mitigation was an attempt to influence their more aggressive comrades of the Chenier cell into taking the same placatory path. It failed to achieve this aim.

Later that day, a Quebec radio station received a call announcing the Chenier cell had executed Pierre Laporte in retaliation for the War Measures Act. The politician's bruised body was found strangled in the trunk of a green Chevrolet abandoned in scrubland near Saint-Hubert Airport. Laporte's murder brought an increase in the number of police raids as authorities chased leads in the hunt for Cross and his kidnappers.

### CROSS RELEASED, ROSE PLUCKED

With the number of arrests of suspected Felquistes steadily rising, the authorities garnered more information on the two offending FLQ cells. On Friday 6 November, acting on an informant's tip-off, police raided the Chenier cell hideout. The Rose brothers along with Francis Simard managed to escape but Bernard Lortie was arrested and charged with kidnapping and murder.

Almost a month later, after weeks of negotiating with the Liberation cell, police managed to orchestrate the release of James Cross. An arrangement had been made whereby the five terrorists would be granted safe passage to Cuba in exchange for the British diplomat. The captive Cross was escorted to the site of the Expo'67 World Fair, which had been declared temporary Cuban territory, and was held there until the felons' flight touched down safely in Havana.

The end of this affair allowed all efforts to focus on the capture of the three Chenier cell fugitives. Finally, on Monday 28 December, police caught up with Francis Simard and the Rose brothers hiding inside an underground tunnel in a farming area on the outskirts of Montreal. A media circus surrounded their subsequent trials which brought life sentences for both Paul Rose and Simard. All the convicted terrorists denied murdering Laporte insisting it had been an accidental death; a struggle during an apparent escape attempt leading to him being garrotted by his religious pendant.

## THE RETURN OF THE NATIVES

The subsequent years after the October Crisis saw a considerable decline in support for the FLQ. With the secessionist Parti Quebecois coming to provincial power in 1976, there was a shift away from change through violence and towards independence via political means. An improved police anti-terrorist unit maintained a deliberate stranglehold on potential activist cells with waves of arrests choking the life out of the movement.

As the Front de Liberation du Quebec lay dying, the five exiled terrorists responsible for Cross's kidnapping began to feel homesick. By 1982 all of these former Felquistes were back in Canada, receiving various short terms in prison on their return.

By the end of this year even Paul Rose was walking free after serving just twelve years of his life sentence. He went on to earn sociology degrees at the University of Quebec and continued to campaign although within the confines of the law. As for the two hostages, James Cross went onto become the Under Secretary for the Department of Trade and Industry and awarded the Companion of the Order of St Michael and St George. Laporte, meanwhile, was honoured with various schools and structures named after him including the Pont Pierre-Laporte – a six-lane bridge over the St Lawrence River in Quebec.

After two referenda assessing the separatist desires of the province in 1980 and 1995, it was found the wish for an autonomous Quebec was still not held by the majority. To date, the closest the province has come to independence was on 27 November 2006 when Canadian Prime Minister Stephen Harper made a token gesture, declaring the Quebecois were a nation within a united Canada.

# THE MUNICH OLYMPIC HOSTAGE CRISIS

With memories of wartime Nazi atrocities and the self-promoting fanaticism of the Berlin Olympics of 1936 which foreshadowed them still vivid in the minds of both athletes and spectators, the Munich Games thirty-six years later was surrounded by an expectant air of hope and change. Yet while the Olympic flame burned eternal, eleven members of the Israeli team were taken hostage by Palestinian guerrillas and held inside their quarters. With the German authorities outwitted at every turn by the armed terrorists, this unscheduled Olympic event would forever mar the medals won in the summer of 1972 and help fuel animosity between the Arabs and Israelis for years to come.

## THE CAREFREE GAMES

Thirty-six years after the propaganda-propelled

Games held in Nazi Berlin, the Olympics returned to Germany with all concerned keen to create an affair free of high-handed salutes and Hitler Youth. Staged in Munich, officials sought to heal old wounds and show the dark times were firmly in the past with an altogether more relaxed and friendly event. This was to be a more positive Games.

Memories of the Holocaust still haunted those who travelled to Munich in 1972 none more so than the members of the Israeli team, many of whom had lost family during the atrocities. Yet they stood defiant and proud behind the Star of David during the opening ceremony parade. In a further bid to supplant the Nazi nightmare organisers had extended an olive branch to the Israeli athletes prior to the curtain-raiser by holding a memorial ceremony at the former concentration camp in Dachau, only six miles from the Olympic Stadium. As Andre Spitzer, Israel's fencing coach, laid the commemorative wreath it seemed to signal a Games founded on peace and unity, devoid of terror and discrimination.

The arrangement appeared flawless. Every aspect of this festival of sport was developed to provide a laid-back atmosphere. Police were prohibited from the Olympic Village replaced by nearly two thousand security officers called Olys dressed in non-threatening pale blue uniforms and white caps.

Athletes were given free rein of the facilities and allowed to come and go as they pleased under this subdued security presence. Nightly sojourns past acquiescent checkpoints and over unmanned perimeter fences for post-event partying in town became the norm during what was quickly dubbed 'the Carefree Games'. But, after ten days of sport and leisurely downtime, the twentieth Olympiad was about to take on a more serious tone.

## BREAKING AND ENTERING

The evening of Monday 4 September had been a welcome rest from competition for Team Israel, attending a performance of *Fiddler On The Roof* at a nearby Munich theatre. By the early hours they were back inside the Olympic Village asleep in their beds dreaming of gold medals.

As the Israelis slept, a group of drunk American athletes returning from a night on the town arrived at the two-metre high perimeter enclosure only to meet eight track-suited figures carrying sports bags. Thinking they were fellow Olympians trying to sneak back into the complex, they helped them scale the fence before saying their goodbyes. Little did they know they had unwittingly helped eight Palestinian guerrillas into the Olympic Village.

The intruders quickly stripped off their tracksuits

and pulled on balaclavas before creeping to the apartment block housing the Israeli sportsmen. Armed with AK-47 assault rifles, they began breaking into the first apartment using a stolen key. This unusual activity woke wrestling referee Yossef Gutfreund who went to investigate. On seeing the muzzle of a gun poking through the door crack, Gutfreund reacted, throwing his weight against the door whilst calling out to his roommates. While some managed to flee through windows or hide from this emerging terror, wrestling coach Moshe Weinberg chose to come to the referee's aid.

Despite the size and strength of the two men, they were unable to prevent the determined gunmen from gaining entry and in the ensuing chaos Weinberg took a shot to the face. Badly wounded but still alive, he was forced to show the trespassers where the other athletes were staying. Thinking the wrestlers and weightlifters in Apartment Three would be able to fight off these men, he took the terrorists to their quarters but, too disoriented from sleep, the strong men were no match for the armed and alert Palestinians.

Down but not out, the Israeli athletes fought back. As the eight guerrillas marched their twelve captives back to the first apartment, Weinberg attacked once again, knocking an adversary unconscious. He was joined by weightlifter Yossef Romano who fought a second gunman allowing wrestler Gad Tsabari to escape through an underground car park. His freedom came at a price; both Romano and Weinberg were shot and killed.

## A BLACK SEPTEMBER DAY

Once inside the first apartment, the nine living hostages were tied down; four on each of the two beds inside the sleeping quarters while Gutfreund – being the largest – was bound to a chair. On the floor between them the guerrillas placed the bullet-ridden body of Yossef Romano as a constant reminder that resistance would be met with extreme prejudice.

While they had chosen the Olympics as their stage, for the eight armed Palestinians this was far from a game. Motivated by a lifetime of poverty within refugee camps throughout the Middle East, these stateless souls saw terrorism as their only way out of their dire existence. Young and impassioned, they had joined this movement to fight for liberation and with months of weapons training behind them they had made their way to Munich ready to make a stand.

It didn't take long for news of the hostage-taking to spread. Those athletes who had successfully escaped capture had raised the alarm and soon Building 31 on Connollystrasse was surrounded by press and police, now a highly visible presence in the Olympic Village. As dawn broke two sheets of paper were thrown from the apartment balcony bearing the terrorists' demands. Two hundred and thirty-four Palestinian prisoners along with the two German revolutionaries, Andreas Baader and Ulrike Meinhof, were to be liberated from their prisons by midday or the execution of hostages would begin.

The communiqué also declared the name of the rebel collective. They belonged to a group called Black September; an extremist splinter cell of the PLO named after an event which took place two years earlier in which over four thousand fellow freedom fighters were killed by Jordanian soldiers.

## DEADLINE

Negotiators quickly made contact with the terrorist leader and spokesman, a man called Luttif Afif but using the name 'Issa', wearing a distinctive white hat and black boot polish to hide his features. Meeting face to face with Munich police chief Manfred Schreiber and Bruno Merk, the Bavarian Interior Minister, Issa, listened to their appeals all the while clutching a hand grenade.

With yet another deadly threat against Jewish life on German soil, the officials were keen to end the crisis as smoothly as possible. After Issa refused an offer of an unlimited sum of money Schreiber and Merk along with other high-ranking statesmen volunteered themselves as substitute hostages. This proposal was also rejected.

As the noon deadline drew nearer, negotiators endeavoured to stall the terrorists suggesting they were still waiting on word from Israel on their decision to free the prisoners. The truth was its Prime Minister, Golda Meir, had already stated no deals would be made with the hostage-takers. With just seconds of the morning remaining, and to the relief of the German authorities, Issa agreed to an extension allowing those countries involved another five hours to release their incarcerated comrades.

## FAILED ATTACKS

Counting down every passing minute of the new deadline, the German negotiators were under increasing pressure to bring the crisis to a close. The strange scene of athletes bathing in the sun and playing table tennis in other areas of the compound brought on by the International Olympic Committee's refusal to stop the competition only added to the day's mounting improprieties.

With three hours remaining on the clock and no solution in sight, the authorities chose to take action. Five large food parcels were delivered to Building 31 by undercover police including the commissioner dressed as a chef. The plan was to overpower the guards or at the very least count the number of hostiles while inside the second floor apartment. Unfortunately the terrorists were wise to such tactics and ordered the food to be left at the front door.

Their first move foiled, the police felt compelled to redouble their efforts and in a bold yet badly planned manoeuvre thirteen West German border guards disguised as Olympic athletes took up positions around the crime scene. With the army unable to engage this hostile enemy due to German law forbidding military action during peacetime, these overwhelmed and under-trained security men prepared to descend on the terrorists via the roof and ventilation system.

In the nick of time realisation dawned on the authorities seconds before the green light was given. Countless news crews set up around the site were broadcasting live pictures and the terrorists, following every move on television, were fully aware of the imminent ambush. Knowing the element of surprise was the key to the mission's success, the German police hastily called back their men, averting a sure-fire disaster caught live and in colour by the world's media.

### AIRPORT TRAP

After this second failure to force the ordeal across the

finish line, the Palestinians, wishing to escape the confines of the besieged building, delivered a new demand to the frustrated German officials. They wanted a plane with enough fuel to fly them and the hostages to Egypt to be made ready by nine o'clock at a nearby airport. Authorities arranged for two military helicopters to take them all to Fürstenfeldbruck, a NATO airbase eighteen miles west from Munich. At ten minutes past ten the nine exhausted captives and their captors boarded a bus which took them out of the Olympic Village and into the unknown.

As the helicopters took on their human cargo and passed over the Olympic Stadium, followed by a third transport containing the German crisis team, yet another trap was being laid at the airbase. Inside the waiting Boeing 727 a body of voluntary policemen masquerading as flight crew was primed to strike. In addition, three snipers were in position on the control tower along with two more sharpshooters at ground level ready to engage the enemy. Assault vehicles would then storm the runway and rescue the nine Israeli hostages to complete what appeared to be a flawless plan.

As the hostage-laden helicopters touched down at Fürstenfeldbruck Airport, the German operation began to unravel. The bogus flight crew inside the plane lost their nerve and voted unanimously to abandon their posts, believing their lack of training would doom them to failure. Consequently, when Issa boarded the Boeing and found the cockpit and cabin empty, he knew they had been deceived. It was then that all hell broke loose.

## GERMAN INEFFICIENCY

The five snipers opened fire on the Palestinians but, without night vision scopes and adequate training, they managed to take out just one of their eight targets. The remaining militants scrambled for cover underneath the two helicopters still containing the nine bound hostages and fired blindly at their surroundings. One such stray bullet took the next life, that of Anton Fliegerbauer, a German policeman, who was standing by a window in the airport building.

The chaotic gun battle laboured on longer than anticipated with the amateur marksmen unable to suppress the terrorist threat. After Mossad chief Zvi Zamir's attempts to contact the hostage-takers via loud haler brought a volley of gunfire, the German forces decided to bring in the assault vehicles. But there was a problem. In all the confusion they had neglected to order the six transport and by the time they had fought through traffic to reach the airbase, their presence was no longer required.

After two hours of relentless conflict a relative quiet descended upon the scene. Then, at midnight, a German spokesman reported the crisis was over. The Israeli Olympians were now safe from harm and all eight members of Black September had been killed by German police. Unfortunately these statements were wide of the mark.

Just minutes after the announcement, one of the terrorists, far from dead, opened fire on one of the helicopters before throwing in a grenade killing all four hostages inside. As snipers gunned down the killer (thought to have been Issa), another hostile discharged his weapon into the second helicopter spraying the remaining five with a hail of bullets. Moments later news filtered through to the world's press exposing the gross inaccuracy of the last bulletin. All the Israelis held captive were now dead.

## THE GAMES GO ON

While the nine dead hostages returned to Israel along with the rest of their team in mourning, the Olympics continued with eighty thousand attending a football match between Hungary and the host nation. The bodies of the dead terrorists were flown to Libya each receiving a hero's funeral; however there were only five. Three of the hostage-takers had endured the mêlée at Fürstenfeldbruck but instead of succumbing to justice, these surviving members of Black September would make it safely back to the Middle East.

On 29 October, less than two months after the horrors in Munich, a Lufthansa Boeing 727 travelling from Beirut to Frankfurt was hijacked by another cell of Palestinian terrorists demanding the release of the three Black September men. In a move steeped in conspiracy, the West German government hastily agreed, handing over the guerrillas who were welcomed into Libya as champions of the cause. It is widely believed the skyjacking had been orchestrated by German statesmen to prevent further attacks within their borders and to avoid details of German incompetence that would come to light during a trial.

While Israel fumed at this perversion of justice, revenge was being exacted upon those deemed by the Israeli Defence Committee and its Mossad associates to be behind the Munich operation. Eleven names of key Palestinian rebels formed a list for assassination by clandestine agents throughout Europe with Operations Wrath of God and Spring of Youth green-lit to prevent future attacks on Israelis. These vengeful attacks continued well into the nineties though to this day both Mohammed Safady and Jamal Al-Gashey – two of the three surviving hostage-takers – remain alive and well, in hiding somewhere in the Middle East.

# PATTY HEARST

In the ultimate tale of rich girl gone bad, this notorious heiress to a media empire was snatched from her Berkeley home weeks before her twentieth birthday and brainwashed by a small band of anti-capitalist terrorists. While her family obeyed the demands of her captors, the high-class hostage transformed from victim to villain and became one with her kidnappers, embarking on a life of crime and rebellion.

## BERKELEY BREAK-IN

Born on 20 February 1954 into an affluent dynasty built by her grandfather and media tycoon William Randolph Hearst, Patricia Campbell Hearst wanted for very little. She grew up in the upscale suburb of Hillsborough south of San Francisco, attended the very best schools and played with best friends from other rich families. Hers was a life used to swimming pools, tennis courts and riding stables.

After completing her elite schooling, graduating from the choice Menlo College, the highborn heiress decided to remain in the state to attend Berkeley University for a degree in art history. By this time she had met and was engaged to college graduate Steven Weed, six years her senior, and the pair lived half a mile off campus in a modest apartment on Benvenue Street. It was here that her fall from the lap of luxury would begin.

At approximately nine o'clock in the evening of 4 February 1974 as the couple relaxed in front of the television the doorbell rang. Before Patty could warn her fiancé to apply the security chain, he had opened the door to an anxious woman in a black coat and hat. She had apparently hit a car in the garage under the house and wanted to make a phone call. With only seconds to wonder whether it was her beloved MG sports car that had been struck, two men barged into the house carrying guns.

In next to no time she was blindfolded, gagged with a knotted rag and bundled into the boot of a white Chevrolet in only her bathrobe. Minutes later her kidnappers stopped to swap cars and she was dragged into the backseat of a green Ford station wagon. Under a blanket and the watchful eyes of her captors she was taken the twenty miles to her first people's prison across the Bay Bridge to Daly City.

Dazed from a blow to her face by a rifle butt and her bare legs bleeding after her forceful extraction from her Berkeley home, Patty Hearst was shoved into a stinking closet crudely soundproofed with layers of carpet. Her makeshift cell was a far cry from the spacious homes she enjoyed as a child measuring a mere two feet wide and only five and a half feet high. In this tiny pen, unsighted by her tear-stained blindfold and her nostrils filled with the malodorous stench of the rotten carpet, she was paid a visit by the leader of her kidnappers. A tall black man by the name of Field General Cinque Mtume, he informed her she was now the prisoner of the Symbionese Liberation Army.

## THE SLA

The grandly-titled leader of this army was in fact Donald DeFreeze a career criminal turned fugitive ever since his escape from Soledad Prison in March 1973. Before his break-out, DeFreeze had discovered some radical beliefs and that summer created the Symbionese Liberation Army along with his fellow freedom fighters Russ Little and William Wolfe.

Influenced by the anti-establishment movements of the time, these rebel soldiers set about starting a world revolution. Together they discarded their slave names, took on aliases and established their manifesto in which it explained the group's name: taken from the word 'symbiosis' meaning a close union of dissimilar bodies.

They proposed an end to what they saw as capitalist creations including prisons and even monogamy, wishing instead for a free, unshackled society.

Their enemy was the state and all those with status and they were quick to make their mark. On 6 November the group ambushed and assassinated Oakland Schools Superintendent Marcus Foster. The official had been erroneously reported as being in favour of school identification cards – an idea the SLA despised. The revolution had begun with deadly force.

Two months later Russ Little and Joe Remiro were arrested for the murder of Foster so DeFreeze, as Cinque, took the movement underground to hatch a plan that would free his enslaved brothers. The band of five women and three men agreed they should kidnap a capitalist foe to exchange for their comrades behind bars and chose the well-bred Patty Hearst as their target.

## FOOD FIGHT

Two days after her kidnapping, the SLA's first communiqué arrived at Berkeley's independent and left-wing radio station: KPFA. It stated that the granddaughter of the newspaper magnate was now a prisoner of war held in protective custody under the terms of the Geneva Convention. Despite no demands being made in the message, it was clear they wanted to cause the release of Little and Remiro. Unable to force this issue, the SLA chose a different approach to highlight their distaste of the corporate enemies of the people. On 12 February an audio tape arrived at the KPFA station upon which Patty announced the movement's wishes. Seventy dollars of high-quality food was to be distributed to every poor person in California by the Hearst family. The food was to be provided for those holding welfare, pension and food stamp cards and even jail and bail release slips and occur over a four week period throughout San Francisco, Oakland, East Palo Alto and Santa Rosa. Accession to this demand would be seen as a gesture of good faith and would prevent any undue harm coming to their captive.

Patty's father was quick to calculate the feeding of California's poor would cost an estimated $400 million including distribution costs; an impossible amount even for his deep pockets. Explaining this, a further taped message from the SLA was issued. Using his daughter's voice once again, Hearst was informed that he should distribute as much food as he could afford. So, on the 19 February, the chairman of the Hearst Corporation announced the creation of People In Need (PIN); a food distribution program which planned to feed one hundred thousand people for twelve months at a cost of $2 million.

The following day was Patty's birthday, however, as she turned twenty inside her cramped cell, she received no gifts. Instead her captors demanded the presents to the state's poor should be increased to the value of $6 million. Unable to stretch his wealth to meet this huge sum, Hearst's hand-out program began two days later. It was an unmitigated disaster as reports came through of West Coast mobs stealing the food from the trucks, causing riots in the city streets. The SLA then reneged on the release of their prisoner stating the food had been of poor quality. As Hearst and his team endeavoured to repeat the delivery of provisions, they struggled to keep hope alive that Patty Hearst would soon be free.

## BECOMING TANIA

While her father spent his millions to bring food to the underprivileged and effect her release, Patty was subjected to appalling conditions, threatened with violence and bombarded with relentless militant rhetoric. Forced to listen to all the members' voices through the closet door pumping the SLA's doctrine into her brain, she underwent an effective brainwashing treatment. Her past high society life was belittled and in her weakened state her identity was broken down creating a different personality; one which rejected her parents and joined forces with her hostage-takers.

After moving hideouts where she was forced to live in an even smaller closet for another four weeks, Patty Hearst transformed from highborn hostage to newborn revolutionary. On 3 April in a fifth audio tape Patty revealed she was now a bona fide member of the Symbionese Liberation Army and had adopted the name Tania after one of Che Guevara's comrades. To fully communicate her conversion to this dark side an accompanying photograph showed Patty posing in front of the movement's insignia – a seven-headed cobra – holding an M-1 semi-automatic carbine.

This communiqué sent shockwaves through the Hearst family and beyond. The general consensus believed she was acting under duress but almost two weeks later another media tremor served to traumatise those involved.

## CROSSOVER TO CRIME

At 9.40 am on 15 April five armed individuals entered the Sunset district branch of Hibernia bank at 1450 Noriega Street in San Francisco. In little over four minutes the bank robbers stole in excess of $10,000 before making their getaway. They were swiftly caught but only on camera. When the CCTV footage was examined, police were amazed to discover one of the thieves was none other than Patty Hearst. Along with DeFreeze and three other female accomplices, the rich girl had gone bad holding up a bank owned by her former best friend's father.

Still in disbelief that she was anything but an unwilling participant in the robbery, the authorities acted cautiously issuing a warrant for her arrest as a material witness. Reports began to circulate, along with the incriminating image, that the gun she wielded was not loaded and that the other members were training their weapons on her at all times. This optimistic outlook was quickly destroyed with the arrival of a sixth audio communiqué from Patty who cleared up any confusion about where her loyalties now lay. Talking as Tania, she maintained she was a keen SLA collaborator, rubbishing talk of any brainwashing and verbally attacking her family and fiancé.

## SIEGE IN SOUTH CENTRAL

Three weeks later Patty was spotted outside a sports shop in Los Angeles firing around thirty shots from her carbine to provide cover for William and Emily Harris who had been caught shoplifting by the store's security guard. The three comrades-in-arms fled the scene in a van which they soon ditched before stealing a series of vehicles to avoid police capture. The abandoned van contained a parking ticket which led Federal agents to the SLA safe house.

On hearing the news of the unearthed evidence,

Field Marshal Cinque and his band of revolutionaries vacated their hideout for fear of being caught. Happening upon a small house on East 54th Street in Compton, South Central, the SLA broke in and took the residents hostage. Soon police, FBI and SWAT teams arrived on the scene calling for the release of the hostages and the surrender of the extremists. Cinque allowed the tenants to leave but ignored a total of eighteen police requests to give up. After a two hour gunfight during which a fire erupted inside the house six members of the SLA perished in the blaze.

For a while Patty was believed to be inside the inferno but in fact she watched the siege live on TV from the safety of a motel room with the Harrises. Fearing they were wanted dead not alive by authorities, the three remaining members of the SLA spent the next sixteen months on the run, seeking refuge as far away as Pennsylvania.

## ARREST AND ARRAIGNMENT

The 300 FBI agents employed in the pursuit of Patty Hearst had found it increasingly difficult to track her down. Unlike most fugitives, she had made no attempt to contact family members or close friends so phone taps had been futile. However, the G-men finally caught a break. She had managed to stay one step ahead of the law until the late summer of 1975 when a red Volkswagen seen near to her safe house in Pocono Mountains provided important clues to her whereabouts.

The compromising car was owned by a Kathleen Soliah who was discovered to be a known SLA sympathiser. Her location was traced to a postal box in San Francisco which, when staked out, disclosed two addresses belonging to those who picked up the mail. Agents descended on the first location: 288 Precita Avenue in the early afternoon of Thursday 18 September and arrested William and Emily Harris returning from a jog in the nearby park. Inside the white two-storey house they found forty pounds of explosives and an assortment of weapons and ammunition but no Patty Hearst.

Empty-handed the FBI headed south-west to the second scene of inquiry making the three mile drive to 625 Morse Street. A little over an hour after apprehending the Harrises, the chasing pack of policemen and agents knocked on the front door of their last potential lead. Thankfully, it proved to be solid. Patty came quietly ending more than nineteen months of investigation.

While looking drained and dishevelled, Patty remained defiant and at ease during her arrest and arraignment. With bail set at $1.5 million the heiress to the Hearst fortune was despatched to San Mateo lock-up where she declared her occupation as urban guerrilla during the booking process. Pumping a clenched fist into the air and fuelled with revolutionary verve she was sequestered in a seven by nine foot cell – larger than either of her closets during captivity.

## THE RETURN OF PATTY

Relieved to have her back safe and sound, the Hearst family hired media-savvy lawyer F. Lee Bailey to defend their daughter during her trial in early 1976. Having dropped her nom de guerre, Patty took the stand as the victim in a plea for mercy from the court. She spoke of physical, emotional and sexual abuse at the hands of her captors suggesting she was intimidated into a life of crime.

Unfortunately the jury agreed with the prosecution which relayed many opportunities during her 19½ months with the SLA when she could have escaped to freedom. Deeming her only a prisoner during her horrific spells in the closets, the San Francisco Federal Court convicted Patty Hearst on 20 March 1976 and sentenced her to the maximum twenty-five years for armed robbery. This was later commuted by judicial review to seven years.

A further act of clemency from President Carter twenty-two months into her sentence saw her released from the Federal Correctional Institute in Pleasanton, California. She then went on to marry her policeman bodyguard Bernard Shaw and moved to Connecticut where they had two girls, Lydia and Gillian. The highborn heiress turned actress in the nineties with a series of small roles in offbeat movies revealing yet another side to her self.

# TIEDE HERREMA

Masterminded by a fanatical fugitive, a renegade splinter group of the IRA abducted Dutch industrialist Tiede Herrema some two hundred yards from his Limerick home. In what became the longest kidnapping in Ireland's history fuelled by a heady mix of politics and romance, police tracked down the secret hideout where a seventeen day siege ensued.

## INDUSTRIAL ACTION

Enticed to the Republic of Ireland by a ten year tax-free exemption period for foreign businesses, Dutch manufacturing company AZKO set up the Ferenka plant in Annacotty, County Limerick in 1972. Making steel cord for tyre walls, Ferenka became the city's biggest employer with nearly one thousand four hundred workers. In the autumn of 1975 the managing director of this factory was fifty-four-year-old Tiede Herrema.

On Friday 3 October 1975 as he left his home in Castletroy less than two miles from the steel works, the industrialist's Hillman Hunter was pulled over on the Monaleen Road by men posing as Gardai – the Irish police force. Within seconds Herrema realised he had been tricked and was quickly bundled into the back of a Ford Cortina. At 8.15 am his abandoned car was found with the keys in the ignition and his briefcase on the passenger seat.

Tiede Herrema had been abducted by a rogue cell of the Provisional Irish Republican Army no longer answering to those at the top. The renegade group was led by Eddie Gallagher, a twenty-eight-year-old left-wing republican, who had become disillusioned with the political direction of the Provos, desiring a more resolute approach to ending British rule in Northern Ireland. However his plan to kidnap the Dutch factory owner had as much to do with affairs of the heart as affairs of state.

## ESCAPE CLAUSE

Several years earlier, Eddie Gallagher met Bridget Rose Dugdale, an English born heiress rebelling against her wealthy background, in an Edinburgh dosshouse. A romance blossomed and together they conceived an audacious plan to strike at the heart of Northern Ireland's law enforcement. On 24 January 1974 the lovers hijacked a helicopter in County Donegal and dropped three milk churns packed with explosives upon the Royal Ulster Constabulary in Strabane. Thankfully the churns failed to detonate and the pair of militant milkmen were later apprehended.

While Gallagher evaded conviction, his beloved Rose was not as fortunate. Authorities had been after the rich girl gone bad following her involvement in the theft of £8 million worth of art from a private collector in County Wicklow. The two crimes brought her a nine year sentence. By the time she took up residence in her Limerick jail cell, Dugdale was pregnant with Gallagher's child.

Later that summer the soon-to-be father found himself behind bars but his stay would be brief. After just one day inside, he led eighteen other inmates on a prison break blasting their way out of Portlaoise prison to freedom. One of the escapees was Kevin Mallon, an IRA man from County Tyrone, who managed to evade the law for several months before being arrested and returned to jail.

Mallon's girlfriend was Marion Coyle, a twenty-one-year-old Derry girl and one-time courier and look-out for the IRA. Now she was a member of Gallagher's renegade gang all of whom had made a pact that if any of them languished in prison, those on the outside would make every attempt to set them free. With loved ones under lock and key Gallagher and Coyle set about planning a rescue attempt with a difference. Instead of using previously-foiled, high-risk methods of rescue, the displaced cell chose to kidnap Tiede Herrema and force the release of their comrades and companions.

## DEMANDS

With their political bargaining chip in the backseat of the Ford Cortina, the breakaway group made for a safe house in the Slieve Bloom hills and from there Marion placed the all-important call to the Dutch Embassy in Dublin. At 11.30 am attaché Eric Kwint was informed that Herrema had been kidnapped and would be executed within forty-eight hours unless certain demands were met.

In addition to the release of their respective partners, the pair called for revolutionary ally James Hyland to be set free and requested the Ferenka plant be shut down. To begin with, the kidnappers seemed to get their own way. The Dutch company agreed to close their factory for twenty-four hours sending its one thousand two hundred workforce home on full pay and was even prepared to hand over an unspecified and unrequested ransom to the hostage-takers. However, the Irish coalition government led by Liam Cosgrave was less accommodating. It refused to release the group's comrades and instead began an extensive search for the criminals, setting up roadblocks and calling in 9,000 free state soldiers to help with the hunt.

As authorities combed the countryside and guarded Ireland's exit points, there was widespread outrage at the kidnapping of Tiede Herrema. Protest marches right across Limerick took place calling for his release. Even Sinn Fein, the political wing of the IRA, denounced the unlawful act with president Rory O'Brady declaring it served no useful purpose.

While audio-taped messages containing Herrema's pleas for his life started to arrive at police head-quarters, Phil Flynn a trade union representative with strong ties to the IRA, was called in to act as an intermediary. A period of restless negotiation began as days turned into weeks without any clue to the hostage's location. Little did they know that Gallagher and company had switched hideouts to remain hidden from the hunting party.

## THE SIEGE AT MONASTEREVIN

Two weeks into the kidnapping the Irish police finally made a breakthrough. They had managed to arrest Brian McGowan, the man who had staked out Herrema's home to discover his early morning routine and who joined Gallagher in snatching the factory owner from his car. After some suspect interrogation tactics, McGowan revealed the location of the new safe house.

Herrema and his captors had relocated to 1410 St Evin's Park; a three-bedroom house in Monasterevin, County Kildare about forty miles from Dublin. As soon as police had coerced the address from their detainee they descended upon the river town to bring an end to the hostage-taking. Unfortunately Gallagher and Coyle had managed to pre-empt the strike and as Irish Special Branch stormed the council house, the kidnappers managed to barricade themselves inside an upstairs bedroom.

The element of surprise had been lost and now a new phase of the kidnapping began. Gallagher and Coyle fired off shots and hurled milk bottles at the surrounding policemen who laid siege to the house. On 24 October Herrema was forced to convey to authorities the gravity of the situation, appearing at the bedroom window to tell police to stay back for fear he would be killed.

In reality Herrema grew less concerned his death would come from the hands of his captors with each passing day. Thanks to some previous psychology training, the industrialist knew it was important for him to develop a rapport with his kidnappers. By befriending Gallagher and Coyle it would be harder for them to make good their death threats. While Marion resisted any attempt to bond with Herrema, Gallagher on the other hand grew more comfortable with his hostage and during the ordeal even consulted him on how best to deal with the police. Psychology was also being used outside the barricaded bedroom. Experts were called in to advise on a strategy that would expedite proceedings. Bright lights were erected to shine in through the windows at night to keep the criminals awake and thus encourage fatigue. Yet still Gallagher and Coyle remained dedicated to their cause. They even foiled a police sabotage plan injuring an officer caught removing a window pane from the bathroom in an attempt to let the freezing cold air into the second storey of the house.

Finally, as the days wore on, the pair's persistence began to falter. Negotiations with Commissioner Edward Garvey and Garda Chief Larry Wrenn were showing signs of progress. Desperate to end the ordeal, Gallagher began to reduced his demands calling for the release of just one imprisoned comrade: the mother of his child, Rose Dugdale. When this was met with the same flat refusal from the government, the two hostage-takers realised they had to consider releasing Herrema.

## BROKEN PROMISES

On Wednesday 5 November the police eavesdropping equipment picked up signs that the stress of the siege was beginning to tell on the kidnappers. Sounds of Marion Coyle sobbing inside the bedroom could be heard and were duly reported throughout the world by the press attending in their hundreds. It was now two weeks since the pair of ex-Provos had shut themselves inside the tiny bedroom along with their hostage and time had come for an end to the standoff.

To persuade Gallagher and Coyle to surrender Herrema unharmed, Garda Commissioner Garvey agreed to sign a document assuring the hostage-takers would receive reduced sentences. The contract stated Gallagher and Coyle would be given a maximum of four and two years respectively. After mulling over the deal, the two kidnappers were united in their decision to give up their prisoner and on 7 November after thirty-six days in captivity Tiede Herrema was allowed to walk out of the Monasterevin house.

The longest kidnapping in Irish history came to a close around eight o'clock on the Friday evening after Herrema complained of neck pains. Thinking their hostage may die and thus negate their deal with the police, Gallagher decided enough was enough and dropped their guns out of the upstairs window. The steel cord manufacturer soon exited the building a free man followed by his two captors who were quickly despatched to Bridewell Garda station in Dublin to be officially charged.

Meanwhile Herrema was taken to the Dutch Embassy and checked over by doctors before attending a news conference where he looked relatively calm and collected. Explaining he feared for his life only during the initial stages of the kidnapping, he showed the world's press a .38 bullet from the gun which had been trained on him throughout his ordeal. This had been given to him as a souvenir by Gallagher as the siege neared its end. The following day Herrema returned to his native Holland arriving at Rotterdam Airport to be met by his three sons; Jelle, Sjoerd and Harm.

Unfortunately for the kidnappers, their deal with the authorities failed to have any bearing on the trial. The four week long court case in February and March 1976 culminated in Gallagher receiving a twenty year sentence while Coyle was given a fifteen year term. Questions were asked about the signed contract but the authorities declared no concessions had ever been made to the kidnappers.

## A MARRIAGE MADE IN PRISON

Eight people were convicted for their involvement in the kidnapping of Tiede Herrema with a total of seventy-one years jail time handed down. This loss of freedom was soon followed by a loss of one thousand four hundred jobs when AZKO closed the Ferenka

119

plant in November 1977. While this Dutch love affair with Limerick came to an end another partnership was going from strength to strength.

On 24 January 1978 Eddie Gallagher and his rebel rich girl Rose Dugdale tied the knot inside a prison chapel becoming the first convict marriage in Irish history. The newlyweds were given a five-hour honeymoon inside a cell before the groom was whisked off back to his Portlaoise lockup. Despite this strong display of commitment the marriage failed to endure.

By 1990 both the Herrema hostage-takers had been released from their respective prisons. Marion Coyle walked to freedom in 1985 having served nine years of her term while Gallagher was discharged after completing fourteen of his twenty-year sentence. Asked to comment on his kidnapper's release, Herrema said it was long overdue considering his abduction to have been purely a stupid act by young people.

The Dutch industrialist had long since left Ireland although during the late eighties, having become something of a celebrity, he did return to host an episode of Saturday Live. He was later made a Freeman of the city of Limerick and along with his wife became honorary Irish citizens. Thirty years after the ordeal on Tuesday 18 October 2005, Tiede Herrema donated his personal collection of diaries, papers and news cuttings – much of which related to his ordeal – to the University of Limerick. His souvenir bullet, however, was not part of the collection. As Gallagher had said on presenting the memento to his hostage: 'This was meant for you.'

# THE DUTCH TRAIN HOSTAGE CRISIS OF 1975

Far from the island paradise known to their parents, a small band of stateless youths frustrated at the lack of aid to their South Moluccan families seized control of a Dutch commuter train in the winter of 1975. Over twelve cold December days the separatists held the passengers hostage, taking innocent lives when authorities ignored their demands. Fears over further deaths were compounded when, two days into the ordeal, a separate cell of South Moluccans captured the Indonesian Consulate in Amsterdam, forcing Dutch authorities to deal with a double Dutch hostage crisis.

## EMERGENCY DISCORD

On Tuesday 2 December 1975 a two carriage train filled with passengers making their daily commute to work was on its way from Groningen to Zwolle in the Netherlands. At ten minutes past seven a group of disaffected youths armed with machine guns, hunting rifles and grenades seized the mustard-coloured train, pulling the emergency cord shortly after leaving the station at Beilen.

As the train came to a screeching halt in the middle of flat, open farmland the hijackers shot the driver, Hans Braam, and took approximately fifty commuters hostage. Six passengers managed to escape before the seven masked terrorists were able to round up their captives and herd them into the forward coach, forcing them to block the windows with newspapers.

Fuelled by adrenaline and passion for their cause the young activists fired at an oncoming train forcing it to apply its brakes. Within minutes the gunmen had blocked all rail traffic in both directions and ensured they had enough human collateral with which to bargain and force their demands upon the Dutch authorities.

Not long after police units had surrounded the stationary train, creating a perimeter 850 yards around the scene, the hostage-takers released two women and a three-year-old child along with a note detailing their initial demands. The seven hijackers called themselves the Free South Moluccan Youths and as well as safe passage to Amsterdam's Schiphol Airport they wanted to bring their struggle for independence to the attention of the world.

## THE SOUTH MOLUCCAN STRUGGLE

These young hijackers were second generation Moluccans; a stateless nation of people originating from an island chain in a section of the Pacific Ocean called the Banda Sea. At the time of the hostage crisis in 1975 their homeland was ruled by the Republic of Indonesia and thousands of South Moluccans were living as second class citizens in temporary accommodation throughout the Netherlands.

Their nation used to be known as the Spice Islands, a Dutch colony popular for its yield of cloves and nutmeg. The natives were converted to Christianity by the Dutch explorers and the islanders soon became loyal to their colonists' Crown. However Japanese occupation of the Moluccas during the Second World War disrupted this harmony. Once the fighting had ceased, the Netherlands were prevented from taking back the islands after the USA threatened a retraction of all its Marshall Plan donations. In order to obtain this much-needed economic aid, the Dutch begrudgingly recognised Indonesia as a republic in December 1949.

Concerned that their new Muslim rulers would not be as friendly as their Christian settlers, the demobilised soldiers from Ceram, Ambon and other South Moluccan islands refused to be absorbed into this newly-created state. On 25 April 1950, to

124

emphasise their discontent, they formed their own independent Republic of South Moluccas and staged a revolt against Indonesia. Despite a reputation as fierce warriors their uprising was quashed and, not wanting to live under this alternative rule, the defeated soldiers agreed to be transported, along with their families, to the Netherlands.

In 1951 shiploads of Moluccans arrived at Dutch ports believing they would be given assistance in gaining their independence. Instead around twelve thousand five hundred Pacific island expatriates were given temporary refuge in ex-army barracks and even an old Nazi concentration camp, isolated from the rest of Dutch society. As the years went by with no help and no repatriation, these stranded South Moluccans grew restless and, overwhelmed by a sense of betrayal, the younger generation decided enough was enough and action had to be taken.

## A HAIL OF BULLETS

After several acts of terror to bring their plight to the eyes of the world the Free South Moluccan Youth now embarked on their most forceful mission to bring freedom and redress to their displaced people. With fifty hostages aboard a train bound for jeopardy, the hijackers presented the surrounding police with their demands. They wanted an admission of guilt from the

Dutch government apologising for the poor treatment of the island visitors over the last twenty-four years and insisted the authorities support the Moluccan claim for independence before a United Nations committee.

These demands were flatly refused by Dutch Foreign Minister Max van der Stoel creating a tense atmosphere as captives and captors alike prepared for their first night aboard the train. Even in darkness the Moluccan militants kept watch for an assault attempt, opening fire on anything that came too close. This continued into Wednesday when Johannes Manusama, the head of the South Moluccan government in exile, attempted to approach the train by car. Called in to act as a mediator, the hijackers' national president hailed his fellow Moluccans via megaphone and promptly received a belligerent reply: three shots narrowly missing him.

Despite not being in the mood to talk, the terrorists soon released another hostage; a Chinese cook who delivered demands of a more pressing nature to the encircling police. Over twenty-four hours had passed since they had seized the train and food and drink supplies were running low. A request for insulin was made for a diabetic hostage and the hijackers ordered a new engineer, a replacement for the one they had murdered.

The provisions were delivered to the train but authorities refrained from supplying the terrorists with another hostage, particularly one that could help them escape. Like the train, the situation was at a standstill and after hours of inaction and the passing of another day, the Moluccan youths savagely asserted their power. Twenty-two-year-old soldier, Leo Bulter, was moved to the forward car's rear door and executed, his body along with the dead driver thrown out onto the tracks.

## THE INDONESIAN CONSULATE

By the third day of the train-jacking the level of terrorism had escalated beyond all imagination. On Thursday 4 December the South Moluccan threat of violence quickly doubled when a second hostage scenario developed one hundred miles west in Amsterdam. Another seven gunmen entered the capital's Indonesian Consulate and took forty-one hostages including sixteen children from a school within the building.

As the terrorists moved their captives to the upper floor a small number of consulate employees managed to climb a rope to freedom. One escapee was not so lucky. In an attempt to avoid capture, he jumped from a window falling thirty feet. Rushed to hospital the man died five days later from his injuries.

With as many as sixty hostages held prisoner inside the consulate, the island separatists put their own set of demands to another collection of police and special forces. The seven gunmen called for the release of several South Moluccan political prisoners and wished for official talks to begin between Indonesian President Suharto and Moluccan leader Manusama. Reaction from the surrounding authorities matched those laying siege to the train near Beilen. Justice Minister Andreas van Agt insisted none of the hostage-takers would be granted safe passage. Even after they released twelve of the children, negotiators refused to consider any demands until all of the school's pupils were set free.

As with the train, non-compliance led to a stalemate and frustration among the Moluccan activists who gathered a number of the hostages onto the third floor balcony, threatening to push them over the edge if demands were not met. Thankfully the terrorists chose not to send any of their captives to certain death. However, back in the remote Drenthe grassland, the threat to the lives of the hostages aboard the two-car train was very real.

## BACK TO THE TRAIN

While no hostages had yet been murdered at the consulate, the death toll aboard the train now stood at two. A group of fourteen passengers not prepared to spend a third night in captivity managed to escape from the rear doors of the train leaving over thirty hostages held at gunpoint.

The following day the number of prisoners was reduced further after reiterated demands were ignored by the Dutch authorities. Feeling they needed to provide another reminder of their determination to have their orders obeyed, the murderous Moluccans brought another victim to the train's front doors. In full view of the press and police, financial expert Bob Bierling was promptly shot in the back of the neck and dumped off the train.

With three dead and no end in sight to their nightmare, the hostages aboard the Zwolle-bound train feared for their lives and not just from a Moluccan bullet. The onboard heating system which had initially staved off the winter cold was now broken and, with their captors refusing to allow a mechanic to make the necessary repairs, the imprisoned commuters ran the risk of hypothermia.

As the ordeal reached the weekend Manusama, the Moluccan government's chief, made another attempt to talk the hijackers into releasing their hostages. Accompanied by three other negotiators, the president spent nearly two hours aboard the train in discussion with the angry youths. Another set of talks took place on Sunday morning but, after ninety minutes of dialogue, Manusama alighted from the train with no guarantees for an end to the ordeal.

Later on Sunday two more passengers made it off the train, this time in good health. Octogenarians Gregory Barger and his wife Ann, the oldest hostages onboard, were given their freedom much to the surprise of the Dutch police. This unexpected release gave hope to all concerned that a positive outcome to this crisis was right around the corner.

## NORMAL SERVICE RESUMED

While it would be another week before the Free South Moluccan Youths surrendered the train and released the remaining passengers, in that time there were at least no more shootings. An anti-terrorist assault upon the train was also avoided thanks to a veto by Prime Minister Joop den Uyl who feared any military strike would risk further casualties.

On Sunday 14 December, after continued negotiations with the separatists, those left aboard the hijacked train were finally released. The hostage-takers' spirit had been broken by the debilitating low temperatures inside the carriages and when they had heard the Netherlands would consider official talks with the South Moluccan government, they believed they had achieved at least some success.

In truth the hijackers had failed in their mission to bring about the end of Indonesian rule in their native islands. Succeeding only in raising the profile of the South Moluccan struggle for independence, the hijackers were swiftly convicted and sentenced to prison terms of up to fourteen years. One of the rebellious youths took the defeat harder than the rest committing suicide in his cell three years later.

Though the train-jacking had been resolved after twelve days, the incident in Amsterdam was still ongoing. The rebel autonomists holding the Indonesian consulate had called for Reverend Semol Metiary to act as their go-between but the clergyman was unable to secure the release of the twenty-five hostages. Two days later on Friday 19 December, after vague assurances from Dutch and Indonesian authorities that they would examine the South Moluccan case, the terrorists surrendered.

# THE HIJACKING OF
# AIR FRANCE 139

In the summer of 1976 as the final days of June ticked by, four anti-Zionist guerrillas hijacked a commercial airline flight bound for Paris. Endowed with the support of two major world dictators, the terrorists were allowed to travel to the heart of Africa where the hostages were holed up in an abandoned airport terminal. Once the rebels began to single out the Jewish captives, Israel were compelled to execute the longest-range assault in its history; an audacious mission which led to the rescue of almost all hostages and Fourth of July celebrations to rival those occurring halfway around the world in America.

## BEN GURION TO BENGHAZI

It was an early start for the four terrorists arriving at Athens International Airport at around six in the morning aboard Singapore Airlines Flight 763 from Bahrain. Their concealed guns and grenades passing unnoticed through an unmanned metal detector, the deadly quartet joined the queue for passport control and, using fake documents, took their seats on board Air France Flight 139 heading to Paris. Minutes after take-off, the armed rebels burst from their seats and hijacked the plane.

While Captain Michel Bacos was forced at gunpoint to make an about-turn, the hijackers planted explosives throughout the cabin and collected passports from the two hundred and fifty-six passengers and twelve members of the crew. Having lost radio contact with the captured Airbus, authorities were unable to glean its destination, presuming it was returning to the flight's origin: Tel Aviv. As Israeli security forces convened at Ben Gurion Airport, the abducted aircraft surprised all diverting across the Mediterranean Sea and landing in Benghazi, Libya.

With Colonel Gaddafi's consent the plane was permitted to refuel and as the tanks filled, the captives grew more anxious inside the stifling cabin. Hostage Patricia Martel, a thirty-year-old nurse from Manchester on her way to her mother's funeral, soon decided enough was enough. Feigning a miscarriage, she managed to fool her captors into releasing her from the mounting claustrophobia. Sadly for the others, she would be the only one to leave with her freedom. After a tense six hours on Libyan tarmac the Airbus took to the skies once more bound for a more unexpected destination.

## AFRICAN AIDE

After more than five hours of southbound flight, the hijacked plane touched down at Uganda's Entebbe Airport at three-fifteen on Monday morning. It would be another eight hours before Captain Bacos received authorisation to move from the runway to an old disused terminal where, shortly after midday, all the hostages were herded inside. The fearsome foursome were then joined by an additional six terrorists already in Uganda, increasing the militant threat as the hostages puzzled over their captors' motives.

Meanwhile, cunning ex-captive Patricia Martel had arrived in London where she provided Mossad agents with descriptions of the hijackers. From these they positively identified both Wilfred Böse and Brigitta Kuhlmann, members of the Revolutionary Cells, a West German activist group with strong anti-Zionist beliefs. The other pair were understood to be members of the PFLP. They were almost right.

The audacious hijacking of Flight 139 was masterminded by one Wadie Haddad aka Abu Hani who, after being expelled from the PFLP in 1973 for striking outside Israel, formed his own splinter cell: PFLP-EO or External Operations. However, he was not without considerable support. Late into the African afternoon those inside the old terminal were visited by the imposing figure of Ugandan dictator Idi Amin-Dada.

Accompanied by countless Ugandan soldiers, Amin blustered into the abandoned building and duplicitously shook the hands of the terrorists before declaring himself saviour to the souls held captive. The medal-bedecked monster responsible for the slaughter of a reported 300,000 of his countrymen throughout his reign had once been a close ally of Israel. However, a refusal to supply him Phantom jet fighters with which to bomb neighbouring Kenya and Tanzania in 1972, led Amin to cut all ties with his friends in Zion and form an alliance with Gaddafi, aligning himself with the Palestine cause.

## DEMANDS AND DIVISION

Before the Ugandan tyrant left the hostages to their continued suffering he spoke of a deadline, though the true extent of its meaning was not made fully aware until Tuesday 29 July; day three of the ordeal. Broadcast via Uganda's Radio Kampala, the hijackers' demanded the liberation of fifty-three political prisoners from jails throughout Israel, France, Germany, Switzerland and Kenya together with a $5 million ransom to be paid by the French Government. Those concerned had until two o'clock on

Thursday afternoon to comply whereupon the terrorists would begin killing their hostages.

Over 2,500 miles away in Jerusalem Israeli Prime Minister Yitzhak Rabin and his cabinet analysed their options. With a rescue mission in such a distant land deemed unrealistic, the statesmen voted unanimously to negotiate, at least until sufficient intelligence could be gathered to assure a successful strike. While Mossad obtained drawings of the old terminal, Israeli military officers focused on potential incursion strategies in case negotiations proved ineffective.

Back in the old terminal, consumed by fear and fatigue, the hostages played cards and other games to take their minds off the excruciating boredom. Some hostages not engrossed in play witnessed the two German rebels begin separating the confiscated passports into two piles. At six o'clock that evening, this division became all too clear. In a chilling throwback to the Nazi selection process, the two German terrorists began calling out Jewish names and had those summoned escorted to a separate area of the building.

## TIME TO PLAN

Over the next two days those singled out for segregation, within what they coined the Room of Separation, saw all the other non-Jewish hostages leave Entebbe for Orly Airport in Paris where they were reunited with friends and relatives. The only non-Israeli captives to remain at the old terminal were Captain Bacos and his crew who had vowed to remain with their passengers until the very end.

Back in Israel, the families of the remaining 107 hostages began to show their frustration at their government's lack of action, insisting more be done to bring their loved ones home. Rabin turned once more to the Israeli Defence Forces for a suitable plan but none was forthcoming. They needed more time.

Fortuitously, their wish was granted. On deadline day of the hostage crisis, the terrorists pushed back their threats of execution to eleven o'clock Sunday morning. The extension had been given at the request of Idi Amin who was due to attend a meeting of the Organisation for African Unity in Mauritius at zero hour. As its president, such high-profile killings on Ugandan soil would seriously undermine his position and the aims of the African coalition.

Recognising there was no way they could accede to the militants' demands and release their list of prisoners even with a three day extension, the IDF began to brainstorm a viable plan of attack. After considering a parachute drop into the crocodile-infested waters of Lake Victoria, the military's top brass submitted their strategy for a hostage rescue to the Israeli cabinet at five o'clock Thursday afternoon.

## OPERATION THUNDERBOLT

The hastily-fashioned and high-risk proposition entailed four C-130 Hercules aircraft to fly over hostile territory and make a direct landing at Entebbe Airport under cover of darkness. Thirty commandos from an elite special forces unit called Sayeret Matkal supported by two hundred infantrymen from the 35th Airborne Brigade would be charged with taking out the terrorists and leading the hostages to safety. While those involved rehearsed every possible scenario upon a full-scale model of the old terminal, Rabin and his leading ministers debated day and night, discussing the ramifications of this audacious mission.

To buy more time, a report was leaked declaring Israel was prepared to release the terrorists' comrades which brought a wave of celebration among the militants at Entebbe. As the hostage-takers chugged from champagne bottles, the imprisoned Jews prepared to observe the Sabbath, lighting matches instead of their usual candles, praying for an end to their suffering.

As the sun came up on Saturday morning, the secret session had yet to come to a decision on whether or not to authorise the operation codenamed Thunderbolt. Time was running out. To strike Entebbe by midnight, the planes needed to be airborne by three o'clock so, to keep the mission alive, the IDF chose to leave for Uganda while the cabinet deliberated.

With the aerial armada on course for Entebbe, its permission to strike as yet undetermined, Idi Amin paid his final visit to the old terminal. In an outpouring of mock sincerity, the Ugandan leader informed the hostages he had tried his best to effect their release. Blaming the Israeli Government for the breakdown in negotiations, Amin confirmed that, thanks to this immovable stalemate and the fast-approaching deadline, he could no longer save them from their inevitable executions.

## SITUATION TERMINAL

Flying under radar in strict radio silence, the battle-ready soldiers within the four military aircraft suffered a terrible seven-hour journey punctuated by bouts of severe vomiting. In this collective air of anxiety only their mission leader, Lieutenant Yonatan Netanyahu, appeared unaffected, sleeping soundly as the Hercules rumbled low over the Red Sea. Then the call came from Jerusalem; Operation Thunderbolt had been approved.

Expecting to have to land in a black-out – a feat never before attempted in a C-130 Hercules – lead pilot Joshua Shani was relieved to see the landing lights on the Entebbe runway were still on. Touching down just before midnight a mere 100 metres from the terminal, one black Mercedes followed by two Land Rovers exited the rear of the first aircraft. The vehicle of choice for African dignitaries such as Amin, the Mercedes was hoped to confuse Ugandan soldiers into firing salutes rather than gunshots.

This cover appeared to fool two sentries who were swiftly taken out by silenced weapons however as they passed their bodies one began to rise. Fearing the survivor would raise the alarm, soldiers in the trailing MPVs opened fire with unsilenced rifles. The immediate threat suppressed, these loud reports alerted the terrorists to their arrival and, fifty metres away, the elite Israeli commandos had to engage the enemy without the element of surprise.

Despite this drawback, the highly-trained Sayaret Matkal managed to secure the main holding area inside the old terminal in a matter of minutes, taking out seven terrorists including the two German rebels in a frenzied assault. Three of the hostages also lost their lives that night. Both Pascal Cohen and Ida Borrovits were caught in the crossfire while a third captive, Jean-Jacques Maimoni, was mistaken for a terrorist. As he jumped to his feet hoping to be saved, the eighteen-year-old prisoner was shot and killed by an Israeli marksman.

As the infantry shielded the hostages to the waiting rescue aircraft, the mission took one final blow. Their attack leader, Netanyahu, had been hit in the back by a bullet fired by Ugandan soldiers in the control tower. Less than an hour after landing, the first hostage-laden Hercules left Entebbe bound for Nairobi. On the short flight to Kenya, doctors worked tirelessly on Netanyahu's wound but were unable to save his life.

## INDEPENDENCE DAY

Once all air transport had refuelled, the rescued Israelis returned to Ben Gurion Airport, welcomed by a sea of loved ones, well-wishers and reporters. The whole of Israel rejoiced, declaring the raid on Entebbe a unequivocal success despite the loss of its leader and hostages who now numbered four. Seventy-five-year-old Dora Bloch had been taken to hospital in Kampala after choking on food during the ordeal and so had not been saved by the Israeli invasion. As the Jewish passengers of Flight 139 touched down in Tel Aviv on Sunday 4 July, news came of Dora's demise. Thirty minutes after a British consul had visited her in hospital, members of the Ugandan secret police, under direct orders from Amin, had dragged her body from the infirmary and executed the old lady.

Aside from this horrific act of reprisal, the day was a happy one. While Fourth of July festivities took place thousands of miles away in the United States,

Israel and its recovered citizens celebrated their very own Independence Day. Two years later, having managed to escape death at the old terminal, the mastermind of the whole affair Wadie Haddad lost a second battle; this one to cancer. In 1979, the oppressive rule of Idi Amin also came to an end and he was forced into exile. This facilitated the recovery of Dora Bloch's remains found twenty miles east of Kampala which were buried with state honours in Jerusalem. Lastly, in a fitting tribute to the man who lost his life so the hostages could live, the triumphant rescue mission was renamed Operation Yonatan.

# ALDO MORO

The 1978 ambush and abduction of one of Italy's greatest politicians in the busy streets of Rome began a chain of events that would turn a political nightmare into a conspiracy theorist's dream. Held hostage for fifty-five days, Aldo Moro would become a Cold War casualty and the victim of an international plot involving the world's major powers in a political hostage crisis which still haunts the Italian nation to this day.

## A CALL FOR COMPROMISE

Born on 23 September 1916 in the small town of Maglie in south-east Italy, Aldo Moro was raised a devout Catholic. Religion continued to play a major part throughout his early years attending church youth groups and, after studying law at the University of Bari, being made president of the Federation of Catholic University Students.

This position was his first foray into politics and, after the Second World War, Moro was elected to the

Constituent Assembly helping to draft the new Italian constitution. A series of cabinet posts including Minister of Justice and then Education followed his membership to the Christian Democratic Party and in 1959 he became the party leader. Four years later Moro led his party to election victory forming the first centre-left government – a coalition with the Socialist Party – and as Prime Minister he sought to create a balance to Italian politics through unity among parties.

During the 1970s, when he enjoyed a second spell as Prime Minister, Aldo Moro developed into a master of compromise. While not the greatest orator, he became a highly-skilled mediator able to help discordant factions find common ground. He forged a strong partnership with Enrico Berlinguer the leader of the PCI – the Italian Communist Party – and together they pursued a project of solidarity between the Christian Democrats and the Communists.

The project became known as the Historical Compromise which called for all political forces to come together during the economic and social crisis of the time rather than persist with personal party struggles. This focused pursuit for stability was to cause widespread discontent and only hours before a major step towards its completion was to be taken, its opponents struck with deadly force.

## THE KEY EVENTS

On the morning of Thursday 16 March 1978 as the Italian Parliament prepared for the start of a new era – the first western European power to invite Communism into its fold – Aldo Moro left his Roman home on the Via del Forte to attend the key event. Riding in the backseat of a blue Fiat 130 along with a police driver and bodyguard in the front, Moro's car was followed close behind by a police escort; three undercover policemen in an Alfa Romeo.

As Moro and his entourage made their way through morning rush hour traffic on the Via Fani, a white Fiat estate pulled out in front of the two-car convoy forcing them to stop. All of a sudden two gunmen burst from the offending vehicle and opened fire on the Fiat killing the front passengers instantly. Next a second group of terrorists dressed in Alitalia flight uniforms who had been waiting at the corner pulled out automatic weapons and targeted the Alfa Romeo. One of the policemen managed to get off three rounds until a well-placed bullet to the forehead ended all resistance.

With his five-man protection all dead, one of the terrorists calmly removed Moro from his car and led him to a light-blue Fiat 132 parked further down the street. Seconds later the former Prime Minister and his kidnappers had vanished and the first calls to the police alerted the world of this vicious ambush. Meanwhile Moro was taken to a secret hideout in the south of the city where his abductors imprisoned him in a rented first-floor apartment behind a crude partition wall. There they revealed their identities; they were members of a revolutionary band of left-wing terrorists known as *Brigate Rosse* – The Red Brigades.

## THE RED BRIGADES

This group was notorious throughout Italy having terrorised the nation during what became known as the Years of Lead; a series of attacks in which countless bullets were fired and many victims were wounded or worse. Founded by sociology scholar Renato Curcio and Alberto Franceschini in 1970, the group was a platform for their fashionable Marxist-Leninist beliefs and together they sought to bring down the imperialist state through an increasing level of violence.

Many young Italians agreed with Curcio and his Communist collective. With unemployment affecting 1.6 million Italians of which half were under the age of thirty, the Italian youth felt betrayed by their government. Those who held the ideological views of Marxism-Leninism found little to lift their hearts in the Italian Communist Party which had become too large and hopelessly compromised thanks to its accord with the Christian Democrats. This disaffected generation needed a champion to fight their corner and found one in the extremist Red Brigades.

The movement began with a wave of machinery sabotage and arson attacks on factories but soon upgraded to kidnapping. Plant managers were abducted and subjected to 'people's trials' in which they were harangued by their extremist captors before being released. Then in September 1974 Curcio and Franceschini were arrested leaving the five hundred-strong resistance movement under the control of their combat unit leader Mario Moretti.

This change in leadership brought a more aggressive tone to the actions of the Red Brigades. A strategy of tension was pursued in which the organisation expanded throughout Italy and began taking more prominent hostages and administering a higher level of brutality. Italy became the terror capital of the Western world as the brigatisti targeted synagogues, political centres and professionals such as lawyers, policemen, judges and junior executives in a bid to foment chaos from which to start a civil war.

## BUSINESS AS USUAL

Incarcerated in his makeshift cell in South Rome, Moro underwent the routine mock-trial, relentless recriminations hurled at him from his radical captors.

A day or two after the abduction the kidnappers sent a Polaroid of their captive along with a typewritten message to the Il Messaggero newspaper and the RAI TV station. The communiqué made no direct demands but informed the press that Moro was alive and under interrogation for crimes against the people.

A further statement finally brought the first specific requirement for the release of Aldo Moro. The Red Brigades wished for thirteen members of their movement to be freed from prison. These included Curcio and Franceschini who were behind bars in a Torinese military camp awaiting trial for a series of kidnappings, assassinations and other subversive crimes.

The abduction of the two-time Prime Minister shocked the nation. Trade unions threatened to strike and even the Mafia issued their own severe warning to the kidnappers: failure to release Moro would bring reprisals against the imprisoned brigatisti. Despite this irrefusable offer the left-wing extremists held on to their captive and continued with their communiqués, denouncing both the Communists and the Democrats and calling for proletarian justice.

Meanwhile the Italian Parliament was forced to decide quickly on what action should be taken. It agreed a tough line against the terrorists was called for and Prime Minister Giulio Andreotti announced there would be no negotiations with the Red

Brigades. With this he called for a vote of confidence and within hours the Christian Democrat leader received the highest majority in post-war Italy. As the parties closed ranks, Andreotti made it clear it was business as usual attending meetings on the economy and even attending a summit in Copenhagen. It seemed this rebel attempt to divide and conquer government had resulted in quite the reverse.

## SEARCH FOR MORO

Instead of bargaining with the terrorists, the authorities implemented the largest post-war manhunt with up to fifty thousand police and Carabinieri drafted in to find the missing statesman. Rome was cordoned off by concentric rings of roadblocks and over three thousand searches were made over twenty square miles focusing on garages and basements. Despite this exhaustive search the Italian mediator remained lost and, as hopes dimmed, the only saving grace to be found was the marked reduction in crime owing to the high police presence on the streets.

After a host of dead-end leads threatened to hamstring the investigation a series of strange events breathed new life into the search for Aldo Moro. On Tuesday 18 April Moretti's apartment was discovered on the Via Gradoli after a water leak was reported by his downstairs neighbour. Moretti was not at home but the raiding party did find weapons strewn about the Red Brigade residence. Ominously, the water came from the bathtub which had been rigged to overflow.

On the same day another communiqué was delivered to authorities stating Moro was dead and his body had been dumped in Lake Duchessa high in the Apennine Mountains. Frogmen were despatched to the frozen lake but their search came up empty. The death-relaying note was a fake. When the kidnappers heard the news of this fraudulent claim they realised someone was trying to undermine their position. Declaring Moro's death subtly removed the Red Brigade's advantage by lessening the impact of the real thing if and when it occurred.

Two days later the hostage-takers released an authentic statement to the press along with another photograph of Moro posing with a copy of a headline reporting his demise. A new deadline of forty-eight hours was given for their comrades to be released or they would execute their captive. The discovery of the Via Gradoli hideout together with the fake communiqué had forced the Red Brigades to make their death threats a grim reality.

## MORO MURDERED

Throughout his incarceration, Aldo Moro had been permitted to write letters to his family and colleagues.

As his government continued to stand firm against any form of deal-making, the veteran master of political compromise quickly realised his fate. After his handwritten pleas to open negotiations with the revolutionary movement were seemingly ignored, he confessed to feeling abandoned by his peers.

Andreotti and his aides had a clear response to these heart-wrenching letters that filled the Italian newspapers throughout the ordeal. They believed the notes were written under duress and even suggested he was being fed mind-altering drugs by his captors. His final letter showed no sign of force but appeared lucid and sane. Resigned to a doomed end, he wrote his last goodbyes to his wife Eleonora and four children, telling them to stay strong.

On Tuesday 9 May after nearly eight weeks in captivity the sixty-one-year-old politician was taken into the garage of their safe house and executed, shot eleven times in the chest by a Czech-made pistol. Later that day authorities received an anonymous call directing them to the Via Michelangelo Caetani, a narrow street off the Via Delle Botteghe-Oscure in Rome. There the police were informed they would find a red Renault 4 containing the body of Aldo Moro. Sadly this was no hoax. As a final insult the corpse-carrying car had been symbolically parked midway between the headquarters of both the

Christian Democrats and the Italian Communist Party.

In the following weeks two separate funeral services were held to honour the life of Aldo Moro. The first was private and attended by family and close friends. In one of his letters from captivity he had requested no members of his political party be present at the village cemetery in Torrita Tiberina thirty miles north of Rome. They observed his request however on Saturday 20 May a televised state funeral was held in Rome's Cathedral of St John Lateran allowing the world to witness their sadness at the loss of one of Italy's political giants.

## PLOT TWISTS

Several years passed until the Moro's abductors were brought to justice. In February 1983 a jury found Mario Moretti and others guilty of the kidnap-murder and harsh prison terms were handed down. Moretti, the leader, who would later confess in his memoirs to being the sole interrogator and executioner of Aldo Moro, received six consecutive life sentences. He would serve just fifteen years securing parole in 1998.

In the thirty years since the killing of Aldo Moro considerable evidence has emerged to shed light on some of the peculiar anomalies that existed during the ordeal. For example, in 2008 former US envoy Steve Pieczenik came forward to admit his involvement in the death of the Italian Democrat. Sent by President Carter, Pieczenik was part of a global crisis committee led by Italian Interior Minister Cossiga which feared Moro would reveal state secrets to gain his freedom. The diplomat confessed to writing the false April communiqué proclaiming Moro's death as part of an international plot to sacrifice the man to maintain a stable Italy.

Moro's mission to provide Communism with a high chair at the top table of Italian politics had met with widespread disapproval. Communist Russia objected to Berlinguer's compromise believing it would weaken their cause whilst the Christian Democrats were loathe to share power. In addition the United States feared their fellow NATO power would pose a severe security threat to the alliance if communists were given authority in the Italian Parliament. Opposition from all these areas have since provided conspiracy theorists with viable proof that the murder of Aldo Moro was carefully orchestrated by higher powers with the fearsome Red Brigades mere puppets in this deadly game.

## THE DEAD BRIGADES

As for the revolutionary movement officially held culpable for Moro's murder, support for their cause fell drastically after the nightmare in Rome. They were forced deeper underground and thus became distanced from their blue-collar following. Attacks became sporadic and after a peak of nearly two thousand five hundred violent offensives in 1978 they had ebbed to 603 in 1982.

Events during this decade proved to spell the end of the Red Brigades. Police had focused their attention on capturing its principal players in an attempt to dismantle the shadowy extremist group once and for all. Those arrested were quick to retract their once firmly-held beliefs and began to give up their comrades in exchange for commuted sentences.

Nearly twelve thousand brigatisti were detained in a hugely successful operation which saw those who slipped through the police dragnet flee to France or South America. Greatly reduced and hopelessly divided, the Red Brigades split into two factions in 1984 and soon after even their imprisoned leaders showed signs their passion for the struggle was abating. Impetus lost and leadership missing, the formerly feared Brigate Rosse dissolved in 1988. While a few random cells remained to execute several attacks into the 21st century, there was nothing quite like the Moro affair to instil terror into the Italian government.

# THE IRANIAN EMBASSY SIEGE

A six day stand-off over the Bank holiday weekend in May 1980 saw half a dozen gunmen take twenty-six hostages at London's Iranian Embassy in a bid to highlight their disaffected country's political plight. During what became essential viewing for millions of TV audiences around the world, a crack team of the Special Air Service was deployed to rescue those inside and bring the ordeal to a successful conclusion.

## EMBASSY TAKEOVER

On the last day of April 1980 at around 11.30 in the morning, six men entered the Iranian Embassy at Prince's Gate in the prosperous London district of South Kensington with guns and grenades under their jackets and political terrorism on their minds. The arrival of these armed activists shattered what had been a quiet Wednesday morning as they quickly took control of the building and those inside.

155

The first to encounter the extremists was forty-one year old Metropolitan policeman Trevor Lock who was on security detail for the Diplomatic Protection Group. Taking a quick coffee break from guard duty outside the embassy he watched the half-dozen hostiles arrive and thought them to be students. All of a sudden machine gunfire filled the room.

In the ensuing chaos some employees were quick to act, escaping through various exits before the six gunmen gained complete control of the building. Twenty-six hostages were taken, predominantly Iranian embassy officials, although there were three other Britons detained along with PC Lock. Ronald Morris, a forty-seven-year-old embassy official, was caught up in the attack together with two members of the BBC: journalist Chris Cramer and sound recordist Simeon Harris who were there to pick up visas for an imminent visit to Iran.

Inside the building the six kidnappers made their hostages sit in a circle on the floor. Dressed in full uniform Trevor Lock was made a figure of authority and told to sit on a Queen Anne chair. Placed reluctantly on this throne, the policeman endeavoured to compose himself after being searched by one of the gunmen. Somehow they had managed to miss the service revolver underneath his jacket. Burdened by this secret, Lock would constantly agonise over when or indeed if he should use his gun in this highly volatile situation.

## THE HOSTAGE-TAKERS

As the twenty-six hostages sat awaiting their fate, they wondered who these six armed men were and what reasons they had for their aggressive actions. Soon all would become clear. The Metropolitan Police quickly established a line of communication with the terrorists and negotiations began to bring the situation to a swift and clean end.

They soon learned the hostage-takers were anti-Khomeini Iranians demonstrating against the oppression of the new ruler or Shah of Iran. They belonged to a small petroleum-rich province located in the south of the Islamic Republic called Khuzestan whose inhabitants desired autonomy. Believing promises of such freedom had been reneged by the Ayatollah Khomeini after he had come to power, this small cadre of revolutionaries now wanted to redress these forgotten pledges.

Calling themselves the Democratic Revolutionary Front for Arabistan (their preferred name for Khuzestan) these six armed men were led by Awn Ali Mohammed who called himself Salim. He was the sole English speaker of the group and so became their contact with police outside. Once trained negotiators had calmed down the excitable Salim, he conveyed their demands for the release of the embassy and those held hostage inside. The Arabistani movement wanted ninety-one of their comrades liberated from Iranian prisons, a bus to transport them to Heathrow airport where a plane would take them to an un-specified destination and to speak directly with ambassadors from Iraq, Jordan and Algeria.

## INTELLIGENCE NEEDED

While negotiators attempted to glean the gunmen's motivation and aspirations, the government's crisis committee named COBRA discussed the various options available to them in dealing with the embassy capture. One of their first decisions was to mobilise an SAS counter-terrorist team from its headquarters in Hereford in readiness for an attack if events got out of control. As the elite squad raced their kit-laden Range Rovers east to the capital, attempts were made to acquire some much needed intelligence.

The authorities knew what the terrorists wanted but little else so the MI5 began drilling holes in the embassy walls through which to insert eavesdropping devices. This surveillance work was soon overheard by the Arab extremists who called for the drilling to cease. Authorities then created a blanket of noise using construction tools and even asking passing aircraft overhead to fly low to hide the sound of the MI5 drills.

Even with the audio bugs in place, the SAS needed more information on what was occurring inside the embassy if they were to mount an effective assault. On the second day of the siege they received accurate details from one of the British hostages. BBC journalist Chris Cramer was suffering from stomach pains during the ordeal and agreed with his fellow Britons to exaggerate his distress. A convincing performance from the pressman bought his freedom whereupon he was able to provide the counter-terrorist force with crucial information on the embassy layout, the hostages and their takers.

Cramer's intelligence brought forward a potential rescue operation. On day three of the siege the SAS squadron performed a reconnaissance operation which discovered a domed skylight on the roof – a potential entry point – and as the terrorists' identities came through from the Foreign Office, an SAS strike awaited approval. The COBRA committee, however, chose to shelve the attack feeling an act of belligerence could occur only after the terrorists had resorted to violence. Until that time the negotiators would lead the way in resolving the hostage situation.

## NEGOTIATIONS DETERIORATE

Soon after the Democratic Revolutionary Front for Arabistan delivered their demands, the British government decided there would be no acquiescence on their part. Likewise, the Iranian Foreign Minister had already made it clear none of the ninety-one political prisoners would be moved from their jail cells. With each passing day the police negotiators managed to obtain the release of a number of hostages including pregnant Hiyech Kanji without providing any genuine assurances to the Iranian militants. By Sunday 4 May – the penultimate day of the siege – five of the twenty-six captives were free and yet the six gunmen were still awaiting completion of just one demand. This poor return was beginning to grate on the now-frustrated activists.

Now into the ordeal's sixth day, Salim knew he had failed in his mission to procure their demands through peaceful negotiation. It was time to bring the situation to a head. At eleven o'clock in the morning of Bank Holiday Monday, Salim forced Trevor Lock to inform authorities that a hostage would be shot if no news about their requested Arab ambassador was forthcoming. Police attempted to mollify the raised level of antagonism with promises that talks were in progress. The attempt failed.

The gunmen singled out Abbas Lavasani, a twenty-nine-year-old press attaché. It had not been difficult for them to choose their first victim. For days Lavasani had been vocal in his hatred of the men and in his support for the Ayatollah. His fellow hostages pleaded for him to remain quiet but his political conviction could not be dampened. Salim's second-in-command, a man called Faisal, grabbed the press attaché and had him tied to a banister on the ground floor. Offering no resistance, a martyr to his own cause, Lavasani was shot three times.

The gunfire had been heard by those outside but without a body authorities could not be sure if anyone had come to harm. Nearly seven hours later the deceased Lavasani was dumped on the embassy steps. Now the British government had proof of murder and could make its move. Prime Minister Margaret Thatcher gave the go-ahead for a show of force; the Iranian Embassy siege had now become a military operation.

## EMBASSY SMOKES

The SAS squadron had been impatiently waiting for a call to arms. At seven minutes past seven the confirmation came; there would now be an incursion on the embassy. Operation Nimrod was a go. While the negotiators stalled the terrorists for time, the counter-revolutionary force would execute their deliberate action plan: five teams through four entry points in a bid to free the twenty hostages.

Within minutes the infamous black shapes swarmed 16 Prince's Gate and, thanks to the constant TV coverage, millions of Britons who had tuned in to watch the Embassy World Snooker Final were now bombarded with live footage of the attack. Instead of black-suited sportsmen holding cues they witnessed black-clad SAS troopers bearing arms, abseiling down the embassy's white exterior.

With Salim busy talking with the negotiators on the field telephone the troopers silently took up their positions. All of a sudden there came the sound of broken glass distracting Salim from his phone conversation. One of the SAS commandos had accidentally put his foot through a window whilst rappelling down the outside wall. With the mission compromised, the need for stealth was over and at 19.23 hours the team at the skylight detonated their explosive charges to disorientate the terrorists within.

All teams on all sides were given the green light to engage the embassy. The power was cut and stun grenades thrown turning the building into a full-scale war zone. Soon fire and smoke could be seen billowing from the windows. Chaos and disorder reigned as the troopers endeavoured to tell hostage from hostile. Highlighting the havoc which played out on TV screens across the world, SAS staff sergeant Tak Takavesi managed to become entangled in his abseiling ropes. Before his colleagues could cut him free, the helpless soldier swung dangerously into the flames that had caught the curtains of the closest window. Escaping with only minor burns, Takavesi dropped to the safety of the balcony.

## SAS RESCUE

Meanwhile, inside the embassy, the SAS teams searched the many rooms for the captives to lead them to freedom. Intelligence told them the majority of the hostages were being held in the telex room up on the second floor. As troopers closed in on the area, two of the terrorists opened fire on the fourteen prisoners killing one and wounding another. When the SAS team burst in on the telex room, their Heckler & Koch submachine guns at the ready, they found the two activists sat on the floor in surrender. Apparently their captives had persuaded them to give up. To the elite soldiers whose only aim was to protect the lives of the hostages, their capitulation meant nothing and the pair of murderous militants were promptly placed up against a wall and shot.

On the first floor Trevor Lock was having his own battle with Salim, the leader of the Khuzestani terrorists. Spotting the chief gunman making a break for a window, the policeman tackled him to the ground and finally drew his revolver which he held to Salim's head. The hostage-taker was stunned at this audacious move but Lock was unable to pull the trigger. All of a sudden SAS trooper Tom Palmer appeared who called for Trevor to get clear. Seconds later Salim lay dead, a line of bullet holes across his body. For his part in bringing down the terrorist threat, PC Lock was later awarded the George Cross.

Whilst one Briton was busy fighting the militant menace, another had managed to make it to the front balcony window, fighting back the flames consuming the room he was in. Simeon Harris, the BBC sound-man, was able to climb across to an adjacent town-house and a waiting SAS team led him to safety.

With five of the six terrorists accounted for, the elite squadron began evacuating the hostages down the main staircase. Forming a human chain, the soldiers passed the embassy victims down to the ground floor. Plastic cable ties were placed around their wrists before being escorted out to the rear garden where they were laid spread-eagled on the grass.

During the mass exodus John 'Mac' McAleese, one of the SAS team at the top of the staircase, spotted one of the terrorists masquerading as a hostage. He was able to signal to his colleague, Pete Winner, who struck the escaping activist with his gun on reaching the foot of the stairs. He was dispensed with in the same blunt fashion; a burst of gunfire ending his life and his bid for freedom. As the body hit the ground, a grenade rolled from the dead man's hand. No explosion followed. The terrorist had failed to remove the pin.

With the embassy clear, the rescue team performed a head count discovering they had one too many hostages lying prone on the grass. While the SAS had successfully prevented one hostage-taker from leaving the building, one Fowzi Nejad had managed to pass by unnoticed. With the world watching it was now too late to return the devious activist to the building to meet the fate of his fellow comrades.

## THE AFTERMATH

In less than fifteen minutes the crack SAS unit had successfully brought an end to the embassy siege, rescuing nineteen of the twenty hostages inside. Thanks to the live coverage of the daylight assault broadcast around the world, the event quickly established the SAS as the world's most able military unit. Retiring to the Regent's Park Barracks, the squadron received a visit from the Prime Minister and her husband who collectively praised the unit's deadly efficiency despite Denis's annoyance at the survival of one perpetrator.

Fowzi Nejad, the sole surviving hostage-taker, was swiftly convicted for his involvement in the embassy attack and sentenced to life in prison for conspiracy to murder, false imprisonment and several other lesser charges. Expressing remorse for his actions through-out his incarceration, Nejad was deemed as no longer a threat to society by his parole board and freed in November 2008. Unable to obtain Iranian guarantees that their released prisoner would not suffer torture or worse if deported back to Iran, the British Foreign Office had no choice but to grant Nejad political asylum. Now in his fifties, the once-radical activist resides in a government hostel under a late-night curfew; his hopes for an independent Arabistan still yet to materialise nearly thirty years on.

# THE IRANIAN
# HOSTAGE CRISIS
# 1979–1981

In November 1979 over sixty Americans found themselves held hostage on home soil yet thousands of miles from their motherland when a band of disaffected students stormed the United States Embassy in Iran. With diplomats and officials tortured and tormented inside the ambassadorial complex for 444 days this shocking violation of international law snowballed into a global crisis which would forever alter relations between the two nations.

## DEMONSTRATION OF FORCE

After a summer made hotter by rising tension in the Muslim nation of Iran, a passionate engineering student named Ibrahim Asgharzadeh began plotting to strike out at the growing foreign interference in his beloved country's affairs. Meeting with four other fervent scholars, a debate ensued to decide which enemy they should target. Should it be their Communist neighbours, the Soviet Union, believed to be a growing threat in Iran or the United States for years of intrusive acts dating back to the Second World War? A vote was cast and a decision was made; their chosen target would be the US Embassy in Tehran, the nation's capital.

Asgharzadeh and his fellow ringleaders gathered a trusted band of over three hundred students in the early hours of Sunday morning – 4 November – for what appeared to be just another student demonstration down Taleghani Street. The mass crowds of academics marched their way down to the American embassy holding aloft their banners emblazoned with anti-Western slogans and the image of the Ayatollah. It was then that Asgharzadeh gave the order to strike.

Immediately a female accomplice, who had been given a pair of bolt cutters, retrieved them from beneath her chador and cut the chains on the embassy gates. Simultaneously, the throng of scholars began to scale the walls forcing the US Marines guarding the compound to raise their rifles. Such was the sheer number of protesters that the American soldiers were unable to fire and the mob quickly disarmed the embassy defence.

Meanwhile the acting embassy chief, Bruce

Laingen, was finishing a meeting at the Foreign Ministry when he was informed of the invasion. Allowing his officials enough time to shred any offending secret documents, Laingen gave the order for the embassy to surrender. Once the chaos had subsided and a number of escaping diplomats were returned to the twenty-seven-acre compound, the ringleaders of the attack stepped forward and introduced themselves as the Muslim Student Followers of the Imam's Line. Planning to hold their hostages for a short period of time, Asgharzadeh and his scholastic cell of activists conveyed their reasons for the demonstration dating back over twenty-five years.

## CIA COUP

Iran's relationship with the United States began during the Second World War when the Allied Powers took control of the country to prevent the Axis alliance prevailing. Mohammed Reza Pahlavi was swiftly installed as a pro-Western Shah, however. When Mohammad Mossadegh and his democratic party took control in 1953 forcing the US pawn to flee to Rome, the United States decided to intervene.

Fearing the Mossadegh government had Communist ties, the CIA were called upon to stage a coup. Codenamed Operation Ajax, Kermit Roosevelt Junior was sent to Iran to create national chaos and overthrow the incumbent regime. After fomenting sufficient insurgent feeling, an angry mob besieged Mossadegh's residence on the night of 19 August 1953 forcing the Prime Minister to flee the country leaving the way clear for Pahlavi to return to the Peacock Throne.

With the Shah back in power, Iran became a strong American ally against the Soviet Union throughout the Cold War period and received billions of dollars' worth of economic and military aid from the United States. However, the Iranian people were living in increasing fear and with considerable hatred of the reinstated ruler whose secret intelligence force, called SAVAK, terrorised and tortured his opponents. As a result, the anti-Shah Iranians despised the United States and blamed its direct association with their dictator for their troubles.

This emergent animosity developed throughout the sixties and seventies culminating in what became known as the Iranian Revolution in January 1979. Once more Shah Pahlavi was forced into exile allowing Iran's spiritual leader Ayatollah Khomeini – himself exiled in Paris for fourteen years – to take control. His return brought millions of anti-Shah nationals out into the streets to rejoice and he quickly declared Iran an Islamic Republic.

That autumn an unhealthy decision made by a

naive US government sparked fear and a need to act in our select cell of Iranian students. The deposed Shah banished from his homeland requested entry into the United States to undergo cancer treatment at the Mayo Clinic in New York. Despite the embassy in Tehran warning against such an impacting entreaty, President Carter chose to ignore the advice and admitted the political friend on 22 October. This sent paranoic tremors through the hearts of many Iranians who feared another US-backed plot to bring back the hated Shah as ruler.

## 'DEATH TO AMERICA'

This fear of a repeat American intrusion and general discontent with the years of oppressive rule by the Shah had led the Iranian students to take action. However, what began as a simple protest demonstration quickly evolved into a revolutionary uprising. From his spiritual throne in the city of Qum eighty miles from Tehran, Khomeini gave the rebellion his blessing calling it the Second Revolution and dubbing the embassy a nest of spies. Busloads of supporters descended on the scene and began burning the Stars and Stripes and defacing the embassy walls, chanting 'Death To America'.

Buoyed by this unswerving swell of public support, the hostage-takers settled in for a lengthy occupation.

They formed committees to handle the custody of their captives and volunteers were hand-picked to stand guard. Others were given the thankless task of reassembling the shredded documents to find proof of an American plot.

Asgharzadeh and his fellow extremists then declared their intentions to the world's press. They had taken a total of sixty-six hostages – three of which were being held at the Foreign Ministry – who would remain in their charge until the Shah was returned to stand trial in Iran. In addition, the students demanded the United States issue a public apology for its interference in Iranian affairs.

## ANTI FREEZE AND OIL PRESSURE

Rocked by this unforeseen assault on their Tehran embassy, the White House attempted to open up negotiations with the Iranian Prime Minister Mehdi Bazargan. However, after just two days of the crisis, the leader of the provisional government resigned, stating his party was no longer in control of the nation; Khomeini and his Muslim clerics were now pulling the political strings. President Carter then sent former Attorney General Ramsey Clark to Iran for talks but on arrival was refused an audience with the Ayatollah.

With all avenues of discussion closed to Carter's administration, the United States was forced to apply some economic and diplomatic pressure upon their former ally. A shipment of military spare parts bought by the Shah for $300 million was prevented from travelling to Iran and on 12 November all US oil imports from the Persian nation ceased. Two days later the President gave Executive Order 12170 which saw $7.9 billion of Iranian assets held in American banks frozen in retaliation for the hostage-taking.

This pressure along with some astute negotiation by Secretary of State Cyrus Vance bought the release of a select number of the embassy hostages. By 20 November the Ayatollah liberated thirteen women and African-Americans, suggesting a bid to garner support from minority groups in the West. Despite this apparent conciliatory move, the Muslim ruler was quick to fan the flames of dissent towards the 'Great Satan' and maintain the surge of patriotism that the attack had created.

## ILL TREATMENT

While the divide between the two nations grew ever deeper, the fifty-three hostages held by the students and their supporters were tormented inside the vast embassy compound. Bound and blindfolded with ragged strips of cloth their only break from the confines of the windowless warehouse basement came when they were paraded before partisan press.

Despite their underground room – dubbed Mushroom Inn by the hostages – being used for communications equipment, they were forbidden to talk to one another, split up into makeshift cells by strategically-placed bookshelves.

Harsher treatment befell the higher-ranking officials. Some were placed in solitary confinement for weeks on end and experienced the thorough interrogation techniques of chief inquisitor Hussein Sheikh al-Islam including regularly-administered strikes from his rubber hose.

Brutality was not confined to physical violence. Sleeping on mats in their improvised cells four months into their imposed prison sentence the hostages were rudely awoken by masked figures who strip searched their disorientated victims before placing guns to their heads. After an agonising pause the guards then withdrew their weapons, laughing. This mock execution was purely for the students' amusement and thankfully was the only occasion this cruel form of torture was applied.

## OPERATION EAGLE CLAW

By the six month mark the White House was coming under increasing attack from its own people, accusing President Carter of a failure to orchestrate a resolution to the ordeal. Rather than the circuitous moves of expelling Iranian students and diplomats from the United States and the banning of commercial travel to Iran, there existed a call for more direct action. Following the advice of his National Security Advisor, Zbigniew Brzezinski, Carter agreed to a military strike codenamed Eagle Claw.

The plan was simple. A Delta Force unit under the command of Colonel Beckwith would fly into Tehran, blow a hole in the embassy wall, overcome the guards and lead the hostages to safety. Unfortunately, the tactical squad never even made it to the capital. On 24 April eight Sea Stallion helicopters flew from the USS *Nimitz* to a remote airstrip in the Great Salt Desert in eastern Iran where the aircraft would refuel. Due to technical faults only six made it to the Hercules C-130 refuelling planes; the mission was beset by problems and would only get worse.

Fully loaded and prepared for battle, the helicopters left the desert the following morning for their flight to Tehran. However, this second leg of the operation was hindered by a severe sandstorm preventing their ability to fly in formation and on schedule. With limited vision and further faulty parts risking the lives of his men, Colonel Beckwith urged his Commander-in-Chief to abort the mission. Carter concurred and the American transport were ordered to return to their desert base.

Back at their arid airfield, the aborted helicopters were in further need of fuel and began to position themselves above the C-130 planes to fill their tanks. As one of the Sea Stallions prepared to be replenished it managed to collide with a fuel-filled Hercules and crash, killing eight servicemen. The failed mission had become a fatal disaster. Forced to return to USS *Nimitz* leaving the burnt corpses of their comrades behind, the ill-fated operation was a tragic blow to the United States. However in Iran the fatal disaster was perceived as divine intervention against their satanic foe. Believing that the mission's intent was to assassinate Khomeini, his Muslim followers felt their leader and the revolution had the backing of Allah, reinforcing their faith and resolve.

## FREEDOM ONE, FREEDOM ALL

Denouncing the flawed operation as an act of war, Foreign Minister Sadeq Qotbzadeh was quick to foster thoughts of American invasion. Five months later the threat of war on Iranian soil became a reality. Realising Iran had lost its ally and protector, Iraq President Saddam Hussein took the opportunity to invade his oil-rich neighbour in September 1980. This was the start of eight years of fighting which impacted heavily on Iran. Draining finances and costing over half a million Iranian lives, the conflict put pressure on the Khomeini-backed student terrorists to negotiate with America.

Helped also by the death of the Shah in the summer, a better climate for talks between the discordant nations had developed. President Carter, who had failed to secure a second term in the White House after the November elections, focused all his efforts on obtaining the release of the fifty-two hostages (one had been released in July due to medical reasons) before his time in office came to an end. With the assistance of Algerian mediators led by Mohammed Ben Yahia an agreement was finally reached on 19 January 1981. In exchange for the immediate and wholesale release of the embassy prisoners, the United States consented to unfreeze Iranian assets, provide immunity from related lawsuits and gave its guarantee to desist from any future interference in Iranian affairs.

The following day brought two major events in United States history. Six minutes after Ronald Reagan was sworn in as the fortieth President, over six thousand miles away in Tehran the hostages were released. Flown on an Air Force Stratoliner code-named Freedom One, the fifty-two embassy officials, attachés and guards arrived at a New York airbase via Algeria to a heroes' welcome.

As for Iran and its hostage-takers, the future was

bleak. With the loss of their Western ally and the continuing war with Iraq, the Muslim nation suffered economic and political pains that took its toll on the Iranian people. With the death of the Ayatollah in 1989 the student ringleaders of the embassy occupation earned spells in prison affording them time to debate the successes and failures of their operation. Today the twenty-seven-acre site of the hostage-taking is home to the much-feared Revolutionary Guard, branded a terrorist organisation by the US, and also contains an anti-American museum. Its exhibits, along with the anti-West graffiti and defaced Statue of Liberty visible outside the compound, serve as a constant reminder of the student action that spiralled into an uncontrollable force majeure.

# WILLIAM BUCKLEY

Lebanon was a perilous place to be for anyone in the mid-eighties not least the station chief of the United States Embassy in Beirut, the country's capital. A relentless civil war between fanatical religious factions had destabilised the country since the mid-seventies and many who fought objected to US presence and involvement in their conflict. To make this point Islamist militants snatched the embassy head and highly-decorated war veteran from outside his home and held him hostage in March 1984.

## SECRET AGENT MAN

William Francis Buckley was born in Medford, Massachusetts on 30 May 1928. After finishing high school he joined the United States Army during which time he attended the Officers Candidate School and became a Second Lieutenant in Armour. Further training including Intelligence School at Oberammergau in Germany preceded service with the 1st Cavalry Division in the Korean War. With the armistice signed and the demilitarised zone in place he returned to America to complete his studies, graduating from Boston University with a Political Science degree. When the troubles in Vietnam erupted several years later, Buckley became embroiled once more in a war effort serving as a Senior Advisor to the South Vietnamese Army. In May 1969 the war veteran was promoted to Lieutenant-Colonel.

As well as this high-profile involvement in global conflicts Buckley had a secret career working for the Central Intelligence Agency. As early as 1955 he was employed on various clandestine assignments for the CIA which found him working in some of the world's most uncompromising political hotspots. Zaire, Cambodia, Egypt, Syria and Pakistan were all visited by Lieutenant-Colonel Buckley on covert missions of political importance to America throughout the sixties and seventies. Such dangerous work brought numerous honours. Two Purple Hearts, the Silver Star, the Meritorious Service Medal and the CIA-conferred Intelligence Star were just a few of the many awards bestowed upon this national hero.

His last post was to take over from Ken Haas as the Station Chief at the United States Embassy in Lebanon. Employed ostensibly as a political officer, Buckley worked under cover to re-establish the CIA station in Beirut after a suicide bomber had attacked the building on 18 April 1983. This assault was just one of the many violent reactions to the unwanted American involvement in Lebanon's Civil War which had been raging since 1975.

## KIDNAPPED

On Friday 16 March 1984 a group of shadowy Islamist terrorists supporting the Ayatollah Khomeini regime in Iran snatched the embassy chief from his apartment in West Beirut. This made Buckley the fourth person to be kidnapped by the Lebanese extremists in what was becoming a regular threat to Westerners in this war-torn and hopelessly-divided country.

The series of political hostage-takings had begun with the kidnapping of David Dodge – the acting vice-president of the American University of Beirut – on 19 July 1982. Despite Dodge being released a year later the militant menace was still very real in the Spring of 1984 when US journalist Jeremy Levin was taken hostage in the Lebanese capital. Less than ten days later Buckley found himself imprisoned in a secret hideaway.

It was a considerable period of time before the United States were given conclusive proof that their covert operative was alive and well. On Monday 28 January 1985 a videotape was released to *Visnews*, an international news agency, revealing he had survived his ten-month ordeal. Lasting less than a minute, the footage showed an ashen Buckley standing before a bare wall holding a copy of a Beirut newspaper dated 22 January 1985. After informing that his fellow hostages – Benjamin Weir and Jeremy Levin – were also doing well, he urged the US Government to take action for their quick release. Unbeknown to the three captives Reagan and his administration were already considering some drastic moves to effect their freedom.

## ARMS FOR HOSTAGES

The US Government had made the release of the American hostages their primary concern. While it wished for them all to be returned safely, the liberation of William Buckley was of paramount importance to United States security. With decades' worth of intelligence residing inside the head of their 'lost man', the integrity of the CIA was in jeopardy. Buckley had accumulated a wealth of secrets which could prove invaluable to the Muslim fundamentalists who held him and America wanted him back.

Three weeks after Buckley's kidnapping, Reagan had taken the first significant step in obtaining his release and those held hostage with him. By signing a breakdown of options called the National Security Decision Directive 138, the President had put into motion a plan that would see America involved in selling military hardware in exchange for the freedom of its captive countrymen.

The Directive uncovered a means by which the American Government could use their resources to coerce the captors into giving up their prisoners. Due to a relentless war of attrition with Iraq, Iran's cache of weapons had become severely depleted however if the United States was prepared to supply them with more stock a deal could certainly be struck. There was, of course, a catch. US Congress had banned the sale of American arms to countries which sponsored terrorism. Using an Iranian arms dealer called Manucher Ghorbanifar as the middleman and Israel as the official selling country, the Reagan administration managed to skirt this issue.

The first consignment of weaponry was shipped by Israel on 30 August 1985. Nearly one hundred American-made TOW anti-tank missiles were handed over to a group of Iranians opposed to the Ayatollah regime in the hope that they would persuade the kidnappers to release their hostages. Two weeks later a second shipment of 408 missiles made its way from Israel to Iran bringing about the deal's first successful release of a hostage. Unfortunately the CIA did not get back their man of secrets. Instead man of the cloth, Reverend Benjamin Weir, was handed over after 495 days in captivity.

## BUCKLEY DEAD

The hopes of effecting the freedom of all American hostages taken by the Hezbollah with the two arms sales in August and September 1985 were doomed from the start. By the time the first batch of sophisticated missiles had been delivered Lieutenant Colonel William Buckley was already dead. Knowledge of his death was limited to his captors who kept silent about his demise until 4 October when they announced they had executed the political officer. The Islamic Jihad said it was retribution for an Israeli attack on the headquarters of the Palestine Liberation Organisation in Tunisia three days earlier. In truth Buckley had been dead for four months almost to the day.

Buckley would have suffered more at the hands of the pro-Iranian extremists than his fellow prisoners. Once the captors found out they had taken an agent of the CIA they would have sought to extract valuable information from him by any means. Torture techniques would have been applied explaining why he signed a four hundred-page statement detailing CIA activities and sources during his captivity.

As the months went by other hostages were released from their incarceration giving accounts of their ordeals to the press. On 2 November 1986 David Jacobsen, director of the American University Hospital in Beirut, was given his freedom and was able to shed light on Buckley's demise. He had spent his first six days as a hostage with the CIA operative in a ten by fifteen foot room full of rubbish in a second floor apartment somewhere north of Beirut Airport.

Jacobsen reported that there had been no execution rather a period of neglect and mistreatment which slowly took its toll on the missing CIA man. Buckley's health gradually deteriorated until his death on the night of 3 June 1985. His last few hours were spent in a feverish state of delirium manacled to the floor with no help coming from the armed guards that kept watch. Despite Jacobsen and the other hostages pleading to their captors to give Buckley some medical attention nothing was done. Left to die from his pneumonia-like symptoms his lifeless body was soon removed from his filthy makeshift cell.

## BUCKLEY FOUND

While the truth concerning Buckley's death was being discovered, his body could not be found. Two years after his death the CIA held an agency memorial service, making Buckley the fifty-first star upon the Wall of Honour at Langley, Virginia. Nearly a year on and still no body had surfaced so a public memorial service was held with full military honours at Arlington on 13 May 1988. Over one hundred friends, family and colleagues including the Director of the CIA William H. Webster attended the event. However, hope for the retrieval of Buckley's body was fading day by day.

Three and a half years later on 27 December 1991 an anonymous early-morning call tipped off authorities to the whereabouts of William Buckley's body. Dumped at the roadside in the Shiite district of Haret Hreik in Southern Beirut a skull and a collection of bones were discovered wrapped in bandages and blankets and placed inside a plastic bag. The human remains were taken to the morgue of the American University Hospital where Lebanon's chief pathologist, Dr Ahmed Harati, identified the bones as belonging to the missing embassy chief.

Buckley's body was flown home the following day via Rhein-Main Air Base in Germany aboard an Air Force jet. His reclamation saw the last of the American captives in Lebanon return home bringing a close to the hostage saga for the United States. William Buckley was buried in Arlington National Cemetery in section 59 lot 346.

# TERRY ANDERSON

From covering the biggest stories in the world to becoming the biggest story, Terry Anderson went from tenacious journalist to humbled hostage stripped of his dignity by his Islamist captors during the bitter struggles of the Lebanese Civil War. After a total of 2,545 days in captivity and after numerous false alarms, the longest-held American hostage in Lebanon obtained his freedom, signalling the end of a ten-year hostage crisis for the United States.

## STORY CHASER

Born on 27 October 1947 Terry Anderson began his connection with big news at an early age. In his early twenties he fought in the Vietnam War with the US Marines as combat correspondent before obtaining a degree in journalism from Iowa State University in 1974. He then began covering global stories with the Associated Press reporting the facts from Asia and Africa and it was in Johannesburg that he first heard about the troubles in Lebanon.

Israel had invaded South Lebanon in the summer of 1982 becoming the biggest story in the world and an ardent Anderson wanted to be where the action was. By the following year his wish was granted. He was made chief Middle East Correspondent and sent to Beirut to cover the conflict. For a man who craved adventure, his assignment would not disappoint.

Following the suicide bombing of both the American Embassy and the US Marines barracks in Beirut earlier in the year a band of Iranian-backed Shiite extremists called the Dawa orchestrated a series of attacks on six key installations in Kuwait. Both the US and French embassies were hit in retaliation for their support of Iraq and lack of assistance to Iran. Fortunately, this well-planned assault managed to take only six lives and after many Shiite Muslims were arrested, seventeeen members of the Dawa were charged and imprisoned in Kuwait.

As the Hezbollah worked to free their comrades, life for any Westerner in Lebanon became yet more hazardous. The US Government began advising their citizens to leave Beirut but the tenacious Terry Anderson was determined to stay. There was a story to be told.

## ANYONE FOR MENACE?

Exactly a year after the kidnapping of Lieutenant Colonel William Buckley, Terry Anderson became the big story. On Saturday 16 March 1985 the chief correspondent was seized by armed fundamentalists in West Beirut and stolen away to a secret Hezbollah hideaway. Earlier that day he had been enjoying a game of tennis with Associated Press photographer, Don Mell, and was dropping him off at his home when the kidnappers struck. They had witnessed a green Mercedes making several passes before pulling ominously to the side of the road. Out stepped a group of bearded Muslims who dragged Terry out of his car while holding a gun to Don's head. There was nothing the paparazzo could do as the men bundled Terry into the back seat of the car and, throwing an old blanket over him, drove off into the labyrinthine city.

As the Mercedes made its way to the 'green line' – the divide between East and West Beirut – one of his kidnappers told their captive not to worry, that this was political. This was true. The militant Muslims soon made their reasons known for the taking of Terry Anderson; they demanded the swift release of the seventeen Dawa convicts from their Kuwaiti prison.

## ISOLATION

Terry Anderson spent his first days in solitary confinement blindfolded and chained in a twelve by fifteen foot cell within one of the many Beirut slum houses. Unaware of his new address he could however tell from the regular rumble of jet engines overhead that his prison was close to the airport. Once the adrenaline had subsided, then came the tears. His desire to be close to the action had resulted in his removal from society to the darkest depths of hell.

Each time his guards came to see him he feared death. Luckily all they wanted at the beginning was information. His captors questioned him constantly, demanding to know the names of all Americans he knew residing in Lebanon. Anderson remained tight-lipped, fully aware anyone he gave up became a potential victim. Lonely as he was this was not something he could do.

Thankfully it would not be too long until he had company. He soon became aware of others held captive in the same building, sectioned off behind plasterboard partitions. One fellow hostage in particular would prove to be significant in helping him cope with the ordeal.

## A RETURN OF FAITH

Growing up in the Midwest, Anderson had been a practising Roman Catholic but once his life was filled with world news bulletins and war reports his faith took a back seat. Held hostage by the Hezbollah with nothing to distract him save the fear of execution he had plenty of time to reflect on his life, regretting bygone mistakes, wishing he could atone for sins of the past. To this end he asked his captors for a bible and one was soon provided; a brand new revised edition which he read regularly from cover to cover. Absorbing the text, hungry for redemption he found his faith returning.

Anderson then discovered one of his neighbours in the crude prison block was a priest. This was Father Lawrence Martin Jenco, a fifty-year-old member of a small Catholic order who had been working with Lebanon's poor providing relief until his abduction in January 1985. Anderson pleaded to the guards to let him see the priest in order to make his first confession in twenty-five years. This was allowed and Father Jenco was brought to visit the reporter in his cell to perform the Catholic custom. The two men were in tears by the end overwhelmed by their situation and the power of their religious conviction.

## MIND GAMES

Despite acquiring a renewed sense of religion, Terry Anderson's faith would be severely tested during the many wretched years of his incarceration. The cruelty of his captors knew no bounds taking to jumping, kicking, poking and generally beating the imprisoned pressman throughout his enforced stay. The brutality extended beyond the physical violence. He was only given fifteen minutes per day to perform ablutions with one chance to visit the toilet. If he missed this opportunity a bottle placed in his cell would have to suffice. Robbed of his dignity he would be forced to sleep on a thin mat and eat meagre meals of Arabic bread, malodorous cheese and rice washed down with tea. Less than three months into his incarceration such maltreatment would soon prove fatal with the death of his fellow inmate William Buckley.

The captors played mind games with their prisoners who struggled to keep their sanity from day to day. After hearing about the hijacking of TWA Flight 847 in late June the chief guard known as Hajj informed them they would be returning home. Anderson and his fellow hostages were filled with hope, elated that their ordeal was almost over. However apart from some improvements made to their living conditions they remained locked in their chains.

A couple of months later and another announcement from Hajj. Bringing good news he informed them one hostage would be released however there was a slight twist; the prisoners would have to decide which of them would be the lucky man. The guard left them to fight it out and after a period of heated debate Anderson won the vote for freedom. On Hajj's return they made their selection only to be told it was just a game, Anderson would not be chosen. Instead

Hajj picked Benjamin Weir who unexpectedly became the first American to be released as part of the notorious arms for hostages deal.

Such constant mental torture coupled with the relentless confinement required considerable mental strength in order to stave off depression. Anderson took to playing his own mind games either alone or with his fellow captives to stimulate the brain cells. Before he was permitted writing materials he made a calendar from dust and saliva to keep track of time and afterwards kept a journal and wrote poetry. A chess set made from tinfoil and a deck of cards crudely fashioned from scraps of paper helped keep his mind alive. When he was not busy cleaning the mats or taking long walks around the tiny cell he also read the various newspapers or listened to the radio to keep up to date with current affairs.

The radio and periodicals became such major links to his survival that when they were all removed one day Anderson decided to go on a seven day hunger strike. This news blackout was surprisingly not one of the hostage-takers' frequent acts of cruelty but in fact a move to prevent him discovering the deaths of both his father and brother back home.

## LAST MAN OUT

As the years passed and fellow hostages came and went

Terry Anderson soon became the longest-held American hostage in Lebanon. Father Jenco was set free in the summer of 1986 soon followed by David Jacobsen a few months later. After spending much of 1987 back in solitary confinement he received a new cellmate, Marcel Fontaine, the vice consul at the French Embassy in Beirut. The pair of them passed the time playing dominoes and chess until one day in May 1988 Anderson is told to get ready for release. This sudden news flash took him by surprise but before he had time to assimilate his fate the guard returned to deliver a sucker punch. Believing his ordeal was over Anderson experienced déjà vu as his captors led Fontaine to freedom instead.

The chief journalist would endure fears of yet another malicious trick when he was told on 3 December 1991 that he should prepare to leave behind his improvised games for good. This time his guards were genuine. Thanks to the Iraq invasion of Kuwait in 1990 the seventeen Dawa convicts had been freed. This issue was now over.

Since the invasion there had also begun a gradual shift in relations between the relevant nations. Both Iran and Syria found themselves in need of American financial aid after a costly war with Iraq and the loss of Soviet sponsorship respectively. This state of affairs provided fertile ground for a successful conclusion to the hostage crisis.

Syria was now in control of Lebanon and used their influence to persuade the Hezbollah to free the remaining hostages. The Shiite group began releasing their captives throughout the second half of 1991 and in return were allowed to remain armed. They also demanded the release of their Israeli-held comrades and consent to this request saw Terry Anderson gain his freedom on 4 December 1991 becoming the last living American hostage to be let go.

## FREEDOM

The reality of his release must have sunk in when he was provided with a fresh set of clothes and a new pair of shoes, the first since his kidnapping six years and nine months earlier. After reading out a statement which was later sent to a Western news agency in Damascus, Terry Anderson began the journey east through the Chouf Mountains to the Syrian capital.

Typically his release did not go quite to plan. While a host of family, friends, diplomats and fellow journalists gathered in Damascus for his arrival, Anderson's convoy was forced to return to Beirut due to heavy snow. What should have been a fairly swift trip to freedom took a protracted nine hours as the release party diverted via Homs in the north. With thoughts of yet another false alarm reducing his family to tears, the Middle East correspondent finally made it to Damascus and the loving arms of his fiancée Madeleine Bassil. Anderson was also introduced to his daughter Sulome whom he had never met having been born three months after his abduction. After a long-awaited press conference in which he thanked the multi-national campaign for his release he was taken to the American military hospital in Wiesbaden, Germany to be examined.

## LIFE GOES ON

After his release Terry Anderson did not shrink into the shadows but used his uninvited fame to positive effect. After writing his memoirs in 1994 entitled Den of Lions he decided to return to the land of his incarceration with a two week, CNN-covered tour of Lebanon in August 1996. There he met face-to-face with the Secretary-General of the Hezbollah Sayyid Hassan Nasrallah in a bid to understand the reasons behind the hostage crisis. With no apology forthcoming he returned to the United States declaring no resentment for the lost years nor towards his captors.

Anderson and his family clearly did feel some bitterness towards the Iranian Government, however, when in March 1999 they filed a lawsuit against the Islamic Republic of Iran and its Ministry of Information and Security. Suing for his hostage years and the emotional suffering they brought to his family the former captive won his case and in 2002 Terry Anderson was awarded a multimillion dollar settlement taken from frozen Iranian assets. The victorious reporter used some of the money to help set up various charitable organisations such as the Vietnam Children's Fund and the Father Lawrence Jenco Foundation in memory of his faith-saving friend who had died in 1996.

Subsequent to running for the Ohio Senate in 2003, losing narrowly to his Republican rival, Terry Anderson settled into semi-retirement to run the *Blue Gator*, a blues bar, back in his home state. This laid-back lifestyle was not to last long and in December 2008 the ex-hostage joined the faculty at the University of Kentucky to teach an international journalism course, providing a new breed of reporters with the benefit of his unique knowledge and experience.

# TERRY WAITE

Throughout the early eighties the name of Terry Waite became synonymous with hostage negotiation. With a soft-spoken style which seemed to win over his contacts, this gentle giant enjoyed great success, bringing home hostages from such danger areas as Iran and Libya. However, when this archbishop's aide turned to rescuing American captives in Lebanon, he suffered a shocking reversal of fortune when he was taken hostage himself.

## EARLY LIFE, EARLY NEGOTIATIONS

On 31 May 1939 in a small Cheshire village just months before the outbreak of the Second World War, Terry Hardy Waite's life began as it would continue; inextricably linked to global conflict. After a childhood dominated by a strict disciplinarian father he weathered a brief stint with the Grenadier Guards before focusing on a more spiritual path.

Following several years as the Education Advisor to the Anglican Bishop of Bristol and his marriage to

Frances Watters, Terry moved to Uganda, travelling throughout East Africa developing relief programmes such as the Southern Sudan Project. Uprooting once again, he took a consultant role in Rome liaising with the Vatican on missionary matters until a return to the UK saw him recruited in 1980 by Robert Runcie, the then Archbishop of Canterbury.

As the prelate's assistant for Anglican Communion Affairs, Terry became responsible for both diplomatic and clerical issues, organising overseas appointments for his spiritual leader to millions of Anglicans around the world. Yet it was in another unexpected role that this lay worker would excel. That summer four Britons were taken hostage in Iran and, after Runcie appealed to the Ayatollah for their release, the archbishop sent his aide to Tehran to negotiate.

Bringing home the British captives proved the decision to have Terry handle the liberation process was the right one and this soft-spoken man was immediately thrust into the limelight, becoming an overnight champion. In 1984 he was asked to repeat the feat by negotiating with Colonel Gaddafi for the release of four Britons held in Libya and after two trips to Tripoli, he brought them home in early 1985.

## TAINTED BY SCANDAL

It was during his third major mission to release

American hostages in Lebanon that this globetrotting trouble-shooter encountered his most difficult and life-changing negotiation process to date. Despatched to Beirut in November 1985 after four Americans held captive by the Hezbollah had sent a letter to the archbishop calling for help, Terry Waite became the first Western envoy to achieve an audience with the Islamic Jihad. Several back-to-back visits to arguably the most dangerous capital in the world brought the release of David Jacobsen, a hospital administrator at the American University Hospital on 2 November 1986. It appeared the six-foot seven Anglican lay worker had built up a real sense of trust with the Muslim militants.

This relationship developed over numerous painstaking meetings with representatives of the hostage-takers was about to be shattered by the breaking news of the arms-for-hostages scandal. A media leak exposing America's illegal sale of weaponry to Iran in exchange for their hostages brought recriminations against the White House and the national security aide who supervised the diabolical pact. Colonel Oliver North, the guilty overseer, had met with Terry Waite many times during his efforts to release the American hostages and, despite asserting he had no knowledge of the illicit arrangement, his good name was tainted by the affair.

The Hezbollah was now suspicious of Waite's ties with the Reagan administration. Together with his association with North, the Anglican envoy had also been photographed on the White House lawn with Vice-President Bush leading the Shiite terrorists to believe he was far from a neutral mediator but a CIA spy. In a bid to clear his name and restore his integrity, Terry chose to return to Lebanon to continue hostage negotiations.

## STOOGE TO HOSTAGE

Terry made his fifth visit to Beirut on 12 January 1987 despite warnings from the Islamic Jihad that he faced death if he returned. With promises of safe conduct from the Druze minority leader, Walid Jumblatt, the emissary pursued leads throughout Beirut refusing to surrender his mission.

Releasing his Druze bodyguards, he travelled alone to meet his intermediary, a Doctor Mroueh, at his office-apartment in West Beirut on 20 January. Terry had been granted a unique opportunity to meet Terry Anderson and Thomas Sutherland, the two remaining American hostages, and had been assured he would not be abducted. On arrival, the doctor immediately excused himself after taking a phone call, saying there was an emergency at the hospital, and moments later a stocky, suited representative of the Hezbollah knocked at the door. Aware of the risk he was taking, Terry accompanied his contact to a safe house, forced to wear a blindfold for much of the journey.

Switching vehicles and swapping his Western clothes for Islamic attire, the lofty legate was driven for miles until they arrived at a basement garage beneath a block of flats. Ordered to jump down through a trapdoor in the floor, he was manhandled into a room. Hearing the reinforced door slam behind him, Terry removed his blindfold to see he was now in a white-tiled cell measuring seven by ten foot and only six foot high in places. His fears had been realised; the hostage negotiator was now a hostage.

## SOLITARY CONFINEMENT

With only cockroaches for company, Terry Waite spent the next four years in solitary confinement. Given only ten minutes a day outside his windowless cell, he combated delirium and maintained his sanity by refusing to give into self-pity, relentlessly pacing his underground chamber and counting the tiles. There could be no room for sentimentality in his prison, forcing thoughts of family and friends out of his mind while, thousands of miles away, they prayed for his safe return.

It was not long until his keepers began to bring more than just hot tea. Still suspecting their detainee of colluding with the Americans, the hostage-takers brought in cables to persuade him to talk. Held down and with pillows pressed into his face, the guards would strike the soles of his feet to obtain the truth about his trips to the United States and his relationship with Oliver North.

With its funding and training received from Iran and its Revolutionary Guards, the Hezbollah tortured the envoy in an attempt to extract information on how to put pressure on the White House. Believing he was fully appraised of the arms deal with Iran, they wanted to force the Reagan administration to resume shipments of military hardware which had ceased since the scandal broke. The problem was Terry Waite had been a unwitting cover of legitimacy for the Americans and could not give his captors the answers they required.

## NEWS ON TAP

After the extensive torture sessions and mock executions failed to break the Anglican attaché's spirit, his interrogators chose to believe his ignorance and the physical harm stopped. The guards began to accede to some small requests from their prisoner, supplying him with occasional books and, lacking spectacles, a magnifying glass with which to read them. These donated tomes served as refuge against the oppressive solitude, however he would not have to wait much longer for human contact.

After three years trapped inside his cell, fruitlessly tapping the walls hoping for participation from the other side, Terry was finally granted a reply. Using a laborious code of one tap for A, two taps for B and so on, he discovered he was conversing through the wall with Thomas Sutherland and Terry Anderson – the two hostages he had come to rescue!

Along with British journalist John McCarthy also in the next cell, Terry managed to provide and retrieve news about life outside. Thanks to his neighbours possessing a radio, he was able to hear about the fall of the Berlin wall in 1989, the end of apartheid and the retirement of his superior, Robert Runcie, as Archbishop of Canterbury in 1991. This communion with fellow hostages helped stave off feelings of loneliness and isolation, a connection that would soon be enhanced.

Suddenly one evening the guards took him from his cell, placed him inside a canvas sack and forced him into a car boot; he was on the move again. This enforced change of address, however, would be markedly different to those in the past. At the end of the journey he removed his blindfold to discover the three hostages with whom he had shared hours of protracted coded conversations. His years of solitary confinement were over.

## LONG WAITE OVER

Being in the company of others after such a long time in isolation was more difficult than he expected. He now had to contend with different personalities and dissimilar behaviour patterns all within a cramped space whilst chained by the ankle. His own failing health was also becoming an issue, suffering regular asthma attacks as a result of the fumes emitted by the electric generator. Thankfully, the attacks were soon controlled by an inhaler supplied by his guards.

With Britain's improved relations with both Syria and Iran creating a better climate for talks, it was not long before the four hostages became three. John McCarthy was given his freedom in August 1991 bringing home news that Terry Waite was alive and well, easing the anxieties of family and friends and raising their hopes of an imminent release.

When the fateful moment arrived, it was surprisingly low key. Freed together with Thomas Sutherland on 18 November 1991, Terry was blindfolded and taken in various vehicles before being handed over to a member of Syrian intelligence who escorted him to his headquarters. Well-versed in the process of hostage release himself, the go-between turned victim was given the obligatory debriefing and medical checks and then placed on a plane to RAF Lyneham where he was visited by his old boss,

Robert Runcie. He then provided a statement to the media inside the hangar of the Wiltshire airbase, thanking the likes of the UN and RAF for their support, before being reunited with his wife and four children. Terry Waite was now a free man.

## LIVING WITH FREEDOM

Having spent 1,763 days in captivity, the majority of which was spent in isolation, the Anglican emissary found it tough adjusting to freedom and opted for a gradual assimilation into the world greatly changed from when he was taken. Invited to join Trinity Hall at Cambridge University, he lived in relative seclusion, devoting his time to handwriting his first book detailing his experiences as prisoner of the Hezbollah.

Once comfortably eased back into normal life, he became more active, spending half each year on the lecture circuit and the other half to a variety of charitable causes. In the years since his release, Terry Waite has co-founded Y-Care International, an agency with close links to the YMCA and Hostage UK, a charity devoted to giving support to victims of kidnapping.

His humanitarian work takes him overseas once more to provide relief to AIDS victims in South Africa, war victims in Kosovo and victims of natural disaster such as the tsunami striking Indonesia and the surrounding areas. His extensive travels also included a return to Lebanon in February 2004 inspecting two of the many Palestinian refugee camps in the north of the country. Lasting a mere nine days, this stay would be considerably shorter than his past extended visit.

# AIR FRANCE
# FLIGHT 8969

In the winter of 1994 the passengers and crew of Flight 8969 would experience a Christmas to remember as they prepared to head home for the holidays. Their festive mood was shattered when an Algerian terrorist group hijacked their plane beginning a fifty-four-hour ordeal of terror that would see death and distress replace the traditional good will to all.

## NIGHTMARE BEFORE CHRISTMAS

At 11.15 am on Christmas Eve 1994 the two hundred and twenty passengers of Air France Flight 8969 settled into their seats for their journey to Paris from Houari Boumedienne Airport in Algeria. As the cockpit began their preparations to leave, the plane took on board four unexpected visitors. Dressed in the blue uniforms adorned with Air Algerie insignia, the four men said they were security agents and began checking passengers' passports. Personal effects were taken and placed in plastic bags and they ordered for all window shutters to be closed. As soon as the doors were locked the official-looking four revealed their true intentions. They were there to hijack the plane.

After placing packs of dynamite in the cockpit and under a seat in the centre section of the plane the hijackers' next move was a brutal one. At around two o'clock they discovered an Algerian policeman among the passengers and promptly led him to the front of the aircraft. Ignoring his pleas for mercy they executed him with a shot to the head before coldly throwing his body out onto the tarmac. Moments later the hostage-takers contacted the control tower for the first time declaring they were members of the GIA; a notorious Islamic terrorist organisation with a ruthless reputation.

## THE GIA

Formed in 1992 to overthrow the army-backed Algerian government, the Groupe Islamique Armé or GIA were made up of Afghan extremists who wanted Algeria to become an Islamic state. They had almost achieved this aim with an apparent victory in the first rounds of elections in December 1991. However the prevailing government made the unprecedented decision to call all ballots null and void preventing the triumph of the Islamic Salvation Front or FIS.

From then on the Islamic radicals pursued a campaign of violence and destruction killing over 100 expatriates in massacres throughout Algeria. Schools were targeted and artists assassinated all in a bid to raise the profile of the country's political struggles. With the succession of a new head or emir, Djamel Zitouni, the level of terror was heightened. At the end of October 1994 Zitouni issued two communiqués announcing attacks on France would begin for their involvement in the conflict.

## THE DEMANDS

The GIA were now making good on their promises having captured their most prominent target at the airport in Algiers; an Airbus A300 with forty French nationals on board. Interior Minister Abderahmane Meziane-Cherif handled the negotiations with the lead hijacker who, refusing to talk directly to the statesman, had Flight Captain Bernard Delhemme relay their demands.

The excitable hijacker called for the release of Abassi Madani and Ali Belhadj, the leaders of the banned political party, the FIS, who were currently under house arrest along with several other comrades languishing in jail. They also expressed a wish to fly to Paris and to hold a press conference during which they would air their political grievances to the world.

The Interior Minister then made some counter-demands of his own insisting the hijackers release some of the passengers if they wished to leave Algiers. Four hours into the negotiations the first wave of hostages were freed. A total of sixty-three passengers, mainly women and children, were given their freedom before the end of the day but the nightmare before Christmas was not over yet.

## SUBTLE TACTIC

As the GIA terrorists were showing their willingness to compromise they then pushed once more for the mobile staircase and wheel chocks to be removed so Flight 8969 could take off. However, the Algerian colonel of the national commando unit nicknamed the Ninjas which surrounded the plane refused to comply. This act of betrayal enraged the leader of the hostage-takers who subsequently ordered Vietnamese attaché, Bui Giang To, to the front of the plane. The sound of another gunshot echoed down the aisles followed by the diplomat's body being ejected from the aircraft.

With two dead passengers dumped on the tarmac the terrorist threat was now very real. Something had to be done to bring this ordeal to an end. As darkness set in the Ninjas used night-vision goggles to identify the lead hijacker. He was Abdul Abdullah Yahia, a twenty-five year old thief and greengrocer from the rough Les Eucalyptus district of Algiers. In an attempt to placate the terrorist, authorities brought Yahia's mother to the scene who implored her son to let the hostages go. At nine-clock that evening shots rang out aimed at the control tower and over the radio Yahia was heard to say: 'Mother, we'll meet in Paradise.' The subtle approach had failed.

## CHRISTMAS CANCELLED

Christmas Day began appropriately with presents as more passengers were released from the stationary aircraft. In exchange for these lives he insisted two more brothers-in-arms – former GIA emir Abdelkader Layada and author Ikhlet Cherati – should be liberated from their incarceration. Along with these two 'gifts' he made repeat requests for the stairs and chocks to be removed.

With no sign of these demands being served a frustrated Yahia summoned Yannick Beugnet, a young cook from the French Embassy, to the front of the plane. At 9.30 pm the terrified passenger spoke to the control tower informing them he would be killed unless the aircraft was allowed to take to the air in the next thirty minutes. Believing this to be a bluff, the authorities did nothing. Half an hour later, as promised, the dead body of Beugnet was thrown from the plane. As those in the control tower and surrounding the plane looked on in horror, the hijackers stated they would kill another hostage every half hour until the plane was allowed to make its way to Paris.

## SECRET TALKS

The hostage situation was now thirty-two hours old and the French government, with its airplane and citizens held captive, demanded a more proactive stance from the Algerian authorities. From the very beginning events had been closely followed by French Interior Minister Charles Pasqua who had convened a crisis team to look into the best method of resolving the problem. However Algeria had no intention of allowing France, a former colonial power, to take over.

With the death of Yannick Beugnet, a French national, the French government applied further pressure on Algeria to allow the plane to leave for France where they would deal with the hijackers. The North African nation finally gave in and at 2 am on 26 December the Algerian colonel ordered the removal of the stairs and chocks. Nearly forty hours behind schedule the flight crew prepared for take-off from Houari Boumedienne Airport.

The terrorists seemed in complete control. However, the cockpit had been in secret communication with the control tower as the drama unfolded. Unbeknown to the hijackers the crew had been given instructions to persuade their captors that there was insufficient fuel to make it to Paris. Due to the extended time at the Algerian airport auxiliary power had been drained. This risky bluff worked and Yahia agreed on an alternative destination: Marseilles. The Air France plane made the 1,375 mile flight across the Mediterranean and at 3.33 am touched down at Marignane Airport.

## DEADLY MISSION

As Flight 8969 touched down on French soil a rescue operation was already in motion. Twenty minutes before the hijacked plane landed at Marseilles an identical Airbus A300 containing around forty highly-trained soldiers had arrived on a nearby runway. These men were members of the Groupe d'Inter-vention de la Gendarmerie Nationale known as the GIGN; a French elite counter terrorism and hostage rescue squad. Unable to gain clearance to land in Algiers, they had been waiting at Palma de Mallorca Airport for the go-ahead.

While the GIGN prepared for attack during the early morning hours practising manoeuvres on their matching aircraft, the hijackers waited in silence, exhausted by their efforts to depart from Algiers. At six o'clock that morning they made their first contact with the control tower. Speaking with Marseilles police chief Alain Gehin, they demanded twenty-seven tonnes of fuel for their ongoing trip to Paris. This request puzzled officials. Paris was less than five hundred miles from Marseilles requiring between nine and ten tonnes of fuel. Why would they need three times the necessary amount?

It was at this time that anonymous calls came through revealing the possible intent of the hijackers. This intelligence unveiled fears of a suicide mission using the fuel-laden aircraft as a flying bomb upon the French capital. With this in mind, Gehin could not permit the plane to take to the air again. Throughout the 26 December he skilfully placated the hijackers with supplies and offers to empty toilets, pushing back imposed deadlines to keep Flight 8969 grounded.

At around four o'clock in the afternoon Gehin managed to orchestrate the release of two more hostages who managed to provide the waiting GIGN with essential information on the state of the plane, the hijackers and their hostages. With Yahia growing more impatient with every passing minute, threatening to blow up the plane if his demands were not met, action had to be taken.

## RESCUE OPERATION

The GIGN team were ready and prepared to move when, at a quarter to five, the aircraft's engines started and the plane moved to within thirty metres of the control tower. While the rescue squad recalculated their approach, the GIA prepared to execute more hostages. Death rituals in the form of passages from the Koran were recited as the atmosphere inside the plane became unbearable, building to a dreadful climax. With Yahia issuing an ultimatum, shots were fired from the plane shattering a control tower window. For the GIGN, this was their cue to move.

With the green light given and with French TV stations broadcasting the action live, the GIGN dressed in black fatigues and ski masks, approached the plane from the rear and sides on three mobile staircases. The first wave attacked the first class section and cockpit tossing in stun grenades to disorientate the hijackers. While a fierce gun battle raged at the front of the plane a second wave extracted passengers from the rear using the emergency chutes.

The incessant firefight ensued between the GIA and GIGN with further grenades thrown by both sides injuring those caught in the blast radius. With two of the hijackers known to be dead the French soldiers focused on the cockpit where the final two terrorists were known to be hiding. The relentless hail of bullets forced co-pilot Jean-Paul Borderie to leap from the cockpit window where he landed on the tarmac sixteen feet below fracturing his elbow and thigh. Soon after the GIGN heard shouting from inside; the voices were French and came from Navigator Alain Bossuat and Captain Bernard Delhemme who were found alive underneath two dead hijackers.

## AFTERMATH

At 17.35 Captain Favier terminated the operation which had lasted a little over fifteen minutes resulting in only four lives being taken, those of the GIA terrorists. Eleven commandos, thirteen passengers and three members of the crew had been injured in the attack but all survived making it the most successful hostage rescue to date. The GIGN had stayed to true to their motto: Servitas Vitae meaning to save lives.

Unfortunately the positive end to the ordeal saw an almost immediate response by the GIA who, on 27 December, attacked the city of Tizi-Ouzou, sixty miles east of Algiers, killing four Roman Catholic priests. This retaliation initiated a period of vengeance which the GIA called the Martyrdom phase. On 30 January 1995 the Islamic cadre committed their first suicide attack. A car filled with explosives driven by a devoted member crashed into the headquarters of the Algerian police killing forty-two people and injuring over two hundred and sixty innocent victims.

# UNITED AIRLINES FLIGHT 93

---

*'We're gonna die. They're gonna kill us, you know, we're gonna die.' And I told her, 'Don't worry, they hijacked the plane, they're gonna take you for a ride, you go to their country, and you come back. You stay there for vacation.'*

*'I'm on United Flight 93 from Newark to San Francisco. The plane has been hijacked. We are in the air. They've already knifed a guy. There is a bomb on board. Call the FBI.'*

*'I want to let you know that I love you. I'm on a flight from Newark to San Francisco and there are three guys who have taken over the plane and they say they have a bomb...'*

*'Mom, we're being hijacked. I just called to say good bye.'*

*'The Lord is my shepherd; I shall not want. He maketh me*

*to lie down in green pastures. He leadeth me beside the still waters…'*

They are some of the most poignant phone calls ever made, the last messages to their families made by the passengers and crew on board United Airlines Flight 93, a scheduled Boeing 757-200 passenger flight from Newark International Airport in New Jersey to San Francisco International Airport in California. On that fateful day, 11 September 2001, when it seemed that the world was coming to a dreadful end, their plane was hijacked by four Islamic terrorists forty minutes into the flight. Their objective, it is believed, was the destruction of the White House or the Capitol building in Washington. The reaction of its passengers would become known as one of the most heroic acts in American history; it was the flight that fought back.

## THE HIJACK

The hijackers checked in for the flight between 7.03 and 7.39 in the morning. They were twenty-six-year-old Lebanese citizen, Ziad Jarrah, a Sunni Muslim who was educated in Christian schools and sent to study in Hamburg in Germany where he met Mohamed Atta, the leader of the perpetrators of the September 11 attacks; Ahmed al-Haznawi, in his early twenties, the Saudi Arabian son of a prayer leader at the local mosque; twenty-three-year-old Ahmed al-Nami, who had studied law at King Khaled University in Saudi Arabia but had vanished, according to his family while on pilgrimage to Mecca and Saeed al-Ghamdi, a man about whom almost nothing is known and who was probably operating under an alias.

Al Ghamdi and Jarrah had no luggage while al-Nami checked in two bags and al-Haznawi one. Al-Haznawi was selected for extra scrutiny by the Computer Assisted Prescreening System but nothing unusual was found and the four men went through to the gate unhindered.

At some point, Ziad Jarrah made a phone call to his girlfriend in Germany, saying only 'I love you, I love you, I love you', before abruptly ending the call.

The plane was boarded around 7.39 and the four men were spaced out throughout the first class compartment of the plane.

The plane was due to take off at 8 o'clock and shortly after that time it had pushed back from its gate. However, it remained in position after that for some time; there was the customary early morning congestion at Newark Airport. At 8.42, it finally sped down the runway and took off.

By this time, the initial phases of the 9/11 attacks were being launched. Flight 11 had already been hijacked and Flight 175 was in the process of being commandeered. Both those planes would crash into the Twin Towers of the World Trade Center in New York, while another plane, Flight 77 would hit the Pentagon, shocking the world and shaping its political future.

Just after nine, as the plane achieved its cruising altitude of 35,000 feet and began to level out, the Twin Tower attacks were taking place. Air traffic officials began issuing warnings to planes in the air, using the Aircraft Communication Addressing and Reporting System. Warnings were sent to all United Airlines flights from 9.19 onwards saying, 'Beware any cockpit intrusion—two a/c (aircraft) hit World Trade Center.' Flight 93 received the warning at 9.23. However, just a minute before, Melody Homer, the wife of one of the plane's crew had had a message sent to her husband, Leroy, who was one of the pilots asking if he was okay. The crew of Flight 93 requested confirmation of what they had been told and then became involved in the regular communications with air traffic control. At 25 seconds after 9.27 they spoke for the last time to air traffic control.

The curious and unexplained thing about Flight 93 is why the hijackers took so long to spring into action. On the other three flights that were seized, the hijackers began their assaults after just thirty minutes, when the seatbelt sign had been switched off. It took the Flight 93 hijackers forty-six minutes to make their presence known.

The first manifestation of the hijacking was evident on air traffic control screens – it dropped almost 700 feet in a terrifying thirty seconds. Then, just after 9.28, a crew member in the cockpit could be heard over the radio shouting, 'Mayday! Mayday!' There was a great deal of commotion in the background but the communication from the plane stopped abruptly. Thirty-five seconds later there was another message. 'Mayday!' the voice screamed, 'Get out of here! Get out of here!'

The hijackers had attacked the cockpit and then herded the passengers towards the rear of the plane. It is thought that three of the hijackers were operating at this time. The fourth, Ziad Jarrah, is believed to have remained in his seat throughout the early part of the attack and then, when the crew and passengers had been overpowered, to have entered the cockpit and taken over the controls of the plane.

At this point, around 9.32, Jarrah's voice can be heard saying, 'Ladies and gentlemen: here the captain, please sit down keep remaining seating. We have a bomb on board. So sit.' An air traffic controller, hearing the announcement, asked for clarification. None was forthcoming. In the background, a flight attendant can be heard begging the men not to harm her.

At just after 9.35, Jarrah turned the plane east in the direction of Washington. As the flight attendant says, 'I don't want to die,' another voice is heard to say in Arabic, 'Everything is fine. I am finished.'

A few minutes later, Jarrah says, 'Ah. Here's the captain. I would like to tell you all to remain seated. We have a bomb aboard, and we are going back to the airport, and we have our demands. So, please remain quiet.' It was the last transmission heard from Flight 93.

## 'WE HAVE TO DO SOMETHING'

It was around this time that the calls began. There were thirty-five airphone calls and two mobile phone calls to family, friends and others. One made by Tom Burnett, explained on the phone to his wife that the plane had been hijacked and someone had been stabbed. He said they had said there was a bomb on board but he did not believe this; it was just something to keep them quiet. Then he was horrified to learn that planes had crashed into the World Trade Center and he realised that these were no idle threats being made by the hijackers of his plane. 'Oh my God,' he said, 'It's a suicide mission.' Critically, however, he added, 'If they're going to crash the plane into the ground, we have to do something. We can't wait for the authorities. We have to do something now.'

Jeremy Glick called his wife at 9.37, telling her what was going on and saying that the hijackers looked 'Iranian' and that they had donned red bandanas and were carrying knives. He told her that the passengers were taking a vote on whether to rush the hijackers.

Todd Beamer tried to get through to his wife at 9.43 but his call ended up with a GTE telephone operator, Lisa Jefferson. In one of the most celebrated phone calls in the history of telecommunications, Beamer told Jefferson that the pilots were dead or dying and that a hijacker had what looked like an explosive belt around his waist. He asked her to tell his family that he loved them and then they recited the 23rd Psalm together.

Meanwhile, three F-16 fighters, armed with heat-seeking Sidewinder missiles, had been scrambled from Langley Air Force Base in Hampton, Virginia. Their orders were to shoot down any civilian aircraft that seemed to be headed towards a target on the ground.

Flight attendant, CeeCee Lyles got through to her husband, Lorne, from the plane. 'Babe, my plane's been hijacked.' He thought she was joking. She told her she was not and asked him to tell their sons she loved them. They prayed together for a moment before she broke in and said, 'They're getting ready to force their way into the cockpit.'

Meanwhile, Todd Beamer was ending his call to

Lisa Jefferson. He put the phone down, although his voice could still be heard.

'Are you guys ready?' he was heard saying. 'Let's roll.'

United Airlines Flight 93 crashed into a field at Stoneycreek Township, near Shanksville, Pennsylvania, one hundred and fifty miles from Washington, killing forty passengers and crew and four hijackers at around six minutes past ten.

# INGRID BETANCOURT

Think of the South American country of Colombia and you immediately think of cocaine barons, kidnappings, rampant corruption and brutal violence. For politicians trying to create change in such an environment, life can be difficult and sometimes downright dangerous. A decades-old civil war waged by the Marxist-Leninist revolutionary guerilla organisation the Revolutionary Armed Forces of Colombia – better known as FARC – has killed thousands of Colombians. The FARC have also kidnapped numerous politicians and officials in order to try to obtain the release of their own people captured by the Colombian army.

It was in such a political environment that the French-Colombian politician Ingrid Betancourt launched a presidential campaign on 21 May 2001, standing next to a statue of the great 19th century South American revolutionary, Simon Bolivar, in the Colombian capital, Bogotá. Little did she know, however, that her campaign would end dramatically in her kidnapping by FARC, a kidnapping that would endure for six and a half years during which she would come close to death and that would ultimately grip the entire world.

## INGRID'S BACKGROUND

Ingrid Betancourt was born in Bogotá in 1961 into one of Colombia's oldest aristocratic families, descendants of Norman immigrants who had arrived from France in the 17th century. Her father was a minister in the dictatorship of General Gustavo Rojas Pinilla who governed the country from 1953 to 1957. He was later Colombian ambassador to UNESCO in Paris and worked in Washington under President John F. Kennedy on the education commission of the Alliance for Progress which was initiated to create economic cooperation between North and South America. Her mother, Yolanda Pulecio, was a former Miss Colombia who went on to represent poor southern areas of Bogotá in Congress.

Ingrid was educated in France and England as well as Colombia and, in 1983, after graduating from university, she married diplomat Fabrice Delloye. Her marriage gave her French citizenship and she travelled with her husband and their two children around the world. In the mid-1990s, they divorced and she remarried, to Juan Carlos Lecompte, a Colombian advertising executive.

Ingrid was motivated to go into politics by the assassination of Luis Carlos Galan, a Colombian presidential candidate supported by her mother. She launched herself with gusto and striking confidence as a Liberal anti-corruption candidate for Congress. She emphasised her stance against corruption with a simple gimmick understood by all. She distributed condoms to the voters as a symbolic protection against government corruption. It was the time when AIDS was high on the world's agenda and it did no harm for her to be able to push the health message at the same time. She won a seat in the Colombian Congress.

However, corruption was endemic in Colombia and it was highly dangerous for anyone to take a stand against it. She was putting herself not just against corrupt politicians but also against the powerful Colombian drug cartels whose tentacles reached to the very heart of the country's political life. She was used to threats against her own life but when threats were also made against her children, she sent them to live with their father in New Zealand, far away from danger.

She formed her own political party, Oxygen, and ran for the Colombian Senate. Having handed out facemasks to equate corruption with pollution, she won, receiving the highest number of votes ever cast for a senator. Her next step was to stand for President in the 2002 election.

Her presidential campaign was extraordinarily vigorous. She travelled widely in Colombia in an old Dodge minibus, even visiting remote parts of the country where no presidential candidate had ever been before. This time her gimmick was Viagra, indicating the type of reinvigoration she believed the country needed.

A demilitarised zone had been created in Colombia where FARC rebels and President Patrana and his representatives could meet to negotiate. The peace talks failed, however, and Betancourt was warned not to travel to the zone. Characteristically, she ignored the advice. When she was denied transport in a military helicopter, she decided to go overland, accompanied by Clara Rojas, her campaign manager. She was stopped and taken prisoner at a FARC roadblock on 23 February 2002.

## NEGOTIATIONS

Within a few weeks, her captors released a tape to confirm to her family that they had her and that she was alive. She seemed to be in good spirits, considering her situation and after her family pursued the election campaign in her absence, she came fifth out of eleven candidates. Meanwhile, shortly after her abduction, a committee of two hundred and eighty activists in thirty-nine countries was organised.

The French expressed great concern about her abduction – she was a French citizen, after all – and just over a year after her capture, the French government staged an ultimately unsuccessful and highly embarrassing rescue attempt, known as Operation 14 Juillet. The participants in the top secret operation who had travelled to South America, failed to even make contact with FARC representatives and in France a major scandal erupted. Towards the end of 2003, another video of her was released by FARC.

In 2004 it seemed that some progress had been made in organising a release of political and military hostages in exchange for around sixty jailed rebels, a proposal made by France and Switzerland. However, the deal stalled when FARC insisted that they were the ones who would name how many rebels should be released. By 2006, Ingrid Betancourt was still being held captive but, according to an interview given by FARC leader, Raul Reyes, to the French newspaper, *L'Humanité* in June of that year she was 'doing well, within the environment she finds herself in. It's not easy,' he added, 'when one is deprived of freedom.'

When Colombian National Police sub-lieutenant

Jhon Frank Pinchao succeeded in escaping from captivity in May 2007, he claimed that Betancourt had been held in the same FARC camp in which he had been kept prisoner. He also gave the news that Clara Rojas, kidnapped with her, had given birth to a son in captivity who had been named Emmanuel. The father was a FARC guerrilla.

The Colombian President Alvaro Uribe reiterated his orders for the use of military means to rescue Ingrid Betancourt and the other hostages. News had leaked out that many of the hostages were becoming ill and Betancourt was said to be in a bad way. In June the Colombian government released thirty FARC rebels as a goodwill gesture, but there was no response from the rebels. Then on 26 July there was worrying news issued by Melanie Delloye, Ingrid's daughter, saying that French diplomats had been unable to gain confirmation that her mother was still alive. It was also reported that she had made five escape attempts for which she had been 'severely punished'. Following her last attempt, she was chained by the neck and forced to remain on her feet for three days. Hopes rose again in August, however, when President Hugo Chavez of Venezuela reported that a FARC leader had told him that Ingrid Betancourt was still alive.

## KEEPING HERSELF BUSY

In interviews after her release, she said that she remained sane in captivity by setting herself activities such as telling stories, teaching French to other hostages, sewing or writing. Sadly, when her notebooks became too heavy for her to carry on the forced marches of up to fifteen miles, she had to burn a number of them. The main thing, she said, was to aspire to some kind of stability in a world where there was none. Her Bible was her most important asset during this time, but the group was given other books, even reading *Harry Potter*. The hostages were kept under the cover of jungle foliage, often not seeing the sun for days.

One of her lowest moments, she later said, came not long after she was captured. She was given a piece of cabbage wrapped in a newspaper. When she unfolded the paper she saw a photograph of a coffin. She read the accompanying article and discovered the coffin to be that of her father who had died a week after her abduction. She said that she felt suicidal at this point.

Later that year, when Colombian troops captured three rebels they had discovered in their possession videos and letters from FARC hostages. The images of Ingrid Betancourt shocked the world. She was shown sitting on a bench in the jungle staring listlessly at the ground. She was frighteningly thin and looked very unwell.

A Colombian Congressman released in February 2008, reported that she was exhausted and that she had also been mistreated. He described how she was chained up in inhuman conditions and that the rebels seemed to be taking out their anger on her. Another reported that she was ill, suffering from Hepatitis B and, chillingly, 'near the end.'

The government now offered to release hundreds of guerrillas but still there was no response. A report came that she had stopped taking her medication and was refusing food.

## AN END TO THE ORDEAL

Her surprise release came on 2 July 2008. For months government agents had been infiltrating local FARC squads and the organisation's command structure. They succeeded in using their now strong influence within the FARC to have the hostages brought from the three different locations in which they were being held to one central holding area. Informing the real rebels that the hostages were to be taken to a place where they would be examined by an international mission, they set out on a ninety-mile march through the jungle.

When they arrived at the designated spot, an unmarked helicopter painted white, landed close to them, precisely guided to the spot by Israeli tracking technology. More government agents, pretending to be FARC rebels, disembarked and announced they were there to transport the hostages to the international mission. The hostages were handcuffed and ordered to board the aircraft. Two of the original FARC rebels boarded with them and the helicopter took off. As soon as they were in the air, however, the FARC men were disarmed and handcuffed. A member of the crew turned to the astonished hostages, including Ingrid Betancourt and announced, 'We are the national military. You are free!'

Ingrid Betancourt emerged from her unimaginable ordeal saying, 'The only thing I've settled in my mind is that I want to forgive and forgiveness comes with forgetting.'

She flew to France to at last be joyously reunited with her children Melanie, twenty-three, but just sixteen when she was abducted, and Lorenzo, nineteen, but just thirteen when she was taken.

# THE NORD-OST THEATRE SIEGE

Nearly a thousand hostages endured a fifty-eight hour ordeal when a team of terrorists with a suicidal determination to seek independence descended on a Moscow theatre in the autumn of 2002. Interrupting a romantic tale of Russian love, these Chechen guerrillas rigged the auditorium to explode, threatening the lives of those inside. Refusing to come to terms with negotiators, the rebels forced Russian elite commandos to use extreme and unusual force, bringing the curtain crashing down on this thriller at the theatre.

## CAUSING A SCENE

On 23 October 2002, after intermission drinks, a packed house of Russian theatre-goers returned to their seats to watch the second act of a popular musical hit entitled *Nord-Ost*. Minutes later in this former Palace of Culture only three miles from the Kremlin, the audience were subjected to a scene-stealing performance as masked gunmen took to the stage with their own lines to deliver.

The audience's reaction was one of puzzlement, unsure whether this departure from the script was a new take on the old Russian favourite. However, when these intruders began to fire their assault rifles and force the performers off the stage and into the stalls, it became all too clear that this was not part of the act. As the frightened patrons were ordered to remain in their seats, further hostages were rounded up from elsewhere in the building.

Only a few members of the cast and crew managed to avoid capture, escaping out of an open window after hearing the gunfire. They quickly alerted the Russian authorities that nearly one thousand men, women and children were now at the mercy of some fifty terrorists inside the Dubrovka theatre.

## CHECHEN CHARADE

The unscheduled interruption was orchestrated by a group of Chechen rebels from a selection of Arab-funded terrorist organisations. Calling themselves the Riyadus-Salikhin Suicide Battalion, this band of activists made up of both men and women occupied the theatre to force the spotlight upon their ongoing conflict with Russia.

236

Chechnya, an oil-rich province in the Caucasus Mountains, had become a thorn in Moscow's side ever since it declared independence from Russia back in 1991. A year-long war ensued after the Kremlin ordered an invasion to bring the area back under their rule but, with a long history of Chechen resistance dating back to the nineteenth century, this proved difficult.

After a wave of Moscow bombing raids in 1999 claiming three hundred lives was deemed to be the work of the rebels, President Putin was forced to re-engage with the separatists and a second phase of fighting broke out. Pledging to the Russian people that he would quash the rebellion once and for all, Putin created a media blackout and persuaded the nation that order had been restored by 2002. This frustrated the Chechen insurrectionary forces who felt the need to put their forgotten plight back in the public eye.

## BLACK WIDOWS

Led by twenty-five year old Movsar Barayev, this cadre of autonomist fighters set about bringing the fight back to centre stage by striking at the heart of their Russian enemy and taking the Moscow theatre under their control. Willing to die for their cause, this suicide squad was determined that ordinary Muscovites would be forced to acknowledge the suffering of their people beyond the Caucasus mountains.

Nineteen of the terrorists holding the captive audience were female, dressed in black burkhas revealing only their defiant eyes. These determined women were known as 'black widows'; wives who had lost their husbands in the Chechen fight against Russian occupation. Fuelled by the deaths of their loved ones, these militants in mourning wore suicide belts filled with explosives. With one hand on their gun and the other on their detonator, they ordered select hostages to help with larger devices. These were set up in row fifteen and up in the balcony allowing the terrorists to bring the house down if their demands were not met.

## STALEMATE

The staged occupation of the Moscow theatre was swiftly surrounded by hundreds of Russian police and members of the FSB – the Federal Security Service – as armoured vehicles and fire engines cordoned off the entire area. Close to midnight contact was made with the terrorists and Russian authorities soon discovered the objectives of Barayev and his fellow separatists.

The rebels demanded complete withdrawal of Russian troops from Chechnya within seven days.

When negotiators informed them this was an unworkable timeframe, an adapted request for a start to the extraction was made. Failure to comply to this demand by dawn on Saturday would result in the execution of hostages and the destruction of the playhouse.

A period of bargaining ensued as each side refused offers made to bring an end to the crisis. Barayev asked for an audience with Akhmat Kadyrov, the pro-Moscow leader of the Chechen republic but no answer came. Similarly, a Russian offer of safe travel to a third country in exchange for all the hostages was met with snubbed silence. Despite this stalemate, the gunmen did show a desire for compromise releasing thirty hostages consisting mainly of pregnant women and young children. They also allowed the captives to use their mobile phones and while some called loved ones, others contacted the media, helping to increase awareness of the Chechen troubles.

Unfortunately the rebels' dark side would soon be revealed. Six hours into the ordeal, a twenty-six-year-old shop assistant called Olga Romanova entered the besieged building from her home which resided inside the police cordon. Once within the main hall, she began loudly ridiculing the rebels, calling them clowns whilst trying to encourage a sense of defiance in the broken-spirited hostages. Refusing to quit,

Barayev ordered her removal from the auditorium and seconds later shots were fired signifying the first fatality and the seriousness with which the hostage-takers were imbued.

## CALL FOR CALM

After further protracted talks and a consistent inability to come to terms particularly over the release of seventy-six foreign hostages throughout the second day of the siege, the Kremlin held an emergency meeting at four o'clock Friday afternoon. A decision to take action against the Chechen rebels had been agreed. With this go-ahead, the FSB deputy director Nikolai Patrushev delivered an ultimatum to the hostage-takers: free those inside and live. This veiled threat only served to anger Barayev who chose to retaliate with a warning of his own; for every member of his team killed by Russian troops, they would execute ten hostages.

With the dawn deadline for executions drawing ever nearer, negotiators focused all efforts on preventing any loss of life. Former presidents and Prime Ministers contacted Barayev to bring an end to the hostilities but all to no avail. At eleven o'clock, an hour after the release of four Azerbaijanis, General Viktor Kazantsev, Putin's special envoy in Chechnya, gave a final plea for calm. He also offered to meet for face-to-face talks the following morning, which softened the mood inside the auditorium. Feeling they had won a decisive battle against their Russian oppressors, the militants relaxed, waiting for the arrival of the diplomat.

This positive atmosphere would once more be broken with yet another trespasser of the police barricade entering the front doors of the building. This time it was a man called Gennady Vlakh seeking his son, Roma. The father was quickly apprehended by the gunmen and brought up on stage where Barayev called out the son's name. No answer from the auditorium confirmed the rebel leader's fears that this man was a possible FSB agent and had Vlakh escorted out the side doors to be shot.

The execution was too much for one young male hostage, who charged the female guard of the main bomb, tossing a bottle at her as he ran along the seat armrests. Two shots rang out, missing their intended target, but found two other audience members. One bullet struck the eye of Pavel Zakharov killing him instantly, and the other hit Tamara Starkova in chest. These unintended victims of rebel gunfire were removed from the theatre by ambulance at three in the morning. In two hours time, the need for para-medics would become all the more pressing.

## SHOWTIME

Half an hour after the wounded Tamara was made to leave her husband and daughter to the deadly whims of the Chechen rebels, loud explosions were heard emanating from within the Moscow playhouse. Believing the separatists had begun to execute hostages ahead of time, the Russian forces prepared for their assault. Knowing a surprise attack was out of the question with such well-defended corridors and stairwells, the Russian Special Forces or Spetsnaz opted for a rare and controversial approach.

With the searchlights cut, the scene plunged into darkness, Barayev and his rebels started to panic, waiting for the Russian offensive. Having rehearsed this moment in an identical theatre across town since day one of the siege, the Spetsnaz soldiers remained calm and focused, fully prepared for their opening night.

At approximately 05:15 hours a mysterious vapour was released by the Russian authorities, pumped through the ventilation system and holes created in the floor. As the hundreds of hostages dozed through the early morning hours they caught sight of a grey-green mist filling the main hall, its foul, acrid odour filling their nostrils. Terrorists and the terrorised slipped into a deep sleep until those still conscious, breathing through their clothes, were aware of loud snoring en masse echoing about the auditorium.

While the Chechen gunmen away from the gas fired wildly out of the windows, the two hundred Russian elite soldiers held fire, allowing this anaesthetic to overwhelm the opposition for a whole twenty minutes. Then three teams made their move. As one stood ready at the front doors, the other two units entered an underground nightclub which shared a wall with the theatre. Breaking through the orchestra pit, the Spetsnaz engaged the enemy and a brutal gunfight ensued.

The female suicide bombers, many of whom were out cold due to the fumes, were despatched with a bullet to the head affording them no chance of waking and setting off the bombs. No quarter was given to the remaining rebels including Barayev who was cornered in a first floor storeroom and gunned down by the Russian commandos and by seven-thirty the building was declared secure.

## SECRET AGENT

With the rebel peril suppressed, attention turned to a new threat on the rain-soaked Melnikov Street outside the theatre. Unconscious bodies of the captives had been removed from the building and left for ambulance staff to treat, however the facts about the mysterious miasma which had knocked out so many had been concealed.

The gas used by the Russian troops appears to have been a weaponised version of an opiate called fentanyl although its exact composition is still not publicly known. Since the paramedics at the scene were not fully appraised of the details, they were unaware a simple dose of Naxolone would have reversed the comatose states of the rescued hostages. Instead the drugged victims laid out on the pavement succumbed to the anaesthetic causing many to choke on their own tongues and vomit.

Hundreds were rushed to nearby hospitals under armed guard for fear that some were terrorists. Distraught relatives who had waited in agony for the crisis to come to an end were prevented from seeing their loved ones, however the victims did receive one visitor. Dressed in a white doctor's coat, President Putin made his rounds at the various infirmaries and publicly praised the attack which had saved so many lives.

The number of dead rose by the hour to a total of one hundred and twenty-six fatalities from gas poisoning. While over eight hundred and fifty survived the controversial rescue, many were scarred for life, left with long-term disabilities, a number of whom filed complaints with the European Court of Human Rights and began seeking $60 million in compensation. Investigations demanded by officials at home as well as from Europe and the US bore little fruit as Moscow shrouded the truth, prompting a wave of conspiracy theories.

# THE BESLAN
# HOSTAGE CRISIS

The Beslan Hostage Crisis remains an incident mired in disinformation and confusion. From day one there have been conflicting versions of events, of who the hostage-takers were and on whose behalf they were working. One account given by murdered FSB defector, Alexander Litvinenko, goes as far as to suggest that the Russian secret services themselves organised the attack. After all, he said in an interview, the hostage-takers had been in Russian custody until shortly before the assault on Comintern Street School Number One (SNO) in Beslan. They would only have been released, he went on, if they were going to be of some use to the FSB.

Of course, the official version – and the likely correct one – states that the attack was carried out by Chechen militants seeking the withdrawal of Russian troops from Chechnya as well as independence for their region. They had already perpetrated outrages in

Russia in pursuit of their goals, including taking hostage a theatre-full of people in Moscow and blowing up two airliners. The Beslan outrage was carried out by the Riyadus-Salikhin Reconnaissance and Sabotage Battalion of the Chechen Martyrs Group, which was headed by warlord Shamil Basayev, although he did not actively take part in the operation.

## THE DAY OF THE SIEGE

The Comintern Street School was a large one, with one hundred and ten teachers and one thousand one hundred pupils. There had been work done on the school recently, a new large gymnasium being added. However, when the work was carried out, the workforce had been infiltrated by Chechens who had concealed weapons and explosives in the building.

The school had something of a history. In 1992, it had been used by Ossetian militia as an internment camp for Ingush civilians, many of them women and children, during the war between Ossetia and Ingushetia. It is also said that a number of male internees were executed at that time. Furthermore, close to the town of Beslan was situated an airfield at which were based Russian planes that were used in air attacks on Chechnya.

1 September was an important day in the school calendar. Also known as the 'Day of Knowledge', it

was a day when parents and their children took part in ceremonies at the school. Consequently, there were a great deal more people in the school than on a normal day.

Early that morning a group of heavily armed rebel guerrillas left their base at a forest camp in Ingushetia. Travelling to Beslan, they encountered an Ingush police officer, Major Sultan Gurazhev. It is thought that he approached them hoping for a bribe, believing them to be part of an illicit oil-smuggling operation. Instead they took him prisoner and took his gun and his badge. He escaped from them and let the local police know what had happened. They did nothing about the incident.

They arrived at the school at around 9.30 that morning, dressed in camouflage uniforms and wearing balaclavas and explosive belts. The people at the school thought initially that they must be Russian police or army operatives on an exercise, but when the terrorists fired their weapons into the air it quickly became apparent that they were serious. Around fifty people managed to escape in the confusion, fleeing from the school grounds and alerting the police to what was developing. Local police officers arrived on the scene and immediately opened fire on the attackers, killing one and wounding several others. The hostage-takers herded their captives into the school building and secured it, making sure that they smashed the windows; their fellow hostage-takers in the theatre in Moscow had been thwarted when the authorities had flooded the building with poison gas. They were not going to let that happen a second time.

Sources differ as to the number of hostages taken. The Russian authorities said initially that it was between two hundred and four hundred but then settled on a suspiciously exact figure of 345. The number was actually later estimated to be 1,128. They were led into the school gym where all their mobile phones were confiscated. They were ordered to speak in Russian and not to speak at all unless one of the hostage-takers asked a question. The seriousness of their intent was callously displayed early in the incident. One man who tried to repeat what they were saying in the local language was executed with a bullet in the head. Another who refused to kneel was also shot. He was left to bleed to death.

They selected around twenty of their captives who looked as if they might have represented the biggest threat – teachers, school employees and fathers – and marched them into a corridor on the second floor. There an explosive belt worn by one of the female terrorists exploded, killing another woman terrorist and a few of the hostages. It was later reported that the leader of the gang, a man known as 'Polkovnik', had himself detonated the explosive belt because the women had objected to capturing children. Those of the twenty hostages who did not die in the explosion were ordered to lie down and were then shot dead.

Outside the school, activity was building. A security cordon was established and three apartment buildings that overlooked the school were occupied by Russian special forces. The situation was complicated, however, by the presence of Ossetian militiamen – the Opolchentsy – and armed townspeople, five thousand of whom had gathered at the scene.

The terrorists took no chances. They placed explosive devices throughout the gym and the building, which would be triggered by tripwires. They sent out a note that said that for every one of their operatives killed they would murder fifty hostages and for every one wounded, they would kill twenty. If the school was attacked, they said, they would blow it up. The note said they would not allow their hostages to eat or drink until the President of North Ossetia, Alexander Dzasokhov, arrived to negotiate with them. The Russian authorities refused, however, to let Dzasokhov anywhere near the school.

Internationally there was outrage and Russia requested a special meeting of the United Nations Security Council which demanded 'the immediate and unconditional release of all hostages of the terrorist attack'.

At the request of the terrorists, Leonid Roshal, a pediatrician who had been involved in the negotiations during the Moscow Theatre siege and had succeeded in having a number of children freed, was brought in. By the second day, however, it was clear that he was making no progress.

Meanwhile, there was unrest at the unrelenting silence from Moscow. President Vladimir Putin was saying nothing at all about the crisis, only making a comment of the second day during a meeting with King Abdullah of Jordan. He would say no more until it was over and would be heavily criticised for it.

Ruslan Aushev, retired army general and former President of Ingushetia, was allowed into the school in the afternoon of the second day, obtaining the release of twenty-six hostages – eleven nurses and fifteen children. He was also given a video tape by the hostage-takers and a note that contained demands from Shamil Basayev. Strangely, the Russian authorities declared the tape to be blank and refused to reveal the contents of the note. Later, it emerged that the note demanded 'formal independence for Chechnya' within the Commonwealth of Independent States (CIS). Basayev also wrote that although Chechens had not perpetrated the recent bombings of apartments in Russia, he was willing to accept responsibility for them if it made things easier.

## A DESPERATE SITUATION

Inside the gymnasium, by this time, children were collapsing due to lack of water and the heat. Many removed their clothing and some are said to have drunk their own urine. Their weakness as a result would ultimately kill them. Many would be too weak to flee when the gun battle erupted the following day.

The terrorists became increasingly edgy during the second day, some of their edginess being accounted for by the fact that twenty-one of them were users of heroin or morphine. One of the reasons they were able later to continue fighting in spite of horrific wounds and unbearable pain was the quantity of drugs in their bodies.

On the third day a number of possibilities arose. The separatist President of Ichkeria, Aslan Maskhadov, had been contacted and he said that he was prepared to fly to Beslan to negotiate with the terrorists. In another initiative, the Chechen Russian presidential adviser, Aslambek Aslakhanov, had gathered the names of seven hundred prominent Russians who were prepared to take the place of the children held in the school. However, it would all end before there was time to put either of these initiatives into action.

It had been agreed that four men in two ambulances would be allowed into the school grounds to remove the twenty bodies that lay there. As they approached the school, at around one in the afternoon, however, there was an explosion from inside followed by gunfire from the terrorists. Two of the ambulancemen were killed while the others scrambled for cover. The explosion, it has been reported, was accidental, a hostage-taker's foot having slipped off a dead man's switch detonator, although some said the government forces were responsible. Nonetheless, the Russian forces seized the opportunity and stormed the school but hostages escaping through the holes blown in the building's walls were caught in the crossfire and many died. There was chaos and confusion as armoured personnel carriers and armed helicopters covered the advancing troops. Flamethrowers and rocket-propelled grenades were fired from neighbouring buildings and a tank rumbled onto the grounds of the school. Two hours after the assault had begun, the Russians had control of most of the school although sporadic fighting continued into the night as pockets of hostage-takers were discovered.

## THE HORRIFIC DEATH TOLL

The death toll was terrible. Three hundred and ninety-six people died during the incident, including one hundred and twenty-two children and thirty-one hostage-takers. However, many hundreds are reported to still be missing.

Russian President Vladimir Putin responded by strengthening presidential power but the government has been severely criticised ever since for its serious mismanagement of the siege, a mismanagement that led to so many casualties.

# MARGARET HASSAN

She was worshipped by the people she helped, poor
Iraqis and, especially, children. They would gather
around her when she arrived, recognising a good soul,
a person who stood up for them and tried to make
their lives better. It was hard to fathom, therefore, how
she came to be kidnapped and held hostage by one of
the numerous shadowy groups that stalked Baghdad's
streets, looking for westerners from whom they could
make political capital. Even the insurgents were
puzzled by her abduction and issued a joint appeal for
her release. A measure of her standing can be seen in
the fact that even Abu Musab Zarqawi, the leader of
al-Qaeda in Iraq, who the Americans would later kill,
appealed on her behalf. He knew that in the 1960s she
had worked in Palestinian camps and he was aware of
the good work in which she was involved in Iraq.

## THE GOOD SAMARITAN

Margaret Hassan was born Margaret Fitzsimmons in
Ireland in 1945 and spent her early years in Dublin
before moving with her family to London where she

completed her education. In 1972, aged twenty-seven, she met and married an Iraqi, Tahseen Ali Hassan, who was studying engineering in Britain. She moved to Iraq with her new husband, obtaining a job with the British Council, teaching English in Baghdad. She learned Arabic and took out Iraqi citizenship which was a condition imposed by Saddam Hussein's government on any foreigners living in the country. She never converted to Islam, however, remaining a Roman Catholic all her life.

In 1979 when Saddam Hussein consolidated his grip on the reins of power in Iraq and then two years later when he declared war on Iran, launching a hugely damaging conflict that resulted in massive loss of life and deprivations for the citizens of each country, she never once considered leaving. She had fallen in love with Iraq and its people.

Meanwhile her career progressed and in the early 1980s she became the assistant director of studies at the British Council in Iraq, being promoted to director a few years later. When the Gulf War following Saddam's invasion of Kuwait brought an end to British Council activity in Baghdad, Margaret found herself unemployed at the end of the war. However, not once during the forty-two-day bombing campaign endured by Iraqis did she even contemplate leaving her adopted country.

In 1991, she took a job with the Brussels-based humanitarian relief organisation, CARE International. As conditions in Iraq deteriorated on the introduction of United Nations sanctions against Saddam's regime, with sanitation, health and nutrition suffering greatly, Margaret Hassan became a prominent critic of the sanctions and their effect on the Iraqi people. She was instrumental in obtaining medicine to help victims of leukaemia in 1998.

In January 2003 she told United Nations officials and British MPs that 'The Iraqi people are already living through a terrible emergency. They do not have the resources to withstand an additional crisis brought about by military action.' Aid agencies, she told one reporter, were only providing 'the proverbial drop in the ocean.' She believed sanctions to be inhuman.

## A POLITICAL PAWN

By 2004 she was in charge of CARE in Iraq but on 19 October, a group of men dressed in police uniforms stopped her car as she was being driven to her office in central Baghdad. Her driver and bodyguard, who was unarmed, were dragged from the car and badly beaten. She tried to intervene, saying she would go with them if they stopped beating the men. However, it was her they were after anyway and they had even tried and failed to abduct her several days previously.

It would be the last time she was seen, apart from her harrowing appearances in some videos sent by her abductors.

The first of these would be sent by her captors – calling themselves only 'an armed Islamic group' – to the Arabic television station, al-Jazeera, just a few hours after her capture. In it she was clearly distressed. Other videos followed, some of which were so harrowing that al-Jazeera refused to broadcast them. One sent on 2 November shows the woman Baghdadis called 'Madame Margaret' pleading for her life before falling to the ground in a dead faint. Her captors then seemed to have thrown a bucket of water over her to bring her round. She was shown lying on the ground, soaked and desperate before raising herself to her feet, weeping pitiably. In the video, her abductors talked about handing her over to the Islamic group led by Abu Musab al-Zarqawi, the same group that had beheaded the British contractor, Kenneth Bigley.

There was an immediate reaction. As she had been born in Ireland and was, therefore, eligible for Irish citizenship, the Irish government took up her case, as it had done with Kenneth Bigley. Her sister, Deirdre, made an emotional appeal for her release, as did her husband. Hundreds of protestors gathered outside the offices of CARE International in Baghdad demanding her release.

In a second video, Margaret appealed to British Prime Minister Tony Blair to withdraw British troops from Iraq. 'I beg of you to help me', she says in a seriously distressed voice and in another released on 27 October, she appears in a confused and understandably emotional state. A fourth video that was never released shows her clearly reading from a prepared text. From off-camera a man's voice can be heard urging her to stick to the text. She says, 'I admit that we worked with the occupation forces...' It is all lies, of course. This woman who loved Iraq and the Iraqis, who was vehemently opposed to the American-led invasion, would never have spied on Iraq.

## THE EXECUTION

The fifth and final tape shows her heartrending execution. Margaret Hassan can be seen standing in a bare room, wearing a white blouse and with a blindfold covering her face. A man wearing a grey and black checked shirt, baggy trousers and with a scarf covering his face, walks into camera carrying a pistol over the barrel of which he sticks what seems to be an apple; a makeshift silencer, it is presumed. He raises the gun to her head and pulls the trigger. However, there is only a click. The weapon has cruelly misfired. He returns, raises the gun to her head again and pulls the trigger. Those who have seen the video say that she uttered 'a tiny sound, a kind of cry, almost a squeal of shock' before falling backwards onto a plastic sheet on the floor. Heartlessly, the camera lingers on her body. There is no blood and little sign of a wound.

Strangely, the videos of Margaret Hassan in captivity did not have the usual trappings of a militant Islamic group. There were no Islamic banners, no Muslim chants and nobody claimed responsibility. However, several men were arrested in connection with her murder. One man, Mustafa Salman al-Jubouri was given a life sentence in June 2006 for the part he was alleged to have played but to the disappointment of Mrs Hassan's husband and family, his sentence was commuted to eighteen months on appeal. The ringleader remains at large, although a twenty-six-year-old English-speaking engineer was arrested in 2008 by British Special Forces and Iraqi troops. The man has confessed to being the interpreter for the al-Qaeda-linked gang who kidnapped Margaret Hassan.

To this date, her body has not been located.

# KENNETH BIGLEY

They rushed him out of the house, giving him an Arab headdress and robe to throw over the orange jumpsuit they had given him to wear that resembled those worn by the prisoners in Guantanamo Bay. Heart beating fast, he leapt into their waiting car. The men freeing him were two of his captors, but they had been given a large sum of money by a couple of agents working on behalf of MI6 to betray their organisation, the Tawhid and Jihad terrorist group and get British hostage, sixty-two-year-old Kenneth Bigley to safety in an American-controlled zone.

The car sped off in the direction of Latifya, southwest of Baghdad. But just five minutes later, they were stopped by a couple of cars filled with other members of the terrorist group. Under the headdress, they immediately recognised the face of Kenneth Bigley. Even if they were not terrorists, they would have recognised it from the hundreds of thousands of leaflets the British had distributed in recent weeks in the city trying to obtain information about his whereabouts. Bigley and his two liberators were returned to the house in which he had been held since his capture. All three men knew that the consequences of their failed escape attempt would be dire.

## THE KIDNAP AND DEMANDS

It had all begun on 16 September 2004. Kenneth John Bigley, from Liverpool, was kidnapped in the up-market al-Mansour district of Baghdad where he had been living. Taken with him were two American citizens, Jack Hensley and Eugene Armstrong. All three men were civil engineers, employed by Gulf Supplies and Construction Services, a company involved in construction projects in Iraq. Bigley was working on one last payday; in a few weeks he would retire and enjoy life with his forty-two-year-old Thai wife, Sombat. He was also looking forward to the birth of his first grandchild. He would not live to see it.

It emerged two days after the abduction of the men that they had been taken hostage by the Islamist group, Tawhid and Jihad ('Oneness of God and Jihad' – 'Jihad' meaning 'holy war'). This group was led by the Jordanian terrorist, Abu Musab al-Zarqawi, a close associate of al-Qaeda leader, Osama bin Laden. A video was released showing the three men kneeling in front of a banner that supported Tawhid and Jihad. It also laid out the demands that they had for the release of the men. If Iraqi women prisoners held by coalition forces were not released within forty-eight hours, the hostages would be killed.

The demand was somewhat confusing as the British government claimed not to hold any Iraqi women prisoners and issued a statement to that effect. The only Iraqi women known to be in custody at that time were held by the United States. The United Nations weapons inspectorate had alleged that British-educated Dr Rihav Taha and American-educated Dr Huda Salih Mahdi Anmash had worked in Saddam Hussein's biological weapons programme. The Iraqi provisional government announced that the two women could be released immediately, adding that their release had been imminent anyway, even before the kidnapping of the three men, as no charges were going to be brought against them.

Four days after the abduction, on the day that the deadline expired, 20 September, a video was posted on Islamist websites showing the horrific beheading of Eugene Armstrong. Twenty-four hours later, Jack Hensley was also brutally beheaded.

In Britain, there was a media frenzy about Kenneth Bigley as the British government turned the issue of his capture into a major political issue, something for which they were later criticised. Many referred to the political disaster that US President Jimmy Carter endured when he did the same during the 444-day

Iran hostage crisis that began in 1979. Many believed that his presidency never recovered from this incident leading to his failure to win re-election for a second term.

Prime Minister Tony Blair and Foreign Secretary, Jack Straw, were in touch with the Bigley family and reassured them that all that could be done was being done, short of direct negotiation with al-Zarqawi and the hostage-takers, but as fears mounted about whether Bigley was still alive, a grim video was released on 22 September in which he pleaded for his life, appealing directly to Tony Blair. 'I need you to help me now, Mr Blair,' he said, 'because you are the only person on God's earth who can help me.'

The Irish government made an intervention when it emerged that Bigley's eighty-six-year-old mother, Lil, had actually been born in Dublin which made her an Irish citizen. It also meant that Kenneth Bigley was an Irish citizen. They issued Bigley with an Irish passport that was shown on the al-Jazeera Arabic television channel. It was hoped that the fact the Irish had not participated in the 2003 invasion of Iraq might have helped his cause. An Irish Labour Party spokesman, Michael D. Higgins, appeared on al-Jazeera and Sinn Fein leader, Gerry Adams, a man with whom it was hoped the terrorists might identify, made a couple of appeals for the release of Bigley.

There were many other appeals, one of the most important of which came from the Muslim Council of Great Britain which condemned the kidnapping, adding that the action was contrary to the teachings of the Qur'an. A delegation was sent from the council to Baghdad to open negotiations for Bigley's release. At the same time, his brother Paul obtained support for their cause from such important figures in the Arab world as Palestinian leader, Yasser Arafat, the Jordanian King Abdullah and Colonel Gadaffi, the Libyan leader.

In Liverpool Christians and Muslims prayed together for his release while fifty thousand leaflets were distributed on 24 September by the British Foreign Office in the al-Mansour district where the abduction had taken place. Another one hundred thousand would be distributed two days later on 1 October.

On 29 September, another even grimmer video was released. This time Bigley was dressed in the orange boiler suit. He was chained up inside a cage made of chicken wire and begged once more for his life. This time, however, there was a hopelessness in his voice as if he already knew his fate. 'Tony Blair is lying,' he said. 'He doesn't care about me. I'm just one person.'

## THE EXECUTION

Kenneth Bigley's execution was first reported on 8 October on a television station in Abu Dhabi. It said that he had been beheaded the previous day. The news was sadly confirmed when a film of it was posted on various websites. Bigley, still wearing the orange boiler suit, is shown reading a statement. A man, later confirmed by voice recognition technology to be al-Zarqawi himself, then steps forward and beheads him.

His body has never been found although it is said to have been buried in a ditch at the entrance to the town of Fallujah, a Sunni Muslim stronghold, where it is believed he was being held.

The chicken wire cage in which Kenneth Bigley was shown was later believed to have been found in Fallujah following the invasion of the town by US forces following the Second Battle of Fallujah. The troops claimed to have found no fewer than twenty houses that appeared to have been used to hold hostages. There were torture chambers, shackles and walls soaked in blood in the buildings. One report said that they also found a number of bodies, believed to be Iraqis, hanging from the walls.

Abu Musab al-Zarqawi was killed by American forces in June 2006.

# ALAN JOHNSTON

12 March 2007 was a beautiful spring day in Gaza City. BBC News reporter, Alan Johnston, had driven across the border into Israel that morning for a dental appointment and was now back in the city from where he had been reporting for several years on the plight of the Palestinian people.

## ALAN, THE REPORTER

Johnston, born in Tanganyika – present-day Tanzania – to Scottish parents, had joined the BBC in 1991 after graduating from the University of Dundee and studying journalism at the University of Wales in Cardiff. During his time at the BBC, he had been widely-travelled and had worked in some very dangerous places, trouble spots such as Tashkent, Uzbekistan and Kabul, capital of war-torn Afghanistan. Gaza was an equally dangerous place to ply the journalistic trade and by 2007 most news agencies and broadcasters had withdrawn their reporters. In fact, Alan Johnston was the only reporter from a major western news organisation still to be based in Gaza City. In this capacity, he had provided vital reports on all of the most important happenings in the region – Israel's 2005 unilateral disengagement plan, Hamas's victory in the 2006 legislative elections, the 2006 fighting between Gaza and the Israelis and the factional violence that had decimated Gaza in 2006 and 2007.

He was respected and experienced, recognised by many in Gaza for bringing the situation in the territory to western eyes. Gaza, however, was a perilous, edgy place and Johnston and his family were well aware of the daily dangers, principal of which was the threat of being kidnapped.

## TAKEN AS A HOSTAGE

He realised immediately what was happening, therefore, when a car suddenly sped past him and then stopped sharply in front of him, forcing him to also brake. A young man leapt from the car and rushed round to Johnston's door, waving a pistol at him. His door was pulled open and he was grabbed and roughly bundled into the back seat of their car where he was made to lie down out of sight. They pulled a hood over his head and the car set off in a southerly direction, through some of Gaza's more dangerous areas.

Alan Johnston was not the first journalist to be kidnapped in Gaza. It had been a regular activity for the disaffected militant factions who used these acts to gain some ground in whatever dispute they were having with the authorities. Traditionally, victims had been held for no more than a few weeks and little would change as a result. Recently, it had become much more serious, however.

Two members of a team from the American network, Fox News, had been taken the previous summer and were released only after they had made a denunciation of the West and its support for Israel, recorded on video and released to the media. The men were also forced to convert publicly to Islam. The kidnappings were becoming increasingly violent and kidnappers were not just settling territorial disputes locally; like their brothers in Iraq and Afghanistan, they were waging Jihad – holy war – on the West. Naturally, the BBC was concerned about Alan Johnston's presence in this dangerously unstable environment and had taken steps to lessen the chance of him being kidnapped. Advice from security experts had resulted in him moving to a new apartment and he made sure that he did not settle into any routines that could be used to capture him. All his movements became random and unpredictable. Ultimately, he believed the work he was doing in Gaza was important and, therefore, worth the risk. He almost made it, too. When he was taken, he was just sixteen days away from the end of his assignment there.

When the car eventually stopped, he was led into a building and pushed down onto a thin mattress in a room. It was the first of his eighty-four days in captivity.

## A BARGAINING CHIP

That first night, he met the man behind his capture when the door opened and a figure dressed in a long white robe stepped into the room, a red chequered headdress covering his face, concealing his identity. In a calm and surprisingly friendly voice, he told Johnston that he was now nothing more than a bargaining chip in a struggle to free Muslims in British jails. Reassuringly he told him that he would not be killed and that he would be treated well. Eventually, he said, he would be permitted to leave when the time was right. The man stood up and left, turning to say with a smile that one day Johnston would write a book about his experiences. The door closed and it suddenly struck Alan Johnston that this could be a very long process.

Shortly after, they returned and placed the hood over his head again. As he was led from the room, he suddenly feared that he was being taken out to be shot. It turned out, however, that he was merely being moved to another cell in another building. He would remain there for some time.

His new room was on the roof of a block of flats. Its furnishings consisted of a narrow bed and a couple of plastic chairs. He was provided with nothing else, had no writing materials and nothing to read. His watch having been taken, he began to learn to tell the time from the call to prayer that rang out five times a day from the muezzins in the nearby mosques.

One of his first problems was his eyesight. As if things were not bad enough, he wore disposable contact lenses that were useless after one day and had to be thrown away. Without them, his eyesight was very poor and the sparse furnishings of his cells became little more than blurred outlines. Avoiding them, he constantly paced back and forward in his tiny cell – just five strides wide and five long.

By 26 March, his kidnapping had become the longest-ever of a foreigner in Gaza. The BBC had finally confirmed that he had, in fact, been kidnapped after a week of no contact from him. Israeli sources speculated that the same Palestinian group that had captured the Israeli soldier Gilad Shalit in June 2006 had taken him. Others said he had been taken by a powerful Gaza criminal family who wanted the release of ten Hamas gunmen. One ridiculous rumour even had it that Johnston had staged his own disappearance, having learned that he was about to be sacked by the BBC.

In the fourth week a tape arrived at the Gaza offices of the television channel, al-Jazeera. It was from a group calling itself the Army of Islam which claimed to have been responsible for the kidnapping. The tape demanded the release of all Palestinian prisoners – including Sheikh Abu Qatada – from British jails.

Meanwhile, the abduction had been condemned by all, including the Palestinian National Authority who demanded Johnston's release. Palestinian journalists held a rally on 17 March outside the Palestinian Parliament. His father, Graham, made an emotional appeal for his release and he was supported in this by BBC Director-General, Mark Byford. BBC staff held rallies to protest, the European Union and United Nations denounced the action and demanded Johnston's release and at the end of a two-day summit meeting, Saudi foreign minister Saud al-Faisal, condemned the abduction, saying that Alan Johnston had merely been doing his job.

### TERMS OF SURVIVAL

Meanwhile, Johnston became ill. The food was palatable Palestinian fare – rice or dishes made from beans or vegetables – but something – perhaps the

*Betty and Barney Hill claimed to have been abducted by aliens on the night of 19–20 September 1961, as they were driving home. Here they can be seen here holding a book written about their experience.*

*Not all terrorist attacks end in tragedy. This is the happy outcome of the hijacking of an Air-France airliner 139. The plane landed in Idi Amin's Uganda and the Israeli passengers were held hostage at the Entebbe airport. The photo shows the crowd lifting the squadron leader of the rescue planes on their return to Israel.*

*The body of former Italian Prime Minister Aldo Moro is discovered in the trunk of a Renault van in the via Caetani in Rome. Moro had been held captive by the militant communist group the Red Brigades for fifty-four days before his murder in 1978.*

*A man carries a young hostage who managed to escape after Russian special forces entered the Comintern Street School in Beslan, which had been occupied by terrorists for three days in 2004.*

*Margaret Hassan, the British-Iraqi head of Care International's operations in Iraq, was seized by kidnappers in Baghdad on 19 October 2004, and later executed after negotiations failed.*

*Marc Dutroux, Belgium's 'most hated' man with a history of violent sexual behaviour, was found guilty of child abduction and murder in 2004, seven years after his arrest.*

*Josef Fritzl, a seventy-three-year-old Austrian, locked his daughter in a cellar for twenty-four years and fathered seven children with her. He was found guilty and sentenced to life in a psychiatric institution, much to the delight of his long-suffering family.*

*On 8 December 1963, Barry Keenan and Joe Amsler, both twenty-three years old, abducted nineteen-year-old Frank Sinatra Jr from a hotel room in Lake Tahoe, Nevada. Above, Mrs Nancy Sinatra embraces her son after being released by the kidnappers for a $240,000 ransom.*

dirty water he had to drink – disagreed with him. He had to do something and realised his best hope was just to eat the potato chips he was often served. He worked out that the hot oil in which the potatoes were cooked would kill bacteria and so requested that his water be boiled. Bread, fruit and tomatoes bolstered this rather plain diet, but at least he was healthy. By the time he left captivity, however, he would have lost 10 kilos.

He had requested a radio but it was only after some time in captivity that they relented and brought him one. At last he had contact with the outside world and something to take away the unbearable isolation that he was feeling. His spirits were raised still further by the news that the world was rallying for his release, especially the news that even Palestinians were condemning his abductors.

Suddenly, however, he was stunned when during a BBC news broadcast he heard the newsreader say that he had been executed. His first thought was for his family and how they would be feeling on being presented with such a report. He also worried that the report would imminently come true. He prepared himself mentally for a videotaped execution, determined to go to his death with courage and dignity. That awful night passed, however, although it was far from the last time that he feared for his life.

Some weeks later, a guard rushed into the room with a set of manacles with which he chained his arms and legs together. He also shut the window and switched off the light. It was being decided, he chillingly told the reporter, whether he was going to be put to death. They would cut his throat if they decided to kill him, the man added.

Again the crisis eventually ended and his chains were removed.

One of the guards allowed Johnston to see his father making a televised appeal to his son's kidnappers. The dignity of his parents in the face of such trauma bolstered his spirits, giving him the courage to hang on. Gradually, the regime slackened still further and he was allowed to make his own meals but the guards, all of them wanted men, were still subject to frightening rages and unsettling mood swings.

When Hamas seized control of Gaza it was good news for Alan Johnston. Hamas was opposed to the kidnapping and his release became a priority for them. However, as his prospects for release improved on the outside, life for him in captivity became worse, and, if anything, even more threatening. They made him wear a suicide bomber's vest with pockets of explosives fastened around his waist. Wearing this, he was forced to record a video message. All around him there was activity as his captors prepared for an assault on their quarters by Hamas.

## A SURPRISE RELEASE

Suddenly one night the hood was placed over his head again and he was taken downstairs to a waiting car. His guards, armed to the teeth in the back seat on either side of him were screaming and shouting. One of them hit him and he tasted blood. They were surrounded by Hamas men and gunfire could break out at any moment, gunfire that he knew could result in his death.

Eventually, the car stopped. He was dragged out and taking off his hood found himself in an alley filled with heavily armed men. For a moment it struck him that he was merely being handed over to a different faction, as sometimes happened in such cases, but as he turned a corner, there in front of him was a familiar face, his BBC colleague, Fayed Abu Shamalia.

A few days later, Alan Johnston was walking in the fresh air of the hills of Argyll with his family, his four months of hell finally behind him.

# PART THREE

# A QUESTION OF INSANITY

# LEON BEARDEN: CONTINENTAL FLIGHT 54

It was 1.50 am on 3 August 1961 and all was quiet on board the Continental Airlines Boeing 707. It was a few hundred miles northwest of El Paso – about sixteen minutes flying time – on its routine flight from Los Angeles to Houston. The flight attendants had finished their service of food and refreshments, the lights were dimmed and most of the seventy-three passengers on board had settled back for the remainder of the flight, reading or dozing in their seats.

Suddenly, towards the rear of the plane, there was a commotion. One passenger recalled seeing one of the stewardesses being shoved along the aisle between the rows of seats by a young man he estimated to be aged around seventeen. What he failed to see, however, was that the young man was pressing a revolver against the girl's ribs. The girl did not appear alarmed and the watching passenger said he thought they were just 'fooling around'.

In the cockpit, however, things were different. Captain Byron Rickards, a veteran of the air with thirty-three years' experience as a commercial airline pilot, immediately understood what was happening when two of the flight crew edged nervously into the cabin closely followed by two men, each carrying a gun. The elder of the two men, a balding man in his late thirties, raised his revolver and put its barrel menacingly against the temple of one of the steward-esses. 'We are going to Cuba,' he snarled. 'Alter your course forty-five degrees to the south.'

## BEARDEN BACKGROUND

The two men were father and son, Leon and Cody Bearden. Thirty-eight-year-old Leon was an un-employed car salesman from Coolidge, Arizona. Life had not worked out well for Leon – his criminal record included prison stays for robbery, forgery and theft. He had never been a very happy man and bore a large grudge against the United States government whom he blamed for all his troubles. He was mentally unstable, having spent time in a mental hospital in Phoenix. He and his son, sixteen-year-old Cody, had come up with the idea of going to Cuba where they would renounce their American citizenship and begin a new life. Needless to say, however, they did not have enough money to buy the tickets they required. The only solution was to follow the example of the many Cubans who had been hijacking planes and taking them to Cuba. Indeed, the words 'Take me to Cuba' had become something of a joke, so frequent had hijackings become. President Kennedy and his administration, tiring of the endless sky piracy had brought out new laws to cover it. Hijacking was now punishable by death. Thus, the Beardens were taking a huge risk in hijacking this plane.

Captain Rickards had seen it all before. A South Dakotan, he had had his first brush with air piracy as long ago as 1931 when as a young pilot for Panagra Airlines, his plane had been captured – along with him and his crew – during a rebellion in Arequipa in Peru. He quickly appraised his situation and decided to play for time, to introduce delaying tactics in order to allow the people on the ground to come up with a plan that would prevent the plane from going anywhere near Cuban airspace.

## DELAYING TACTICS

Captain Rickards calmly announced to the Beardens that the plane did not have enough fuel to make it all the way to Cuba. They would have to land in El Paso to take on board the extra fuel needed. Leon Bearden gave his permission for the refuelling stop and Rickards made contact with the control tower at El Paso, letting them know what was going on in the sky above them. 'We want gas to go to Cuba,' he told them.

As the plane landed ten or so minutes later, FBI operatives, border patrolmen and police officers, summoned from their beds, were rushing to the airport. Word was spreading that another couple of crazy Cubans had skyjacked a plane. Two Air National Guard F-100 fighter planes were scrambled from Albuquerque's Kirtland Air Force Base and flew in the direction of El Paso International Airport. Meanwhile, Continental Airline's President, Robert Six, issued an order to stall the plane in any way possible and for as long as possible.

Leon Bearden had told Rickards before they landed to pass on an order to El Paso ground control that no ramps were to be brought out to the plane. Only the refuelling vehicle was to approach it. As soon as the 707 rolled to a halt, a fuel truck drove out to it, stopping under its wing where the ground crew went about its business, hooking up the fuel line and beginning to pump in fuel. They deliberately moved slower than usual, however, heeding Six's order to delay the flight as much as possible.

On board the plane one of the stewardesses announced to the confused passengers that, 'We may be flying on to Havana.' They had already got the message when they had spotted Cody leaning on the doorway of the cabin, casually swinging his revolver.

One of the passengers, a pregnant woman became hysterical and others were seriously distressed by the situation they found themselves in. Leon could see the situation getting out of hand. There were only two of them, after all, to control more than seventy people. The best way, he resolved, was to let all of them go except four who would stay on board as hostages and would be much more easily managed during the trip to Cuba. He announced this to the passengers, allowing them to nominate the four who would remain on board. Continental employee, Jack Casey elected to stay, as did Luis Evrives of Los Angeles. The other two could prove difficult for the hijackers, however. Army Private Truman Cleveland surreptitiously swapped his army uniform for civilian clothing and volunteered, as did Leonard Gilman who, as luck would have it, was an off-duty United States border patrol officer. He kept that fact to himself, however.

The other passengers were allowed to leave the plane but as the first of them leapt to the ground, the waiting law officers believed them to be hijackers and one was knocked to the ground and handcuffed. The stewardesses quickly restored order, explaining to the agents what was actually going on.

Meanwhile, at the airport perimeter, some of the thousands of onlookers who had gathered were leaking through the road blocks set up by the police to keep them away. Some reporters and photographers had even made it on to the runway and were waiting expectantly close to the plane. It was a chaotic scene.

Captain Rickards continued to delay take-off as dawn crept over the mountains around El Paso Airport. He told Leon Bearden that the 707 was too large to land at José Marti Airport in Havana, that they would have to wait for a smaller DC-7 that had already taken off and was on its way to El Paso. The delay only made the hijackers increasingly nervous.

In Washington, meanwhile, President Kennedy and his security advisers were being kept informed about developments. Still convinced that the flight had been hijacked by Cubans, the president ordered that there should be no exchange of planes. He wanted the affair to be ended by the law officers on the scene.

Eventually Leon had had enough. He had been arguing with Rickards and the control tower for hours. It was time to go. He ordered the pilot to take off, emphasising his determination dramatically with a bullet into the floor of the cockpit between the feet of the Second Officer. His point was made. Rickards called the control tower and told them that the refuelling had to be finished and the plane readied for take-off. 'Things are getting desperate on this plane,' he informed them calmly.

## DESPERATE TACTICS

The ground crew at last finished the refuelling, unhooked the fuel pipe and drove away from the plane. Rickards released the brakes and the plane started to taxi forward to the start of the runway. At that moment cars poured out of the area around the terminal building, officers hanging out of the windows wielding rifles and machine guns. A fusillade of bullets was poured into the plane's undercarriage and it jerked to a stop, its eight large tyres blown out and one of its engines shot up.

On the plane the Beardens were becoming increasingly desperate and when FBI agent Francis Crosby came on board to negotiate with them, Leon became hysterical, threatening to kill himself rather than be arrested or shot. At that moment, Leonard Gilman suddenly swung his fist in a powerful uppercut, knocking Leon out with a shuddering blow to the chin. So powerful was the punch that Gilman's hand was broken. The others leapt on Cody, easily disarming him.

After ten hours it was over and for the foreseeable future Leon and Cody Bearden would be spending their time as guests of the United States Federal Government rather than Fidel Castro.

# COLLEEN STAN

The inherent dangers of hitchhiking are well known to those travelling by thumb but when Colleen Stan climbed into the backseat of a blue Dodge Colt in May 1977, she was blind to her fate. This particular ride would see her consigned to seven years of torture and humiliation at the hands of a brutal sadomasochist. Forced to become his slave and sexual toy, the young hitchhiker was confined to a wooden box beneath her captors' bed and subjected to unspeakable abuse; her nightmare ending only after a confession to a priest brought the tragic truth out in the open.

## THE ROAD TO HELL

In 1970s America, hitchhiking was a common way of moving around the country particularly for the youth of the time. However when twenty-year-old Colleen Stan decided to thumb her way to the Westwood area of Northern California to visit a friend, she could not have imagined the terrible fate that would soon befall her.

On Thursday 19 May 1977, her roommates Bob and Alice took her to the nearby highway in Eugene, Oregon, from where she planned to hitch her way south four hundred miles to the Golden State. Thanks to the kindness of strangers, the blue-eyed Colleen managed to make it all the way to Red Bluff, California without any problems. Now only fifty miles from her destination, she waited on the I-5 overpass for her next ride.

Forever cautious, Colleen refused to accompany a carload of men who had stopped to pick her up and when the next vehicle was only going a few miles, she chose to hold out for a better offer. When a blue Dodge Colt pulled over at the sight of her extended thumb, she was happy to see it contained a clean-cut couple in their twenties. The woman was even holding a baby in her arms. What could be safer?

Climbing into the backseat, disregarding the strange wooden box beside her, the young traveller settled in for what she hoped would be the final stage of her journey. By the time they stopped for gas half an hour later Colleen was beginning to doubt her judgement. She had spotted the man staring at her in the rear-view mirror and so, alone in the station restroom, she wondered whether to ditch the couple and find another ride. Telling herself that the man, while creepy, would not do anything with his wife and child in the car, she returned to the Dodge Colt to continue her road trip.

Discussing the local sights of the area, the driver suggested they make an impromptu stop at the nearby ice caves. Making good time and not wanting to rock the boat, Colleen agreed and it was not long before they turned down an isolated dirt track. Coming to a halt, the mother and child exited the car but before their passenger could get out, the man pounced. Holding a knife to her throat, he bound, gagged and blindfolded Colleen before turning to the strange wooden box next to her.

The plywood contraption measuring fifteen by fifteen by eighteen inches was placed over her head and served to block out all sights and sounds. Suffering this sensory deprivation, she could just make out the car moving once again and descend down a winding mountain road; a road to hell.

## A MARRIAGE VOW

Colleen's clean-cut attacker was one Cameron Hooker; a man possessing some dark and sinister fantasies. Despite being born in 1953 to a hardworking and devout working class family, he was to develop a disturbing predilection for sadomasochistic pornography. In 1973 he met Janice, a fifteen-year-old epileptic, who was quick to succumb to Cameron's kinky desires.

Endless acts of degradation continued unabated for the young Janice even when the pair married two years later. With a live and compliant victim, Cameron was able to play out his fantasies and soon his appetite for sexual malice began to grow. It was then that the couple made a pact: if she allowed him a love slave, he would give her a child. When Janice fell pregnant soon after, she hoped her husband had forgotten about her side of the bargain. Unfortunately, he had already began planning how to capture his second live victim, constructing the 'head box' which would soon cage the face of Colleen Stan.

Fast forward to 1977 and, under the cover of darkness, Cameron and his subservient wife brought the snatched hitchhiker back to their rented home on Oak Street in the rural town of Red Bluff. Once inside, Colleen's head was removed from the stifling box. However before she could express any relief, she was dragged down to the basement, cuffed to pipes running along the ceiling and the ice chest on which she stood was kicked away. Suspended in the air, a dazed and disorientated Colleen hung in fear, waiting anxiously for unknown tortures to commence.

## TORTURE TECHNIQUES

Eager to break in his new-found slave, Cameron pulled down Colleen's jeans and began to flog her bare legs, front and back. Once he had whipped up a frenzy, the perverted kidnapper stopped, pausing only to bring his partner in crime down to the cellar, and beneath the dangling, welted body of their victim, the Hookers proceeded to have sex. Once they had had their fun, Colleen was cut down and forced inside a coffin-sized box so cramped her breathing was severely restricted. This was just the beginning of a series of actions designed to tame the abducted slave.

Over the next few months, Colleen was subjected to a depressing variety of sadistic torture techniques. She was half-drowned in water, stretched out on a rack, electrocuted by wires linked to the mains and burnt with matches and light-bulbs all for the sexual gratification of the merciless Cameron Hooker.

It was not long before these incessant physical and mental torments began to take their toll on poor Colleen. Living on meagre rations, she lost over twenty pounds in weight and stopped menstruating. She soon realised in order to survive these ordeals, she had to remain silent. Any pleas for mercy only served to encourage her captor and before long the once-vivacious young woman had become with-drawn; a broken shadow of her former self.

## THE CONTRACT

Eight months into her captivity, after missing her

twenty-first birthday and New Year celebrations, Colleen Stan was removed from her wooden box on 25 January 1978 and handed an official-looking document. Entitled 'This Indenture' and copied from one of his underground S & M magazines, Cameron demanded his captive sign what amounted to a slave contract. Her soul suitably beaten into submission after months of torture, Colleen – rechristened K – willingly provided her signature, agreeing to devote her mind and body to Hooker whom she was to call 'master'.

To add weight to this deed Cameron invented a secret society of slave traders known as 'The Company', to which he told her he belonged. He informed Colleen that members of this clandestine group were always watching and were prepared to inflict even greater harm on both her and her family if she failed to act as his model servant. Worried for the safety of her loved ones, the beguiled hostage committed herself to the perverse whims of her master, obeying his every order, observing every rule.

## INVISIBLE CHAINS

In 1980, Colleen's complete dedication to her captor over three long years of confinement built a level of trust. She was rewarded with longer periods outside the wooden box now kept underneath the marital bed and allowed to perform a range of chores around the house. Still very much a slave, Colleen worked as the Hookers' maid, gardener and nanny to their two young children, Christy and Angela.

Proving she could handle this newly-acquired freedom without taking advantage, Cameron granted Colleen yet more independence and allowed her to go jogging, visit the local store and even attend church. She never thought to run for the hills for fear of reprisals from her vengeful master or his fictitious 'Company' associates, always returning to the Hooker home like a loyal and obedient pet, an invisible leash around her neck at all times.

Later that year, Cameron permitted his slave to go out on the town with his wife. Satisfied Colleen and Janice belonged to him in every way, he gave his consent for both women to pick up men from the bars in Red Bluff and have sex with them. They both dutifully obliged, wishing to please their master. Enjoying the fruits of his complete subjugation of both his wife and hostage, Cameron decided to set Colleen the ultimate test of obedience.

## HOME AND AWAY

After nearly four years as his prisoner and slave, Cameron chose to let Colleen visit her family in Riverside, nearly nine hours drive down the I-5 into Southern California. While it was a welcome return home, there were conditions. She was forbidden to discuss the existence of 'The Company' and, when questioned about her own whereabouts, she was to give only vague answers. Still under her master's control, a frail Colleen arrived on her father's doorstep, a thin portrayal of her old self.

Concerned an intense grilling would send their child away again, Colleen's surprised parents made a concerted effort not to cross-examine her but to simply focus on the happy fact that their daughter was now home after so long. However, after just two days, Cameron called pretending to be her fiancé and said he was coming to pick her up. As quickly as she had arrived, Colleen disappeared once more from her parents' lives and back into slavery over five hundred miles upstate.

This brief homecoming would signal the end of her rewards for compliance. Once back in Red Bluff, Cameron took away all her privileges of semi-freedom and, after a year's relief from the cramped wooden coffin, she returned to the box beneath the bed to spend twenty-two hours of every day for the next three years.

During this second term of incarceration, Cameron started to yearn for more excitement beyond what was provided by either his wife or Colleen. Such was the extent of his sadomasochistic desires, one submissive sex slave was not enough and he began to plan further abductions. Dreaming of an entire harem of dutiful women, he built a dungeon in the backyard in the autumn of 1983 and moved Colleen into it. Fortunately for Colleen and any forthcoming victims, the underground chamber flooded killing any immediate hopes of a slave collective, and his one solitary hostage was placed back underneath the bed.

## CONFESSIONAL RELEASE

Approaching her seventh full year under the complete control of her sadistic captor, Colleen was once more afforded some semblance of freedom. In May 1984 the twenty-seven-year-old hostage was released during the day to work as a maid at the nearby King's Lodge Motel, her wages set aside for a place of her own. Even with this prospective arrangement Janice Hooker knew her husband would never surrender the hold on his slave.

Over the passing years, Cameron's insignificant other had grown tired of this disturbing love triangle and so that summer, her conscience stained with guilt, Janice paid a visit to Frank Dabney, the pastor at her local Nazarene church. Omitting the finer points of Colleen's abduction and ongoing sexual assault, the complicit wife unburdened herself, confessing to the long-held secret of their ménage a trois.

Advised to leave home with Colleen, Janice Hooker picked the slave girl up from the motel and, on the 9 August 1984, told her 'The Company' was but a figment of her husband's imagination; a simple ruse to keep her confined. With this sole restriction to her freedom destroyed, Colleen decided to leave her master the following day, calling him from a bus station to break the bad news. More than three years after her last fleeting visit, the estranged daughter was back on her father's doorstep but this time free of Cameron's invisible chains.

## NO LONGER A VICTIM

Since Colleen wished to forget about her seven year ordeal and had no wish to involve the police, Cameron Hooker's sexually deviant crimes appeared as if they would go unpunished. However, Janice made another trip to Pastor Dabney to disclose the whole truth about her husband's slave in a box, which brought the police to the Hooker home. Despite Cameron having torched the majority of his incriminating material, enough physical evidence was discovered to arrest the thirty-one-year-old sadomasochist.

Charged with kidnapping, false imprisonment and a series of sex offences, Cameron Hooker stood trial a year later with both his wife and his former slave taking the stand to testify against him. His defence lawyers urged the jury to perceive the sexual acts as consensual not criminal. They also called into question her imprisonment, highlighting the numerous occasions on which Colleen could have escaped. However, bolstered by a solid testimony from psychologist Dr Chris Hatcher who explained how she still remained under the control of her master despite the lack of a leash, the prosecution was ultimately successful in gaining a full conviction.

After a five-week-long trial, it was now Cameron Hooker's turn to take orders. The jury at San Mateo Court found him guilty and Judge Clarence Knight sentenced the heinous hostage-taker to a total of one hundred and four years behind bars. As he served his time in a Folsom prison cell, ineligible for parole until 2023, Colleen Stan strove to live a normal life after her seven year crucible of pain and suffering. Married twice and now with a daughter in her twenties, Colleen refuses to remain a victim beyond her ordeal, spending much of her time as a volunteer counsellor for a crisis hotline helping fellow sufferers of domestic violence and sexual assault.

# GARY HEIDNIK

There were five of them. Chained, manacled and filthy, clad only in flimsy blouses and socks. Blood was caked on their bodies from his beatings and there was terror in their eyes. The horror they had experienced was indescribable.

At first the police had refused to believe Josefina Rivera's story. As she showed them the marks on her body and the sores left by the manacles and chains, however, they realised that there might just be some truth in what she was saying. She told them of a man who had kidnapped her four months previously and had then taken a further four women prisoner. He had held them captive in a room with a deep pit excavated in the middle. He had raped them repeatedly and beaten them when they had broken one of his rules, or even when they had not. He told them of his perverted dream. His ambition was to have ten women in the house to do with as he pleased. By the time she escaped, astonishingly, he was halfway towards achieving his goal.

Police officers followed him from his house to a petrol station where they took him into custody. They then went to his house at 3520 North Marshall Street in a northern suburb of Philadelphia where the full story of the horror that he had unleashed began to become clear. They found the surviving girls, Agnes cowering in the pit where he had recently thrown her, the others chained to a beam. An industrial food processor stood ominously in the kitchen, blood caked around its edges and bits of unspeakable material drying on its sides. It had been used very recently. An oven dish sat on a work surface. Inside it was a human rib. One officer opened the fridge door to be confronted by a human forearm.

Gary Michael Heidnik would go down in history as one of the most brutal kidnappers in American criminal history. Not, strictly speaking, a serial killer – the FBI stipulates that to fall into that undesirable category you have to kill three or more people – Heidnik was responsible for two murders. Nonetheless, the acts he perpetrated place him in a category all of his own.

## A DISTURBED INDIVIDUAL

As is often the case with such people, his life had been a series of disappointments and he had suffered from mental health problems. After what can only be described as a disastrous schooling, it had seemed as if enlisting in the army as a medic might give him some stability and a career. Even there he had failed, however, being discharged after just fourteen months due to a condition diagnosed as schizoid personality disorder.

In 1978 he kidnapped a woman for the first time, signing the mentally ill sister of his girlfriend out of the institution in which she was being cared for and imprisoning her in the basement of his house. He raped and sodomized the girl before she was discovered and he was arrested. He was convicted of kidnapping, rape, unlawful restraint, false imprisonment, involuntary deviant sexual intercourse and interfering with the custody of a committed person. His sentence of three to seven years' imprisonment was overturned on appeal but he was sent to a mental institution for three years, being released in 1983.

In 1985, he married a woman called Betty whom he had met through a matrimonial service. She soon learned to her cost what sort of man she had become involved with when she came home one day to find him in bed with three women. He forced her to join in and the marriage began to fall apart with Heidnik beating and raping his new wife. After only three months she left him. She went to the police and he was charged with assault, indecent assault, spousal rape and involuntary deviant sexual intercourse. He was lucky, however. When Betty failed to appear for the preliminary hearing, the charges were dropped. He left her an abiding memory of himself, however. Betty gave birth to his son after she left him, a son he would never see. He was not Heidnik's only child. He later told Josefina Rivera that he had fathered four children by four different women, but had lost touch with all of them for various reasons. Perhaps it was this fact that made him conceive his twisted plan to create a family of women who would bear his children; perhaps, after all, he was, in his own perverted way, searching for love.

## A RIDE TO HELL

Josefina Rivera argued with her boyfriend on 26 November 1986 and stormed out of the apartment they shared. Out on the street, as she stood fuming in the rain, a silver and white Cadillac pulled up beside her. Rolling down his window, a bearded man asked her if she wanted a ride. She thought he looked okay and climbed into the warmth of the car's interior. They went and had a coffee and she studied the expensive watch and jewelry he wore. They then drove to his house, a run-down building in a rough area. Parked in front of the house, however, was a 1971 Rolls Royce. In spite of the neighbourhood he lived in this man clearly had money, Josefina thought to herself.

She was curious about the strange key he used to open the door – he had cut the key in half and the other half remained in the lock. No one could get in without his half of the key. He started to show her round the house, but as they walked from room to room, he jumped her from behind and began to choke her. Terrified, she fought back but he was too powerful. He grabbed her hands and handcuffed them together before pushing her into a damp basement room where he clamped manacles around her ankles and chained her to a large pipe fixed to the ceiling. He pushed her down onto a dirty mattress, ordered her to sit up and lay his head on her lap, immediately – and incredibly – falling asleep.

When she woke, he was gone. Enough light was coming in through a small window, allowing her to examine her prison. In the centre of the room a shallow hole had been dug through the concrete and into the earth below. He returned with a shovel and began to work on the hole, widening and deepening it. While he dug, he told her of his plan to kidnap other women. He then raped her for the first of many times.

When he left again, she approached the window and began to scream for help, hoping to alert a neighbour or a passer-by to her plight. All she succeeded in doing, however, was to enrage her captor who came running into the room carrying a large stick with which he viciously beat her. Dragging her over to the pit, he threw her into it, bending her head down onto her chest and covering the hole with wood that he weighed down so that she could not escape.

A short while later when he removed the wood and allowed her out of the pit, there was another woman in the room, manacled and chained to the pipe. Sandy Lindsay had been a fellow patient at the Elwyn Institute, a local hospital for the mentally and physically disabled. When she had become pregnant with Heidnik's baby, but had decided to have an abortion, he had been furious. He had even offered her a thousand dollars to have a child with him, but she refused. So, he had kidnapped her.

Her family had begun to search for her, but Heidnik forced her to write a note to her mother saying that she was going away for a while. He posted it in New York to make them believe she had gone there.

The weeks passed, the horror and their terror unrelenting. He raped and beat them, threw them in the pit and suspended them by one arm from the pipe in the ceiling for hours at a time.

Sandy's mother, in the meantime, remained suspicious about her daughter's disappearance. She went to the police and told them that she thought Sandy was being held against her will by a man called Gary. An officer visited the address she gave them – Heidnik's house – but when he received no reply to his knocks at the door, he went away and the case was forgotten about.

## THE 'FAMILY' GROWS

Another girl, nineteen-year-old Lisa, arrived in late December and shortly after, twenty-three-year-old Deborah Dudley joined them. Deborah was feisty, fighting and arguing constantly with Heidnik. He responded by beating her savagely. In the middle of January, Jacqueline, a petite eighteen-year-old turned up.

He was halfway to his total.

He began to play games with the girls, appointing one to be in charge while he was gone. It was her duty to report on the other girls when he returned and beat any of them who had misbehaved. If no one had misbehaved or the leader refused to say, he would beat them all, anyway. He fed them very badly, resorting eventually to a diet of tinned dog food.

## A FOUL DEATH

In early February, when Sandy became ill and died, he dragged her out of the room and upstairs. Shortly after, to their horror, the girls heard the distinctive sound of a power saw. They could imagine what it was sawing up. A little later, one of his dogs walked into the room carrying a long, meaty bone, unmistakably human, and their worst imaginings were confirmed. What they did not know, however, was that he was grinding up Sandy's flesh in the food processor and mixing it with their meager dog food rations.

When the house began to smell of Sandy's rotting flesh, Heidnik's neighbours complained. A police officer visited to investigate the source of the smell, but Heidnik cheerfully apologised, claiming that he had merely overcooked a roast dinner. Satisfied with his answer, and with more important things to do, the officer left.

Heidnik's paranoia that the girls were conspiring against him led him to try to stop them communicating. His method was horrific; he tried to deafen them by gouging inside their ears with a screwdriver, stuffing gags into their mouths to stop their dreadful screams.

One day, when Deborah had been stirring up trouble as usual, he unchained her and took her upstairs. When she returned, she was unusually silent. He had taken her to the kitchen where he had lifted the lid of a cooking pot to reveal Sandy's head. He also opened the fridge to show her other parts of her body. He told her that this was the fate awaiting her if she persisted in causing problems.

Soon after, he took care of the problem she had presented. He had introduced new punishments, electrocuting the girls with bare wires, all except Josefina who was his favourite and now slept in his bed and spent time alone with him. One day, he ordered her to fill the pit with water and threw the other girls in. He then touched Deborah with the exposed wire and she writhed in agony before collapsing into the water, dead. He wrapped up her body before putting it in his freezer.

## FREEDOM AT LAST

On 24 March, Josefina had won his trust to such an extent that she managed to persuade him to let her visit her family, on condition that she would bring back another woman. Naturally, as soon as her astonished boyfriend opened the door, she blurted out her story and the police were called.

Gary Heidnik was found guilty on two counts of first-degree murder, five of rape, six of kidnapping, four of aggravated assault and one of involuntary deviate sexual intercourse. He was sentenced to death but, as he had done throughout the trial, showed not a flicker of emotion as the sentence was read out.

He was finally executed by lethal injection on 6 July 1999.

# THE INCARCERATION OF ELISABETH FRITZL

Finally he cried. She had slipped into a seat as her videotaped testimony played to a hushed courtroom. She wanted to be sure he would be made accountable for his despicable acts and, above all, she wanted revenge for the years she had lost – twenty-four years locked in the basement of a house in the Austrian town of Amstetten.

## FATHERLY LOVE!

The case had been revealed to a shocked world the previous year, a world scarcely able to believe that a father could do what Josef Fritzl had done to his daughter, Elisabeth. He had locked her in the cramped space under the house, raped her some three thousand times and had fathered seven children by her. The question on most people's lips was 'how could such a thing happen?' How did he get away with it for so long without anyone finding out – his wife, the authorities or his neighbours?

Elisabeth Fritzl's unimaginable nightmare began on 28 August 1984 when her father asked her to help him carry a new door down to the basement of their well-appointed three-storey house at Ybbsstrasse 99. Eighteen years old, Elisabeth had already suffered at the hands of her stern disciplinarian of a father, having been raped for the first time by him when she was just eleven years old. She had already tried to run away from the horror of life in the Amstetten house but had been picked up by police in Vienna after a month. Now she had it in her head to once again get away. Her father knew it and was determined to stop her.

That day was the last time she would see the sun for more than two decades. He drugged her and handcuffed her while he put the finishing touches to his dungeon. He had been working on it for some time, extending it some years previously and concealing it behind walls. Eventually, the windowless dungeon was fifteen feet square but only five and a half feet high. As the years passed, however, and Elisabeth began to have his children, more room was needed. At that point, he put Elisabeth to work, cruelly forcing her to extend her own prison cell.

He brought his skills as an engineer and electrician to bear, installing electronic locks on the doors which could only be opened with the proper access code.

They were designed in such a way that if he died, the doors would open automatically after a certain amount of time had passed. Through time he provided her with an old television, a video recorder, hotplates on which to cook and a refrigerator, but it was a charmless, uncomfortable and stifling place in which to spend so many years.

And every night, Fritzl would visit, to eat with his second family and repeatedly rape his daughter, claiming to his wife that he was downstairs working on mechanical drawings and should not be disturbed.

Fritzl later claimed that he did it to protect his daughter but she had been nothing more than a normal teenager who was behaving the way teenagers across the world behaved. She had been sneaking out of the house to sit in bars with her friends but given what her father got up to when she was at home, she can hardly be blamed for that. At the time of her initial incarceration she was waiting to hear about a waitressing job in Linz. She had already enjoyed her first taste of freedom when she had spent six months training to be a waitress at Strengberg and was anticipating getting away for good.

## MOTHERLY LOVE!

Josef Fritzl had never been allowed to rebel. Born in

Amstetten in 1935, he was brought up by his cold, authoritarian mother after his father had abandoned his young family. His life had been miserable, his mother beating him viciously until he was bruised all over, even kicking him when he lay on the ground. They were difficult times, the Nazis having annexed Austria in the Anschluss and instilled rigid discipline and militarism into Austrian society. Following the war, Fritzl was the epitome of the Austrian bourgeois, driving a Mercedes and dressing well. He was a highly secretive and private individual, however, and people from that time describe him as someone it was impossible to get to know.

In 1967, he gave an indication of his future crimes when he was convicted of rape in Linz, serving eighteen months in prison. The Austrian system came to his aid, however. Crimes in Austria are expunged from the record after fifteen years. By the time Fritzl was adopting and fostering his children with Elisabeth, there was no trace of the rape in his records. It is also claimed that he raped his wife's sister and police have reopened the case of the murder of a young girl, killed near an inn that he once owned.

He married seventeen-year-old Rosemarie, a kitchen helper, in 1956. She was a plain, submissive woman who complied with whatever her imposing husband wanted. She never protested when he went on holiday to Thailand to indulge his sexual urges and when he stopped having sex with her she did not complain. Neither did she question her daughter's disappearance.

Elisabeth had, of course, helped Fritzl concoct a vaguely believable story by already having run away from home. She was reported missing the day after he had locked the door to the basement for the first time and several weeks later he took a letter from her to the police, postmarked from the Bavarian town of Branau-am-Inn. In it she told them that if they searched for her, she would vanish for good. They obliged by not making much of an effort to find her, something for which they would be severely censured twenty-four years later. She wrote further letters, on her father's orders, saying that she had joined a cult but again the authorities did nothing.

Elisabeth's first child was born in 1988, a girl, named Kerstin. In 1990, Stefan was born and two years later, Lisa. Fritzl audaciously smuggled Lisa out of the basement when she was still very young and claimed that Elisabeth had abandoned her and asked them to care for her. The local social services swallowed his story without actually doing much to verify it. The Fritzls adopted Lisa and brought her up as their own.

When Monika was born in 1994, she too was brought upstairs and adopted. Twins, Alexander and

Michael arrived in 1996 but when Michael died shortly after birth, his body was disposed of in the household furnace by Fritzl. Alexander was brought upstairs and joined the growing family. Felix was born in 2002 but stayed downstairs with his mother and sister, Kerstin who, at fourteen years of age, had never seen daylight.

## THE SECRET IS OUT

Josef Fritzl's secret world came crashing down in April 2008. Kerstin, by this time nineteen, fell seriously ill. For a long time she had suffered bad health, both physically and mentally which is hardly surprising. She had pulled her own hair out and bitten so hard on her lips and tongue that she made them bleed. Elisabeth pleaded with her father to let this girl, who had never in her life ventured outside the confines of the tiny windowless cell, go to hospital. To her surprise, he agreed.

At the hospital, Fritzl pretended once more that Kerstin was an abandoned child of his runaway daughter, that he had discovered her outside the house with a note from Elisabeth. This time, however, the authorities became concerned and issued an appeal to Elisabeth to make her whereabouts known so that they could find out what was wrong with her daughter. The police became involved, re-opening the case of her disappearance, a case that had barely been opened twenty-four years earlier.

Astonishingly, Fritzl let Elisabeth hand herself in, possibly exhausted by the years of pretence or resigned to that fact that the edifice of lies he had built was crumbling around him. The plan this time was to say that she had finally left the cult. However, as soon as she met with investigators and was re-assured that neither she, nor her family, would have to see her father again, she revealed the truth of the last twenty-four years. The investigation into Josef Fritzl began.

Meanwhile, Kerstin, seriously ill, was placed in a medically-induced coma from which she would recover some months later. The others were mentally and physically damaged, malnourished and suffering problems from incarceration in such a cramped space. Stefan, for example, had developed spinal problems.

Rosemarie and the children from upstairs joined Elisabeth and the others in a psychiatric hospital as the authorities tried to socialise them again and get them used to the outside world. They later moved into an apartment, but Elisabeth threw her mother out after a short time, possibly questioning Rosemarie's claims that she had no idea what had been going on beneath her feet.

Fritzl initially pleaded guilty to charges of incest, coercion and the deprivation of liberty, pleading not guilty to further charges of enslavement, rape and the murder of his son, Michael. After Elisabeth's appearance in court, however, he changed his plea and declared himself guilty of those crimes as well.

His lawyer had tried to blame his behaviour on his brutal childhood, but the jury rejected this, taking only four hours to find him guilty of all charges. He was sentenced to life in a psychiatric institution, but, under Austrian law, could, conceivably be paroled in fourteen years if it is believed he will not re-offend.

Elisabeth Fritzl and her children now live, it is said, in a fortress-like house in an unnamed village in northern Austria. All the children are undergoing therapy.

# THE ALTA VIEW
# HOSPITAL INCIDENT

When a devoted father of eight discovered his wife had undergone a procedure ending their chances of adding to the family, it left him with wounds not even time could heal. Two years later and the distraught daddy felt compelled to exact revenge. Armed with guns and sticks of dynamite, he broke into the maternity annex of a Utah hospital to find the doctor responsible. After a fruitless search, he took several hostages including an expectant mother. Over the next eighteen hours those inside and out would participate in a story of life and death in its truest form.

## BIRTH CONTROL ILLS

In the summer of 1989 a heavily-pregnant Karen Worthington was admitted to Alta View Hospital in Sandy, Utah for a routine delivery. With her husband Richard at her side, she had become a regular visitor of maternity wards over the years for this was to be the couple's eighth child. It would also be their last.

Following her doctor's counsel, Karen was advised to undergo a birth control operation known as a tubal ligation preventing the couple from conceiving further children. While consent was given, it is believed they later recanted but not before the procedure had been performed. Wishing to avoid a protracted legal battle, the hospital agreed to waive the costs of delivering the pair's newborn as well as the unwanted sterilisation. Those at Alta View hoped this would spell the end of their association with the Worthingtons.

Returning to their home on Little Cottonwood Drive in the suburban town of Sandy, the couple celebrated their new addition to the family, however, Richard could not overcome feelings of sadness. The father of eight fell into a deep depression, distraught that he would sire no more and began to focus his deep-seated frustration upon one man: Dr Glade Curtis, the obstetrician who had tied his wife's fallopian tubes.

The normally quiet churchgoing Mormon embarked on a rage-fuelled fixation on the doctor and his associated hospital, regularly threatening the medical man following the rejected operation. Two years on and the inconsolable Utahn had not shaken off his hatred towards Alta View. Realising her husband's resentment still posed a serious threat to the staff there, Karen demanded he hand over his cache of weapons. Unfortunately, this domestic disarmament was only sufficient to temporarily halt Richard's actions.

## AN EYE FOR AN EYE

On the evening of Friday 20 September 1991, Richard Worthington was at home showing baby pictures to a neighbour when he decided it was time to take action. Maybe these past memories of fatherhood inflamed his emotional wounds and led to his desire for violence, nobody knew. What is known is that he demanded his wife return his hoard of guns and, armed to the teeth, drove the short four mile journey to Alta View hospital.

Seeking an 'eye for an eye' form of justice, the angry father arrived at the community clinic with the express intention of murdering the man who had killed his hopes of future progeny. After vandalising Dr Curtis's car, Richard made for the Women's Health Centre, a 24-suite annex assisting in over 1,800 births per year, linked to the main building via a covered skywalk.

At a quarter to midnight, the madman shot out a ground floor window and climbed inside, tearing through the clinic's hallways for the focus of his anger. The first to come face-to-face with the intruder was a maternity nurse named Karla Roth who had only been a member of staff for two weeks. As she attempted to placate Mr Worthington, Susan Woolley, the centre's charge nurse, overheard the man's hunt for Dr Curtis and managed to warn her colleague. Fearing for his safety, the obstetrician fled the hospital but not before calling the police.

## A MATTER OF LIFE AND DEATH

As over seventy police officers and members of special weapons teams from the neighbouring cities of West Valley and Salt Lake descended upon the scene, Richard Worthington began to take hostages. While thirty-two patients along with staff evacuated the hospital, he forced Karla and Susan to wheel two babies into a patient's room where, unbeknown to the armed invader, Dr Curtis had been only moments before.

The room belonged to twenty-two-year-old expectant mother Christan Downey who was only hours away from having her first child. With her was father-to-be Adam Cisneros, her sister Carre and the attending nurse, Margie Wyler, who was preparing for the imminent delivery. Far from a conducive environment for childbirth, Richard brought his anger and mental turmoil to the scene, firing his .357 Magnum into the floor, insistent he would see the doctor.

When their search for Dr Curtis came up empty, the gunman forced Karla and Susan out of the building and into the visitors' car park. Heading for Worthington's car, Nurse Roth saw a chance to grab the shotgun trained on them. Failing to wrestle the weapon from his grasp, she turned to run and, gripped by panic, the Mormon father opened fire shooting Karla in the back as she fled. Frozen in fear only feet away from her wounded colleague, Susan Woolley was then hastily dragged back inside the building.

While paramedics were quick to respond, they were unable to save the nurse and she died from her injuries in an emergency room leaving behind a husband and two children. The hospital siege had now become a matter of life and death; the murder of Karla Roth outside the building and the imminent arrival of a child within.

## AN EXPLOSIVE DELIVERY

Shocked by this brutal slaying, the growing crowds of onlookers and reporters gathered at police barriers to watch the hostage incident play out. Richard Worthington now held seven victims captive inside the ground floor hospital room while two mothers and their daughters were trapped in another part of the maternity wing. Cheryl Bowen and Cindy Adamson had chosen to hide instead of fleeing Alta View with their babies and were now forced to wait until the situation was resolved.

As those laying siege to Alta View waited, Richard Worthington was preparing to tilt things further in his favour. Holding a gun to his girlfriend's distended belly, Richard ordered Adam Cisneros to go outside and retrieve a toolbox which he had hidden in the bushes near the front door. When the father-to-be exited the building, the surrounding authorities pleaded for Adam not to return. Unsurprisingly, the police were unable to convince the twenty year old to abandon his family and, toolbox in hand, he rejoined his fellow hostages.

Once back inside, Adam delivered the box to his captor and quickly discovered the reason for his assignment; contained within the box were forty-two sticks of dynamite. With more than enough explosives to obliterate the entire building, Richard Worthington had now become an even more dangerous villain in this hospital drama.

## THE EIGHTH HOSTAGE

As SWAT commandos and police snipers searched for viable lines of sight into the delivery room, an already paranoid Worthington began to feel exposed and decided it was time to move. Forcing his seven victims upstairs to a windowless third floor office area, the gunman told Adam and the two nurses to barricade them all inside.

Meanwhile Christan persisted in delaying the birth, feeling her baby was safer inside her than out in the open and in the line of fire. It had been a traumatic move for the pregnant twenty-two-year-old. Far from the comfort of her room downstairs, she had been wheeled at gunpoint to their new hiding place and now lay on sheets inside an office; her bed too large to fit through the doorway.

As the expectant mother held on, Richard showed no signs of composure. Waving his guns around, he ordered his captives to search for his wife's medical records. When they could not be found, he made them ransack the entire office, breaking furniture and computer equipment, creating a vision of disorder that matched the gunman's frame of mind.

By 3 am his hostage with child could not wait any longer. Without proper equipment and supplies Susan Woolley and Margie Tyler helped deliver the baby amid the strewn files and sporadic gunshots. Twenty minutes later Christan gave birth to Caitlin, a seven pound and one ounce little girl who became Richard Worthington's eighth hostage.

## POST-NATAL DEPRESSION

Throughout the remainder of the early morning, as Christan recovered from her overdue exertions, a relative calm descended inside the barricaded hideaway.

Worthington was able to confide in Margie Tyler with whom he had developed a clear bond, reflecting on his misdeeds both past and present. Confused by the imposed castration yet remorseful of the chaos he had caused, their captor fell into a deep sleep.

With his hand still on the detonator switch, none of the hostages dared emulate the heroism of their murdered colleague and try to disarm their keeper; instead they chose to write what they believed to be goodbye letters to their families. Often kneeling in prayer, hoping they would soon be reunited with their loved ones, the captives were unaware their relatives were being held at the local fire station two miles away.

Kept away from media scrutiny, distressed family members like Ross Woolley and Dale Wyler, the husbands of the two nurses, were provided with few clues as to what was occurring inside Alta View Hospital. The truth was simple: the authorities camped at their command post a block away from the scene had a dearth of information to give. Lacking any contact with the hostage-taker, they were unable to deduce the stability or even the intentions of the armed intruder.

## AN END TO THE SIEGE

After fifteen hours of silent standoff, a line of communication was finally established between the police and the unstable father. He quickly informed those outside that he was carrying eighteen pounds worth of dynamite and would not hesitate to detonate the explosives if any attempt was made to storm the building.

With the SWAT teams holding fire on an incursion, Sergeant Don Bell and Detective Jill Candland of the Salt Lake City police department engaged in a period of negotiation with the disturbed father. Their aim was to bring the crisis to a swift and satisfactory end and so denied any request that might prolong the ordeal. This included misinforming the gunman that his wife was not at the scene after his repeated demands to see her.

Three hours of intense, studied talks passed by before police and prisoners received the news they had prayed for. Thanks to the additional persuasive powers of the nurses inside, Richard chose to surrender all weapons to his hostages and allow them to break out of their third floor prison.

Believing he would be gunned down once clear of the maternity annex, Richard had one last request to make of Margie Wyler; asking her to cut off one of his fingers to be given as a morbid memento to his wife. The nurse and mother of eleven refused forcing the defeated murderer to exit the hospital with a full count of all fingers and hostages.

As those inside stepped out of the besieged building, the hostage-taker was immediately separated from his detainees. The two nurses carrying babies along with the extended Downey family were led to safety and after initial checks were allowed to join their loved ones at the command centre. After eighteen hours the deadly encounter had come to an end however, for some, the nightmare was not over.

## THE FINAL SETTLEMENT

The terrible hours incarcerated inside the Alta View Women's Centre left deep-set emotional scars on those involved. Some were affected worse than others. Already traumatised by the events, Susan Woolley was forced to relive the worst moments during a forty-five minute interview to a Sandy City detective at the nearby Cottonwood Hospital. Recalling the memories of Karla Roth's death served only to augment her traumatic state and led to her suffering from Post-Traumatic Stress Disorder for years to come. So severe were the symptoms that she even considered stepping out into traffic while on a trip to Los Angeles.

Richard Worthington was also beset with a desire to take his own life. Placed on a suicide watch inside his cell within the mental health unit of Salt Lake County Jail, his first attempt took place the morning after his arrest. At 6 am on Sunday 22 September, he climbed on top of his prison table and allowed himself to fall backwards. Surviving this act of self-destruction the prisoner lived to be granted a sentence of thirty-five years to life.

After Karen had filed for divorce, a move to ensure she remained solvent, she later was hit with a lawsuit issued by David Roth, the husband of the murdered nurse. Believing she was aware of her husband's plan to endanger the lives of those at Alta View, the widower maintained Karen was in breach of a civil duty to warn the would-be victims. Unable to prove this negligence in court, the Roth family agreed to a $97,000 settlement from the Worthington's insurance company.

By the time this case came to a close, Richard had managed to succeed in his unending wish to commit suicide. On Thursday 11 November 1993, after numerous attempts, the troubled taker of the Alta View hostages hanged himself between the hourly guard checks at Ely State Prison in Nevada.

# STEPHANIE SLATER

The banal-looking, bespectacled man had already murdered one unsuspecting young woman when Birmingham estate agent Stephanie Slater turned up alone to an empty house one winter Wednesday to show him around the property. Held at knifepoint and whisked eighty miles to an known hideaway, she was enslaved for eight torturous days often inside a makeshift box, her body and mind stretched to the very limits of their endurance. Fearing for her life with every passing hour, she hoped her hostage agony would end not in death but with a chance to live again.

## THE HOUSE VIEWING FROM HELL

For twenty-five-year-old Stephanie Slater, 22 January 1992 was just another ordinary Wednesday morning as she arrived for work at Shipways, a firm of estate agents in the Great Barr area of Birmingham. The young sales negotiator had only been with the company for six weeks when this red letter day came around to change her life forever. Checking the diary, she noticed an appointment for a house viewing that morning which had been requested by letter. Despite no follow-up phone call to confirm, Stephanie decided to keep the appointment and make the mile drive north to meet a Mr Southall. This diligence to her work was to be her downfall.

Waiting for her outside the address in Turnberry Road was the prospective buyer; a scruffy, bespectacled man in his mid forties. Introductions made, she began the routine tour of the end of terrace house and quickly surmised her client was not paying a great deal of attention. Allowing him to wander at his leisure about the unheated upstairs rooms, she yearned for the warmth of the office only minutes away. As Stephanie was about to head back downstairs, Mr Southall drew her attention to something on the bathroom wall. Moving inside for a closer look, she gave him the chance to strike.

Blocking her exit, this mild-mannered man suddenly pounced on the estate agent, his face wildly contorted in a mad grimace. Instinctively, she fought him off and the pair struggled inside the bitterly cold bathroom. Flashes of metal then caught her eye and she quickly realised her attacker was armed. Unaware that the man's knife had already cut her face, Stephanie grabbed the blade and refused to let go. Her assailant simply pulled the weapon down hard slashing her hand and shoved her into the bath, pinning her down, the knife to her throat.

After a fifteen minute struggle, she eventually gave in, allowing her subjugator to place a noose around her neck. Initial fears of hanging were then dismissed as she was led down the stairs by this makeshift leash and out to the man's car. Bound and blindfolded, Stephanie Slater lay on the backseat as she travelled on her journey to a destination unknown. While she strained her ears for sounds to reveal her where-abouts, the abducted estate agent was unable to glean a single clue why this strange man had stolen her from her daily routine.

## KIDNAPPED BY A KILLER

Driving his captive over seventy miles northeast to Newark-on-Trent in Nottinghamshire, Stephanie's kidnapper relaxed in the knowledge that his house viewing ruse had worked. The deadly Mr Southall now looked forward to the next phase of his premeditated plan. Pulling over into a quiet lay-by, his young hostage was soon acquainted with the awful truth of her abduction. Leaning in close and ordering her not to scream, he informed her she was to be held for ransom.

Any relief Stephanie might have felt on hearing his intentions were financial would soon evaporate on her arrival at her journey's end. Little did she know her captor was a killer with considerably more than money on his mind. Mr Southall was in fact one Michael Sams, a fifty-year-old, one-legged toolmaker from the East Midlands who had cut his teeth as a kidnapper on eighteen year old working girl Julie Dart the previous summer. Plucked from her solicitations upon the dark streets of Leeds, the part-time prostitute was taken to his tool repair shop in Newark from where she tried to escape. Angered by this act of non-compliance, Sams strangled her to death and, wrapping her body in a dirty sheet, dumped her in a Lincolnshire field.

Six months later and Stephanie Slater was to visit the very same workshop in which the murdered teenager lost her life. Dragged over the gravel driveway and cobblestones of Swan & Salmon Yard, she finally arrived inside the glorified tool shed and was immediately bound to a chair. Still wearing the sweat-stained blindfold, the kidnapped estate agent found herself lifted from her seat and forced onto a mattress where Michael Sams proceeded to rape and abuse his victim. Consumed with dread all through the initial attack and car journey, the physical violation abruptly altered Stephanie's outlook. Believing this was the worst that could befall her, she began to lose her fear. But the feelings of sheer terror were to return all too quickly.

## BOXED IN

While poor Stephanie processed her shocking assault, her work colleagues back at Shipways had raised the alarm of her kidnapping. Somewhere along the route to Newark, Michael Sams had telephoned her manager, Kevin Watts, informing him she was being held for ransom and that he should expect a package in the post. West Midlands police officers were quick to the scene of the original crime, finding signs of a struggle within the vacant house. Now the search was on for the missing estate agent.

Back in the Newark workshop, Stephanie's nightmare continued. Her fate lay inside a custom-made wooden box built to fit inside a large wheelie bin fashioned by her captor to keep her out of sight. Unable to see the impossibly cramped space, Sams guided her in feet first, cuffing her hands above her head and chaining them to a metal rod across the top of this makeshift coffin.

With barely enough room to breathe, Stephanie was given redundant incentives not to move whilst inside her box within a box. As well as several large boulders placed on top of the wheelie bin threatening to crush her if disturbed, her sadistic keeper placed a sharp electrode down her trouser leg to further restrict her movement. Her back severely twisted inside the box, Stephanie fought the urge to shift her body to alleviate the pain. Her limbs fell numb, as lifeless as the dead feeling inside since her defilement, losing hope of rescue with every passing minute.

## BONDING WITH BOB

As Stephanie suffered inside her casket, the police investigation into her kidnapping uncovered the package sent to Shipways estate agents. Not wanting to waste time waiting for its delivery, they intercepted the parcel at the sorting office in Birmingham. Inside the envelope they found a letter and a tape on which Sams had forced Stephanie to read out the ransom details. With less than an hour remaining of her first day in captivity, the police visited Stephanie's adoptive parents, Warren and Betty Slater, and played them the recording. On receiving confirmation that it was indeed their girl's voice, the investigation began to analyse the letter for potential clues.

When certain similarities to an extortion letter following the Julie Dart murder became apparent, Detective Chief Superintendent Bob Taylor of the West Yorkshire Police was brought in to lead the investigation. He had been chasing the evidence on the Dart case for the last six months but was still no closer to finding her killer. Focusing on the matching phraseology of the two letters along with identical errors in spelling, it was quickly deduced they were dealing with the same man. Hopefully, they could catch Julie's killer before he elected to take the life of poor Stephanie Slater.

Over the next seven days, the Birmingham estate agent was subjected to continual physical and mental torture. Yet despite her pain and suffering, Stephanie knew compliance was the key to survival. She managed to build a rapport with the man whom she knew only as Bob and this undoubtedly saved her from following Julie Dart to an early grave.

Growing displays of compassion such as bringing her chocolate bars and cups of tea or warming her up when she complained of the cold led to her being allowed to sleep on a mattress outside of her coffin. This, however, brought new dangers. With Sams sleeping right alongside her, Stephanie was open to further violation but such was their new-found bond, her captor asked for permission. Refusing his polite advances, she was relieved when Sams respected her decision.

## THE MONEY DROP

After several phone calls to both the Slater household and the estate agents, arrangements were made for the delivery of the ransom. Sams had requested £175,000 to be couriered to a place of his choosing by Stephanie's boss, Kevin Watts, and on Saturday 29

January – eight days into the ordeal – he was given his first set of instructions. At seven o'clock in the evening, Kevin was directed to a telephone booth at Glossop railway station where he was given a series of convoluted directions intended to lose any unwanted police shadow. Nearly two hours later, miles away from home, the ransom courier was completely alone, fighting through a thick fog that had rolled down from the nearby Pennines.

Unable to stick to Sams' tight schedule, Kevin began to panic as he crept along a narrow country lane somewhere in the South Yorkshire area. It was then he spotted a traffic cone in front of him attached to which was a note informing him to swap the money into a bag sat on a nearby wall. Obeying this final instruction, Kevin Watts departed the scene, his terrifying role as courier now thankfully complete. Unbeknownst to the Shipways man, sixty feet below on the other side of the wall stood Michael Sams holding a piece of string. This line was attached to a tray upon which the money now rested high above him. One swift tug brought the cash-packed bag falling to him concluding a perfectly-orchestrated ransom drop.

## A PROMISE OF FREEDOM

While Sams was collecting the money fifty miles away, Stephanie was spending some of her worst hours trapped inside the makeshift casket. Believing she had been left to die inside the Newark tool shop, she tried to suffocate herself with the blankets in which she was wrapped. Fortunately, this suicide attempt failed and at around ten-thirty that evening, after an entire day twisted into a misshapen pose, her kidnapper returned.

Releasing her from the box, Sams made good on his promise to set her free once he had acquired the money but not before politely asking if she would like to stay with him for one more week. While still maintaining an air of friendship, Stephanie told him she should return to her parents who would be worrying about her welfare. Without forcing the issue, Michael Sams loaded her into his car and made the drive back to Great Barr, dropping her off outside 54 Newton Gardens with an expression of remorse.

Taking forever to answer the door, one of the Family Liaison Officers looking after the Slaters finally let the missing estate agent inside. The arrival of this weak and feeble figure on the doorstep had come as a complete shock to all concerned. All Stephanie wanted to do was embrace her loved ones but, aware she could be carrying precious evidence, the officers stopped her from touching her parents for fear of contamination.

There was no time to rest for the poor victim.

Despite her eight days of captivity, Stephanie was immediately sent for various tests and interviews including long sessions with a sketch artist to ensure an accurate likeness of her attacker was obtained. This description would prove vital in the hunt for Michael Sams.

## PHOENIX RISES

Three weeks later the police made a TV appeal via the BBC's *Crimewatch* programme. Both the sketch and a voice recording taken from one of the phone calls made by the kidnapper produced a phenomenal response from the public. Over five thousand calls were received in connection with these memory-jogging aids, but it was one call in particular that pointed the finger squarely at Michael Sams.

Watching the broadcast at home, Susan Oakes recognised the voice on the recording as that of her ex-husband and contacted police. This led detectives to a tool repair company in Swan & Salmon Yard. The moment they stepped inside they knew they had their man. Thanks to Stephanie's accurate descriptions of both Sams and his workshop they were able to make a swift arrest and received a confession soon after.

On 8 July 1993, following a twenty-two day trial at Nottingham Crown Court, Michael Sams was sentenced to consecutive life sentences for the murder of

Julie Dart, the unlawful kidnapping of Stephanie Slater and an attempted blackmail of British Rail. Even jail was unable to halt his hostage-taking ways when in 1995, he took probation officer Julia Flack hostage inside Wakefield Prison. This stunt to air personal grievances earned him an additional eight years and he is currently not due for release until 2017.

The tragic days held at the whim of a disturbed killer left Stephanie Slater a woman forever changed. Finding her freedom hard to handle, she withdrew from society into voluntary isolation, nailing down her curtains to keep out the world. In a bid to separate herself from the hostage ordeal and banish the memories altogether, she chose to change her name becoming Phoenix Rhiannon. Today she lives with her best friend surrounded by a menagerie of pets in her Isle of Wight home, each day striving to cope with the past, to rise out of the ashes of her abduction and live again.

# DAVID KORESH AND THE SIEGE AT WACO

David Koresh was an extraordinarily manipulative human being who held people's minds hostage as well as their bodies. The people living with him in the Mount Carmel Center, near Waco in Texas, would undoubtedly have insisted that they were not hostages but were instead living a holy life in the company of a man they believed to be so close to God that he might even have been God, as he had begun to claim.

## STRUGGLE FOR LEADERSHIP

Koresh was the leader of the Branch Davidian religious cult, a radical spin-off from the Seventh Day Adventists. His rise to the top of the cult had not been without its difficulties. Handsome, assertive and claiming to have the gift of prophecy, he had always harboured ambitions to be a leader. Aged twenty-four, he had even entered into a sexual relationship with the cult's leader, Lois Roden, then in her sixties, in order to further his ambitions. But there was one major obstacle to him – Lois's son, George. Realising the danger represented by Koresh, Roden evicted him and his coterie of followers from Mount Carmel. A struggle ensued between the two men for supremacy. At one point George Roden challenged Koresh to a contest to see which of them could bring a dead person back to life. A corpse was exhumed, but there are no reports of any miracle occurring. Things turned violent when Koresh and some followers attacked Mount Carmel, firing at Roden and his followers in the compound. Only police intervention prevented a serious incident.

In 1988, however, Roden was convicted of the murder of one of Koresh's supporters and sent to prison. Koresh moved into Mount Carmel, assuming the leadership of the Branch Davidians. He was already behaving like a religious leader, anyway. He had made a pilgrimage to Israel a few years previously where he had experienced what he described as a vision. He returned to America, proclaiming to his followers that he was a reincarnation of Cyrus the Great, the king who had delivered the Jews from Babylon. He also announced that he was the 'Son of God' and as such he would henceforth be permitted to indulge in polygamy, sleeping with any of the women and girls in his group. Some were as young as twelve years of age.

## THE FORMATIVE YEARS

He had been born Vernon David Howell in Houston, Texas, in 1959 to a fourteen-year-old mother. He never knew his father. Soon an abusive stepfather arrived on the scene and the remainder of Koresh's childhood was miserable.

He changed his name in 1990 to 'David Koresh'. David, already his middle name was selected in order to establish a link with King David. He said that he was now head of the biblical house of David and it was from this house, it had been said in the Bible, that the messiah would emerge. Koresh was a version of the name 'Cyrus'. Taking this name, he emphasised his belief that he was the messiah.

He began to establish a code of behaviour for the Branch Davidians, creating strict guidelines which he changed on a whim. The rules were administered brutally, even the most trivial of breaches being punished with food deprivation, isolation and savage beatings. In the basement of the compound's main building was a 'whipping room', in which children could be beaten out of earshot of their parents or anyone else. Branch Davidians believed in the purity of the body, believing the Holy Spirit to live there and they had strict rules, therefore, regarding what they could eat and drink. Naturally, most of the rules did not apply to Koresh as leader. He ate whatever he wanted, drank alcohol – forbidden to his followers – and slept until noon if he wanted while they were roused at the crack of dawn. Cult members' days were filled with long, rambling sermons that he delivered no matter the hour, day or night.

His sexual activity was relentless and he fathered numerous children at Mount Carmel. One woman later told how she had been sexually molested by Koresh for the first time at the age of only ten. Following the molestation, Koresh made her sit and listen as he read long passages from the Bible. Sometimes he did not require the written word; he had learned the New Testament by heart at the age of twelve. This was something of an achievement as he suffered from learning difficulties at school, his schoolmates cruelly nicknaming him 'Mister Retardo'.

Branch Davidian girls were groomed in a manner that made them believe that not only was sex with Koresh natural, it was also desirable. Meanwhile, normal familial relationships were eradicated, marriages being annulled as soon as couples arrived at Mount Carmel. Children were taught to call their natural parents 'dogs' while Koresh was known as 'father'. Children that he had not fathered were 'bastards', his paternity being the only legitimate one. They were brainwashed into relying solely on him and God, being led to believe that there was really not much difference between the two. A girl, who was set free during the later siege at the compound, was distraught to learn of Koresh's death. It meant that she could never become one of his many wives.

## LESSONS IN WEAPONRY

When they were not listening to one of Koresh's frequent sermons, laced with biblical references and threats of dire consequences if his rules were not adhered to, the children learned about Koresh's other main interest, guns and weaponry. He had for some time been stockpiling an arsenal of guns and food that he told them would be necessary in the battle with the enemy – the defectors, dissidents and especially the government agents for whom he had a special biblical name – the 'Babylonians'.

The Branch Davidians' interest in guns had not gone unnoticed by the US Bureau of Alcohol, Tobacco and Firearms. By 1993, it had come to their attention that they were selling weapons and ammunition, an activity not illegal in the United States. What was illegal, however, was the sale of rapid-fire automatic weapons that the Branch Davidians had been engaged in. Their interest escalated when, one day, the packaging on a parcel that was addressed to the Mount Carmel Center, fell apart. Grenade casings fell out and the delivery company reported it to the police.

As a result, BATF agents had been carrying out surveillance on the compound for some time, even managing to infiltrate some of their agents into the compound. The fortuitous discovery of the grenade casings was the last straw and it was decided to move in and bring their activities to an end.

## SAFETY IN NUMBERS

On 28 February 1993, more than seventy BATF agents approached the compound as a Blackhawk helicopter from the local National Guard hovered overhead. An agent knocked at the door to the main building in which around one hundred people waited. As he called out that he had a search warrant, Koresh slammed the steel door in his face. Immediately, gunfire erupted.

One report later stated that the agents were shooting the dogs in the compound and those inside, believing they were under attack, returned fire. Inside, women lay on their children to protect them from the bullets but when the shooting subsided some two hours later, four BATF agents and five Branch Davidians lay dead. Koresh was himself wounded in the hip as well as in the wrist. The raid – an unmitigated disaster – led to a fifty-one-day siege of the Mount Carmel Center. It was a moment for which Koresh had been waiting. He had introduced the concept of martyrdom to his followers, questioning them on how far they were prepared to go in defence of their faith. He told them now that the only way to serve God was to die.

Although the people inside the compound sent out a videotape explaining that they were there of their own free will, the authorities chose to treat the situation as a hostage crisis. They broadcast radio messages but Koresh's response was a reading from the scriptures. Many feared a Jonestown-like situation, believing that Koresh would persuade his people to kill themselves as Jim Jones had with his congregation in Guyana. Koresh, meanwhile, bleeding badly and saying that he expected to die, was already giving interviews to the media by telephone.

When he released ten children, including a baby, hopes rose that he might give up, but, as one psychologist correctly surmised, God was not going to prison. When the FBI cut the phone line, Koresh was furious. He then told them that if they let him broadcast his message to the entire nation, he would let everyone go. He released a few more of the children as a sign of good faith.

On 2 March, the hour-long tape he sent out was broadcast on a number of Christian radio stations. The waiting agents prepared for the release of the Branch Davidians, but it did not happen. Koresh merely told them that he had been instructed by God not to do it that day.

For days the waiting agents had to listen to his rambling sermons relayed from inside the compound while they responded by directing tapes of dying animals, dentist drills, bagpipes and chants at him. As ever, his response was always a reading from the Bible.

## BRUTE FORCE

He continued to find excuses for not releasing everyone – the feast of Passover, or the fact that he wanted to complete the writing of a manuscript about the meaning of the Seven Seals. Eventually, new Secretary of State, Janet Reno, deciding enough was enough, and issued the order to bring the siege to an end. At dawn on Monday 19 April, a couple of Combat Engineering Vehicles approached the building, punched several holes in the walls and inserted CS gas canisters, as the Branch Davidians fired volleys of shots at them. Shortly before noon, however, the agents were horrified to see flames coming from the building, accompanied by loud explosions and still more gunfire.

Only nine emerged alive from the burnt-out shell of the building. Inside investigators found eighty bodies, twenty-three of them children under the age of seventeen. David Koresh had fathered fourteen of them, it was later learned.

There were rumours that Koresh had managed to get away, perhaps through a set of underground tunnels but his body was identified from dental records. He had died from a bullet wound to the head.

# MARC DUTROUX

It was a case that rocked Belgium, almost bringing down the government, implicating powerful people in despicable acts and showing up the shortcomings in both the Belgian judicial system and in the methods used by its police force. At the heart of it, however, lay the horrific abduction, imprisonment, torture and sexual abuse of six young girls, aged from eight to nineteen between 1995 and 1996. Dutroux murdered four of them personally; the other two died of starvation.

## THE BIRTH OF A KILLER

Marc Dutroux was born in 1956 in Brussels, the oldest of five children. His early years were spent in the Belgian Congo where his parents, both teachers, had emigrated. Back in Belgium, in 1971 they separated and Dutroux was looked after by his mother. He worked briefly as a male prostitute before marrying and fathering two children. Divorced in 1983, he began a relationship with Michelle Martin and the couple would get married in 1989 while they were both in prison and go on to have three children.

Dutroux had trained as an electrician but was unemployed, earning money from drug dealing and trading cars stolen in Poland and Slovakia as well as by trafficking girls and young women across Europe to be used in prostitution. Although he was drawing welfare from the state, he would come to own seven houses in Belgium, most of which were vacant. The only ones that were occupied were the three in which he held captive young girls that he and his associates had kidnapped who were either to be sold into prostitution or used in the filming of pornographic videos. He lived principally in a large house in Marcinelle near Charleroi underneath which was located a large basement accessed by a massive concrete door, disguised as a shelf. This dungeon was seven feet long, less than three feet wide and about five feet high.

Dutroux, well-known to the police, possessed an extensive criminal record, mostly involving car theft, mugging and drug dealing. Finally in February 1986, he and his girlfriend, Michelle Martin, were arrested for the abduction and rape of five young girls. He was sentenced to thirteen and a half years in prison. During his incarceration, however, the Belgian Justice Minister, Melchior Wathelet, announced the release of a large number of Belgian sex offenders from prison. Dutroux benefited from this leniency towards some of the country's worst offenders and, having displayed good behaviour in prison, was released after serving just three years.

## FREE TO START AGAIN

After his release, young girls began to disappear from around some of the areas where he owned houses. On 24 June 1995, he abducted two eight-year-old girls, Julie Lejeune and Mélissa Russo, imprisoning them in his basement dungeon and making porn films featuring them.

A couple of months later, on 22 August, he kidnapped two girls, seventeen-year-old An Marchal and nineteen-year-old Eefie Lambrecks, who had been enjoying a camping trip to Ostend. They were abducted by Dutroux and his associate, Michele Lelièvre who helped him in return for drugs. As the dungeon was occupied by his first two abductees, he chained his latest victims to a bed in one of the rooms in the house. Several weeks later, he is believed to have killed these two girls, but the circumstances of their deaths have never been made clear.

A few months later, Dutroux was in trouble with the law once again on a car theft charge. On 13 December they searched the house in which Julie Lejeune and Mélissa Russo were still alive in the basement, but as the search was in relation to car theft and not kidnapping, they did not use sniffer dogs or any specialised equipment. They also failed to notice that the wall that concealed the dungeon had been freshly painted and plastered. Worse still, while searching in another part of the basement, police officers later reported that they had heard children's cries but believed that they had come from outside on the street.

The police failed in their duty in several other instances. Dutroux had offered money to a police informer for the provision of girls, telling him that he was building a secret dungeon in his basement to house them. The informant tipped off the police but they failed to act until a year had passed – too late for Julie Lejeune and Mélissa Russo. Incredibly, Dutroux's own mother wrote to prosecutors to tell them of her certainty that he was keeping young girls in one of his houses. Sadly, once again, nothing happened.

Meanwhile, vital information about the disappearance of young girls was withheld from investigating officers. One magistrate involved in the case even forgot to tell the magistrate replacing her that there were children going missing.

## LEFT IN CHARGE

Dutroux went to prison for two months on the car

theft charge, leaving an associate, Bernard Weinstein to feed the two girls locked up in his secret dungeon. Bernstein failed to do so, however, and the two girls died a horrific death from starvation and lack of water. When Dutroux was released from prison in March 1996, he was furious when he unlocked the dungeon to find the girls' bodies. He overpowered Weinstein, crushed his testicles until he revealed the location of some money he had hidden and then drugged him with barbiturates. He buried the girls' bodies in the garden and, digging a grave for Weinstein next to them, buried him alive.

## SABINE DARDENNE

On 28 May 1996, Dutroux and Lelièvre kidnapped twelve-year-old Sabine Dardenne and threw her into the dungeon. She later recounted how Dutroux told her that she had been kidnapped by a criminal gang who had demanded a ransom, but that her parents had refused to pay. He allowed her to write letters home, but he read them and never posted them. On 9 August, she was joined there by fourteen-year-old Laetitia Delhez who had been taken as she walked home that night from her local swimming pool. This time there was a witness, however, who remembered part of the number plate of the vehicle Dutroux had been driving. For once the Belgian police were efficient and they succeeded in matching it to a vehicle owned by Dutroux. On 13 August Marc Dutroux and Michelle Martin, who was fully aware of her husband's activities, were arrested. His houses were searched but nothing was found and the two girls languished in their cell at Marcelline. Two days later, however, both Dutroux and Martin cracked under intense questioning. They both confessed and Dutroux led police officers to the concealed basement dungeon. Sabine Dardenne and Laetitia Delhez were found alive on 15 August.

On 17 August, Dutroux took investigating officers to another of his houses, in Sars-la-Buissière where he showed them the graves of Julie Lejeune and Mélissa Russo. Next to them lay Bernard Weinstein's body. An Marechal and Eefie Lambecks were found buried under a shed at another house he owned on 3 September.

The public outcry began almost immediately and when Jean-Marc Connerotte, a popular judge involved in the case, was dismissed for attending a dinner organised by the girls' parents to raise funds, a huge protest march – known as the 'White March' – was staged. Some three hundred thousand people demonstrated the strength of feeling in Belgium. Demands were made for urgent reforms in the country's judicial and police system.

## THE CASE WOULD NOT GO AWAY

However, there were shadowy figures in the background of the case and Dutroux claimed to have been working for a paedophile ring that involved prominent people. It was suggested that the investigation had been deliberately hampered by people in the government afraid of being exposed as paedophiles. After a seventeen-month-long investigation, however, a report was issued concluding that Dutroux had no accomplices in senior government posts.

The case would not go away, however, and there was even more public outrage and disbelief when Dutroux escaped from custody while being transferred to a courthouse from prison. Astonishingly, in another example of police incompetence, he had not been wearing handcuffs and had managed to overpower a guard, stealing his gun and getting away. Fortunately, he was re-captured a few hours later but both the Interior Minister and the Chief of Police subsequently resigned.

Marc Dutroux's trial did not begin until 1 March 2004, more than seven years after his arrest. It took place in the town of Arlon and four hundred and fifty people were called to testify. He was charged with three counts of murder, all of which he denied but his charge sheet also included a long list of other crimes – car theft, abduction, attempted murder and attempted abduction, molestation, and the rapes of three Slovakian women who had come forward.

He, Martin, Lelièvre and another associate, Jean-Michel Nihoul appeared in a bullet-proof glass cage in court to protect them from attack by angry members of the public. Nihoul was there because Dutroux had claimed that he was the brains behind the paedophile network. It was also rumoured that he had organised an orgy at a Belgian chateau, attended by several government officials, some police officers and a former European Commissioner. Seven other people would later be arrested in connection with the network.

After a trial lasting three months, all apart from Nihoul were found guilty of all charges. They were unable to reach a verdict on the role played by Nihoul. He would later be acquitted on the murder and kidnap charges but was sent to prison for five years on drug-related charges.

Michelle Martin was sentenced to thirty years in prison, Lelièvre to twenty-five years and Marc Dutroux was, as was expected, given the maximum sentence of life imprisonment.

# NATASCHA KAMPUSCH

On a March morning in 1998, as she stomped her way to school following a row with her mother, ten-year-old Natascha Kampusch was stolen from the streets of Vienna and hidden below the garage of a disturbed IT technician. With every aspect of her life under his complete control, the young girl fortified her mind against the suffering, feeding her brain with knowledge gleaned from the radio, TV and assorted books allowed down in her dungeon. Held hostage for more than three thousand days, the abducted Austrian would be eighteen by the time she found the strength to escape her keeper's clutches.

## PARTED IN ANGER

Monday 2 March 1998 was just the start of another school week for ten-year-old Natascha Kampusch, shaking off sleep as she rose from her bed. The previous night had been a late one after returning from a trip to Hungary with her father, punctuated by yet another row between her parents, now separated and living apart. As always she had been caught in the middle of their feud and, that morning, was still smarting from its effects.

Petulant stares and cold snaps were thrown at her mother, Brigitte Sirny, as she got ready, storming out of the house, slamming the door as she sulked off to school. Refusing to turn and wave back to her mother at the window, Natascha left home in anger, unaware she would not return for another eight years.

Walking through Donaustadt, Vienna's 22nd and largest district in the northeast of the city, little Natascha endeavoured to shrug off her frustrations, hoping life would become less of a struggle. As her mood improved she noticed a white minivan parked up ahead and began to feel uneasy. A little voice inside her head was telling her to cross to the other side of the road but, dismissing this impulse as silly, she pressed on.

The moment she pulled level with the van, its side door slid open and she was grabbed, disappearing inside the belly of the metal beast. Petrified with fear, Natascha was unable to let out a scream and, as the van violently sped from the scene, the kidnapped child was tossed about the back of the getaway vehicle, wondering where she was headed and what her abductor wanted with her.

## SEARCH FOR NATASCHA

After hours of driving around in circles, the minivan arrived at a house. Swathed in a blanket, Natascha was manhandled inside the property and thrown into the darkness of a small basement. The windowless space was a mere five square metres in size and soundproofed against her calls for help. With no idea she was only twelve miles from home, the abducted Austrian tried in vain to attract attention, throwing bottles against the wood-panelled walls. She soon realised nobody was coming to save her.

With Natascha failing to turn up at school later that morning, her estranged parents were united in fear for their daughter's safety. Her father, Ludwig Koch, had thousands of missing posters printed and put up around the city even before police began their investigation. Diving teams dredged the Danube and helicopters swept the surrounding landscape in what became the most extensive search in the country's history.

After widespread media coverage, police were inundated with information from the public, much of which led to dead-ends. Amongst the endless false leads and crank calls, authorities did manage to locate a potential witness to the kidnapping; a twelve-year-old girl who identified the white Mercedes van. More than eight hundred vehicles matching the description were stopped and checked in and around Vienna but to no avail. Police would later discover they had come face-to-face with Natascha's abductor but, supplying a solid alibi, officers had let him go.

## UNDERGROUND FEARS

The man who had slipped through the net was one Wolfgang Priklopil, a forty-four-year-old communications technician who lived a lonely, inconspicuous existence, fifteen miles northeast of Vienna. His house resided in the quiet suburban neighbourhood of Strasshof an der Nordbahn and had been built by his grandfather, Oskar Priklopil, just after the Second World War. It was here in the old bomb shelter – now doubling as a dungeon – where poor Natascha was being held against her will.

For the first six months of her incarceration, she spent every hour of the day down in her makeshift cell, unable to sleep for fear her captor would enter her prison and take advantage. Over time, her fear evolved beyond what he might do to her. Confined behind a 150 kg steel door weighed down with a concrete block and with no means of escape, Natascha grew concerned for her keeper's welfare. If anything were to happen to him, she would be trapped in this hellhole and left to rot.

After the six months of solitary confinement, Natascha was given some semblance of freedom. At various times throughout the day she would be allowed to spend time above ground in Priklopil's house, forced to work for food. However, once these daily chores were complete, it would be back down to the basement below the garage, where she was left alone with nothing but her thoughts.

## MASTER CONTROLS

During her time spent in the company of her keeper, she would be bombarded with lies about her parents and the outside world. To authenticate his fiction, Wolfgang would follow the regular news reports on Natascha's disappearance and even stalked Brigitte Sirny, leaving his poor captive believing her mother and father were not concerned with her safe return.

Her spirit sufficiently broken by these falsehoods, Priklopil filled her head with horror stories of drugs, cigarettes and the evil of man to make her so in fear of the outside world that she would want to stay with him. All of these despicable acts were part of the one aim: to dominate his captive. Even while Natascha was in the underground cell, he would impose his authority upon her. Possessing the means to regulate the temperature and air supply into the dungeon, Priklopil was able to make the room hot or cold and the air unbearably thin.

Controlling every aspect of her life, from the food

she ate to the air that she breathed, Wolfgang began to provide Natascha with a few 'luxuries'. Two years into her captivity, she was allowed access to a radio which she had tuned to Ö1 – a public station which played mainly cultural programmes. This access to affairs outside of her house of horrors would begin a hunger and thirst for knowledge that would rival the stomach aches and dry mouth she would suffer day after day.

## SURVIVAL STRATEGY

Listening avidly to the radio, soaking up every piece of information, kept Natascha's mind strong and agile, helping her to endure her years of captivity. As time passed, Wolfgang agreed to let her read the newspapers, though only after he had read them first, censoring any unsuitable material. It was the same with the television which was later permitted inside her subterranean home. Programmes were recorded on to videotape and thoroughly checked before she could view them.

This level of regulation spread into other areas. Priklopil would dispose of all rubbish miles from the house, having rooted through all the detritus to ensure nothing would give him away. He even avoided shopping locally to keep his secret safe. Natascha's survival strategy, meanwhile, was taking shape.

Schooling herself, developing her mind with books and cultural radio and TV shows, she went from being a little, lost girl to a young, intelligent woman.

As her intellect grew, so did her power in her relationship with Priklopil. With dogged determination, Natascha managed to claw back some control and soon the abject slavery indicative of her earlier years of confinement matured into a more normal existence. They began to eat breakfast together and she would provide him with shopping lists. Even gifts were exchanged when captor and captive celebrated birthdays and national holidays. This change to their relationship afforded Natascha the belief that one day she would escape.

## CLEAN GETAWAY

After Natascha had turned eighteen, Priklopil felt she could be trusted sufficiently to accompany him on various errands about town. Yet despite her budding influence over her gaoler, she was too traumatised to flee. Forced to walk in front of him, all she could do was scream with her eyes and mimic the smile worn in her much-publicised photo in the hope that someone would recognise her and come to her aid. With no outside help, her freedom would come down to her own sharpness of mind.

On Wednesday 23 August 2006, eight and a half

years since her abduction on her way to school, Natascha finally believed she possessed both the physical and mental strength to orchestrate her own escape. The opportunity arose while cleaning her abductor's burgundy BMW 805i outside the front of the house. Just before one o'clock in the afternoon, Wolfgang took a call on his mobile phone. Deafened by the sound of the vacuum cleaner working on the car's interior, Priklopil moved away from the teenager to conduct his conversation.

This was Natascha's chance to run. Leaving the Hoover running to mask the sounds of her footsteps, she bolted out of the front garden and, climbing fences and scaling walls, she endeavoured to put as much distance between herself and her keeper as possible. Whenever she came across someone in the street, she screamed at them for help but her appeals were met with indifference. Finally she managed to gain sanctuary inside the home of an elderly neighbour who called the police with the news that Natascha Kampusch had been found.

## END OF THE LINE

Police officers arrived at her safe haven just after the hour and, after she was positively identified by a surgical scar, the self-liberated slave gave authorities directions to her nearby prison. By the time they discovered the underground lair beneath the garage of the Strasshof residence, Wolfgang Priklopil was long gone. Finishing his phone call to find his hostage of more than eight years had deserted him, he had got into his freshly-cleaned BMW and taken off.

Driving around aimlessly, panicking over the loss of his victim, Priklopil ended up at a shopping precinct in downtown Vienna. From here he placed a call to his only friend and business partner, Ernst Holzapfel, who agreed to come and meet him. Sold the lie that he was wanted by the police because of a drink driving offence, Priklopil's friend took him to the city's Wien Praterstern train station.

What happened next would have come as no surprise to Natascha. Her captor had always insisted he would not be taken alive if she ever managed to escape his clutches. So, with the net closing in, Priklopil felt there was only one option open to him. At around nine o'clock that evening, he chose to end it all, throwing himself underneath an approaching commuter train.

## HOSTAGE TO HOST

When the media discovered Austria's famous missing girl had been found, there was a frantic clamour for her exclusive story. Natascha was astutely aware of this inevitable spotlight and made it clear she would tell her tale on her own terms. After eight years of being under someone else's rule, Natascha, quite rightly, wanted full control of her own life. Five days after her escape, helped by a team of media consultants, she issued a letter to the press appealing for more time. A little over a week later ÖRF aired her first TV interview, the sales of which were donated to help victims of kidnap and poverty around the world as per her wishes.

As part of her ongoing psychiatric help provided for by the city, Natascha visited a Vienna morgue to say goodbye to the man with whom she had spent eight of her most formative years. On 8 September 2006, Wolfgang Priklopil was then buried under a false name during a low-key ceremony south of the capital with his mother the sole family member in attendance.

Following her long stay in captivity and the unimaginable torments she endured during this time, Natascha was later awarded over £450,000 by the Austrian Criminal Injuries Compensation Board. In addition to paid medical care and an apartment in the city, she also received two-thirds of the property under which she was incarcerated for those eight years. With the spotlight still firmly focused on the ex-hostage, Natascha chose to develop her media skills with her very own chat show which debuted on 1 June 2008.

Left with light-sensitive vision thanks to her endless days and nights confined to the darkness of her dungeon, Natascha Kampusch still manages to look on the bright side of life with her captor. When questioned about the many things she missed out on while hidden away from the outside world, she has always focused on the positives; that she avoided many of the negative distractions of youth such as smoking, drugs and bad company.

# JOSEPH PALCZYNSKI

In March 2000 the quiet suburban communities of East Baltimore County were rocked by the wild actions of a schizophrenic spree killer intent on winning back the heart of his estranged girlfriend. Following a lifetime of physical and mental abuse dished out to a series of young girls, this murderous madman held the family of his latest lover hostage, expecting his life to end as he lived it; in a haze of violence and chaos.

## TROUBLED UPBRINGING

When Joseph Palczynski went on a murderous rampage through the towns of east Baltimore in March 2000, many of those people aware of his past were far from surprised. Born into trouble in 1968, his parents' marriage on the verge of collapse, young Joseph's childhood was anything but normal. Moved from school to school in an attempt to reverse sliding grades, he was diagnosed with attention deficit hyperactivity disorder (ADHD) and given special tuition. However, at the age of fourteen, following a traffic accident in which he sustained a head injury when his school bus crashed, his behaviour began to deteriorate.

Less than a year later he received his first of many entries on his juvenile charge sheet when he was caught stealing a firearm from a friend and by 1985 had begun visiting a steady stream of psychiatric centres to analyse what appeared to be a severe case of depression. Exhibiting considerable anger at the world, exacerbated by the death of his older sister, Joseph made his first prediction that he would die by the bullet; a prophecy he persistently repeated throughout his troubled life.

## BAD BOY

Beleaguered by routine visits to mental institutions and forced to take a variety of prescription drugs, Palczynski desired a control over his life that often seemed out of reach. Spending hours at the gym pumping iron, he developed an impressive physique which, together with his clean-cut good looks, began to attract the opposite sex. Much like his idol James Bond, he quickly saw himself as a ladies man; a self-confessed bad boy driving around in a flashy sports car, he was every teenage girl's dream.

The first to fall for his ample charm was fifteen-year-old Amie Gearhart. She was already smitten by the time this dashing senior sent her balloons on Valentine's Day, however after five months together the early sheen upon the relationship had begun to fade. His controlling nature led to an increasing level of intimidation and violence culminating in a beating that summer so severe it left her with multiple lacerations, contusions and bruises.

Having beaten the living daylights out of this poor, victimised sophomore, the OO7 wannabe moved on to a new impressionable young woman. There seemed to be an endless supply of teenage girls eager to be swept off their feet by this perfect catch. Even two years in prison for the assault on Amie Gearhart only served to intensify his bad boy image and a few months after his release in April 1991, Joseph – or Joby to his throng of admirers – began dating seventeen-year-old Sharon. She, too, was to learn his secret; that beneath an attractive exterior lay an unstable and dangerously-split personality, a ticking time-bomb waiting to explode in disaster.

## THE MAN WITH THE GOLDEN CHARM

After Sharon had pressed charges, following a vicious assault outside her school in which he threatened to kill her parents, Joby was released on bail and soon ended up back inside hospital for evaluation. Various conflicting diagnoses followed until 16 December 1991 when he managed to escape from the Spring Grove State Psychiatric Facility, fleeing Maryland altogether.

The fugitive mental patient went on the run crossing the entire country, settling in Gooding, Idaho where he returned to his old habits, picking up and then assaulting a fifteen-year-old girl. In January 1992, he was finally apprehended from an apartment after a sixteen-hour standoff in which a SWAT team hit his barricaded hideout with tear gas. Joseph was then brought back east to face further charges and psychiatric assessment. Deemed legally insane, he was able to avoid further jail time and, after focusing the next fifteen months on improving his mental fitness, he was back in east Baltimore cruising the streets in his convertible.

Over the next three years this man with the golden charm lured two more unsuspecting teens into the life of a sociopath. Bestowing gifts of love with one hand and inflicting black eyes with the other, Joby intimidated his girlfriends into silence. However once they realised the man they loved would never change, both spoke out when it placed themselves and their families in mortal danger. Thanks to these courageous confessions their schizophrenic ex-boyfriend was back behind bars by November 1996 unable to inflict his brand of charm and harm offensive upon the naïve maidens of Maryland.

## THE FINAL FLAME

By the time Joseph Palczynski was released from prison in 1998 he was approaching his thirtieth birthday. Gone were his youthful good looks and he had developed a bald patch that not even hair plugs could hide. Such insecurities over his appearance only added to his volatile behaviour ensuring the next girl he found would undoubtedly suffer his black and belligerent moods.

The inevitable new flame came in the form of twenty-year-old Tracy Whitehead whom he met at a local supermarket in downtown Middle River. Reacting favourably towards his advances, this high school dropout and drug addict would become Joseph Palczynski's last girlfriend. In the beginning she was in paradise. Her Joby could not do enough for her, helping to improve her quality of life; saving the day just like his hero James Bond. Yet this waking dream would lead inexorably to a living nightmare.

Once threats turned to violence Tracy knew she had to escape the relationship, but every time she tried to leave, the persuasive Palczynski convinced her to stay. Eighteen months down the line, the now drug-free and upwardly mobile Whitehead found the nerve to move out of their shared apartment. Accepting an offer of refuge from her work boss, Gloria Shenk, she moved in with the fifty-year-old and her husband but their Bowley's Quarters home would provide no sanctuary from an enraged Joseph.

## UNSAFE HAVEN

After a spate of vicious threats failed to scare Tracy back into his lethal arms, the jilted Joby decided to use extreme force. Unable to purchase a firearm thanks to his convicted felon status, he somehow persuaded his mother's neighbour, Constance Ann Waugh, to buy him a 12-gauge shotgun and rifle. Armed and unstable, he descended upon the Shenk residence on the evening of 7 March adamant he would get Tracy to come back to him.

As Tracy relaxed in front of the television with Gloria and George, content at the distance she had placed between herself and her abuser, Joseph Palczynski burst through the front door, demanding she leave with him. When her two protectors refused, the violent felon opened fire on them both killing them instantly and, grabbing her by the hair, dragged Tracy from her unsafe haven. Once outside, David Meyers, a curious neighbour, dared to intervene in the abduction and became Joseph's third victim of the evening. Without his hero's licence to kill, Joby had now become a murderer on a violent spree of death and destruction.

Now a law unto himself, Joseph drove his kidnapped girlfriend into the woods of east Baltimore and subjected her to endless torment. Pressed to the ground with a gun to her head, he threatened to cut off her limbs and pull out her teeth before forcing himself on her during a night of unfathomable pain and suffering. The following morning revealed his schizophrenic side; racked with remorse, pleading an undying love for Tracy, Joby pulled out a wedding ring and proposed to his captive. Fearing the return of the monster, she took the ring and surrendered to further sexual advances all the while praying for her nightmare to end.

## A CHANCE TO ESCAPE

Managing to persuade her affianced to leave the woodland marshes to seek out food and water, Tracy and her captor tore through the nearby town of Chase carjacking their way to El Rich Motel on Pulaski Highway. Turning on the TV, Joseph discovered his bout of auto theft had taken another life; that of Jennifer McDonel, a mother of two, who had been struck by a ricocheting bullet. News bulletins on all four deaths and the hunt for their killer caused Palczynski to panic; he had left the murder weapons in the last stolen car parked outside. As Joseph went to retrieve them, he noticed a police unit pull into the motel. This gave Tracy the chance to escape and as she ran into protective custody, her deranged fiancé fled back into the vast Maryland marshland.

His disappearance then sparked an intense manhunt the likes of which had never before graced the Old Line State. Countless roads were blocked, bloodhounds unleashed and state of the art technology employed to locate the schizophrenic fugitive all to no avail. As the local community armed themselves in fear, Joseph slipped past blockades and escaped to Virginia by train. There he forced fifty-three-year-old William Louis Terrell to buy him food and survival equipment before driving him back to east Baltimore. The hostage was later picked up by police in the early hours of Saturday 11th March unharmed but in shock. Palczynski was nowhere to be seen.

## I'VE BEEN EXPECTING YOU

Nearly a week later, the renegade sociopath resurfaced in a suburban area of Dundalk just off the Baltimore Beltway. Passing unnoticed through police cordons on Friday 17 March, Joseph made for Lange Street and the home of Tracy's mother. His unwavering hopes of being reunited with his betrothed led him to knock on Lynn Whitehead's door at 9.30 that evening. Her boyfriend's twelve-year-old son, Bradley, went to answer, unaware he was opening the door to a deranged killer.

In next to no time, Lynn, Andrew McCord and young Bradley were bound and verbally beaten into submission. Armed with a cache of weapons, Joseph settled in for a long standoff with surrounding police who quickly formed a restricted area around the crime scene, evacuating residents to a local elementary school. Meanwhile the enraged hostage-taker made his first demand; he wanted Tracy. The negotiators held firm even when Joseph threatened to shoot his captives. They wanted to keep the focus of his fury out of harm's way.

While Tracy was placed under police guard in a nearby motel, police aided by a psychiatrist endeavoured to calm Palczynski's volatile mood swings. Flattering his ego helped to make him feel in control. Any time he felt his power undermined, he would fire out at the windows and risk the lives of his hostages. This explosive situation continued for four whole days with his mother and even his lawyer making appeals via the media calling him to surrender.

As night fell on the fourth day of their incarceration and with no end to their ordeal in sight, both Lynn and Andrew McCord decided they would take matters into their own hands. Spiking their captor's iced tea with a sedative, the pair climbed out of a window while Joseph was fast asleep on the living room couch, his guns across his chest. Strangely, they chose not to bring little Bradley with them compelling the attendant SWAT team to enter the house and rescue the boy.

At ten minutes to eleven, the elite squad crashed through the front door just as Joby was waking up. Before he had time to reach for his assorted weaponry, they opened fire, peppering his muscular frame with a total of twenty-seven shots. At five minutes past the hour, Joseph Palczynski was confirmed dead. His long-held death-by-bullet prophecy had finally come true allowing his past victims and their families to breathe an overdue sigh of relief.

# THE ABDUCTION OF
# ELIZABETH SMART

It was around two in the morning of 5 June 2002 in
the Salt Lake City house of Ed and Lois Smart and
their daughter, nine-year-old Mary Katherine Smart,
had been in a deep sleep. Something had roused her
from her slumber, however, and she strained her eyes
in the darkness to see what it was. As her vision
became accustomed to the dark, she saw figures. One
was her sister, fourteen-year-old Elizabeth, who had
climbed out of the bed the two girls shared. Also in
the room, however, was a man who did not look like
her father or one of her brothers. Elizabeth stubbed
her toe on something and cried out as she moved
around the room and Mary heard the man say in a
hushed voice that he would kill her if she made
another sound. It was a voice she thought she
recognised but could not quite place. Through half-
closed eyes she saw that he was wearing a light-
coloured cap and jacket and appeared to be carrying

something that looked like a gun. When Elizabeth asked in a whisper why he was taking her, he hissed back at her something that sounded to Mary like 'for ransom or hostage'. After putting on a pair of sneakers, Elizabeth and her abductor left the room.

Mary immediately got up and went to the door, just in time to see the man and her sister emerge from the room of one of her brothers. But terrified of being seen, she sneaked back into bed and lay there for two hours before waking her parents. Of course, they did not believe her at first, thinking she had probably had a bad dream, but when they could find no trace of their daughter and noticed a hole cut in a downstairs screen window, they knew something was very wrong. They phoned 911 and family and friends, regretting the fact that they had not switched on the alarm that night. One of the kids would often get up in the night and set it off, waking the entire house. Within minutes the house was flooded with people, everyone willing to help, but unwittingly making the job of the police more difficult by contaminating what was effectively a crime scene.

## THE SEARCH FOR CLUES

The search began at once, bloodhounds being brought in to try to find some trace of the missing girl. Unfortunately, the trail the dogs lighted upon ended just a few feet from the house. The morning news bulletins were taken up with news of the abduction and by nine that morning a team of one hundred police officers and local volunteers was combing the area, helicopters hovering above them, scanning the ground. Everyone tried to help. Using its network of churches, the Church of the Latter Day Saints distributed Elizabeth's photograph across five neighbouring states, asking its members to join in the hunt for the missing girl. The Laura Recovery Center, set up to find missing children, sent someone to advise the search operation.

Thousands of posters were printed and flyers were distributed via the internet, to be printed out and distributed. Meanwhile, the authorities extended the area of their search into Idaho and Oregon where two children had recently been abducted. They checked Elizabeth's computer to make sure that she had not been groomed by a sexual predator. Contractors who had worked on the Smart house in recent months were questioned and a $10,000 reward was posted for information leading to her return. Ed Smart spoke to the media later that day, making an emotional plea to the kidnapper to let his daughter come home.

## THE FIRST BREAK

The first break in the case came when police interviewed Chris Miller, the neighbourhood milkman. He reported having seen a green car cruising around the area two days before the abduction, its driver wearing a white baseball cap. When the car had started following his truck, he became worried that he was about to be robbed, made a note of the vehicle's license number and reported it to the police. Eventually, the car had driven off.

At a vigil for Elizabeth held at a Salt Lake City park, police officers checking car numbers found a green sedan with the number 266HJH, not an exact match to the one the milkman had seen, but close enough for the car to be watched until its owner returned. As a man approached the car, two police officers approached him, but he jumped in before they had reached him and sped off. Later that day the vehicle's registration plates were found by a boy at the side of a road and fingerprints on them provided a match with those of Bret Michael Edmunds who was wanted for assaulting a policeman.

Although he was much taller than the man described by Mary Smart, he had worked in the area and immediately became a suspect. There were others, however. Richard Albert Ricci had done odd jobs for the Smarts in 2001. They had liked him but when his background was examined, it emerged that he was a heroin addict and alcoholic with a criminal record for theft. He had also shot a police officer in

1983 in the course of a robbery. He was around the same height and build as the abductor described by Mary and had been on a day off on the day of the kidnap. When his home was searched, items stolen from the Smart house were discovered, as well as a machete and a light-coloured hat of the kind worn by the kidnapper. He was arrested on a parole violation charge and taken into custody. Shortly afterwards, however, Ricci collapsed with a brain haemorrhage and died. His death devastated the Smarts who worried that they had lost their last chance of finding out what had become of their daughter. Meanwhile, Bret Edmunds was apprehended but it soon became clear that he had nothing to do with the crime. The police were back to square one.

## A NEW LEAD

In the October following the kidnapping, there was an extraordinary break for investigators when Mary Smart suddenly remembered where she had heard the voice that threatened to kill her sister that night. It belonged, she claimed, to a man called Emmanuel who had done a day's work at the Smart's house in November 2001. Lois Smart had encountered him begging in town and he had told her he wanted to become a minister to the homeless. She had given him odd jobs to do around the house. Police were sceptical at first, but when a sketch of the man appeared in the media, he was recognised by his family as Brian David Mitchell.

Mitchell's upbringing had been a difficult one. His social worker father had taught him the facts of life by leaving pornographic material around the house. Aged sixteen, he had exposed himself to a child and was sent to live with his grandmother. Before long, however, he was experimenting with drugs and alcohol and dropped out of school. Married at nineteen, he fathered two children but the marriage was short-lived and he moved to New Hampshire with his children. Back in Utah in 1980, he became involved with the Mormon Church and married again to a woman who already had two children. As his religious views became increasingly extreme, he was warned by the church to show more restraint during services. His private life, too, was in trouble. He divorced his second wife, accusing her of cruelty to his children while she, in turn, accused him of abusing her children.

Undaunted, he married for a third time. Wanda Barzee was six years older than him, a divorcee with six children. The children were horrified by Mitchell's religious practices, however, and soon moved out of the house. Wanda, on the other hand, idolised him, treating him like a holy man as they begged for money on the streets of Salt Lake City. By this time, the Mormon Church had had enough of their bizarre behaviour and excommunicated the pair of them. Mitchell responded by concocting his own gospel, *The Book of Immanuel David Isaiah* in which he claimed to have been sent by God to restore the fundamental values of the Church of the Latter Day Saints. One of those fundamental values was polygamy and Elizabeth Smart was the first of the 'seven times seven sisters' he urged Wanda to accept.

On the night that she had been taken, Elizabeth had been forced to walk four miles into a canyon where he had built a makeshift shelter. She was given the same type of white robes that Mitchell and Wanda wore and was tied to a tree. They remained there until 8 August and then returned to their old haunts in Salt Lake City, the lower parts of Elizabeth's and Wanda's faces covered by veils. Elizabeth showed no signs of being held against her will.

Mitchell, Wanda and Elizabeth were finally spotted on 12 March 2003 in the town of Sandy in Utah. An elderly couple recognised them from the television programme, *America's Most Wanted*, that they had watched the previous night even though Elizabeth was wearing a disguise of a wig, sunglasses and a veil. When officers arrived on the scene, they asked the girl if she was in fact Elizabeth Smart. 'If thou sayeth,

I sayeth', she replied, enigmatically.

When Mitchell was taken into custody, he was asked for his address. 'Heaven on earth,' he replied. When asked for an emergency contact, he replied, 'God'.

Mitchell and Barzee were charged with burglary, kidnapping and sexual assault, but neither was found competent to stand trial, a situation that persists to this day. Mitchell has regularly disrupted hearings by singing hymns and has become increasingly delusional. Barzee has divorced him.

Meanwhile, Elizabeth's experiences as a captive of this strange pair remain a closed book. She refuses to discuss them and the details remain known only to her, her parents, and her captors.

# THE ABDUCTION OF KATELYN KAMPF

Maine couple, Nicholas Kampf, fifty-four, and his fifty-three-year-old wife, Lola, were more than a little upset when their nineteen-year-old daughter, Katelyn, announced to them that she was five months pregnant and that the father of her baby was her twenty-two-year-old black boyfriend, Reme Johnson. The couple probably took matters a little too far, however, when they abducted Katelyn and tried to take her to New York or Massachusetts so that she could have an abortion.

## KATELYN AND REME

Katelyn had left Boston College the previous year and had entered into a relationship with Reme. She was staying with Reme's mother in Portland when she phoned one Thursday night to give them the news that they were going to be grandparents. Although they had met Reme before and had been pleasant enough to him, Katelyn spoke later about a change in their attitude when she announced her pregnancy. Her mother, she said, would refer to the baby as a thing and not a person, using the word 'it' and a lot of other unkind comments were made that referred to the colour of the child's skin and disparaged the baby's father for being black.

Katelyn and Reme were from very different sides of the tracks. Reme had arrived in the United States from South Africa, an aspiring rap star who went to ordinary schools. Katelyn, on the other hand, came from a wealthy background – her parents were both real estate developers from North Yarmouth in Maine – and graduated with honours from a prep school that cost in the region of £20,000 a year. Katelyn, however, had always had a difficult relationship with her parents, frequently spending the night at the houses of friends rather than go back to her parents' house, a luxurious eleven-room mansion in North Yarmouth, worth an estimated $850,000.

It is unclear how this upmarket young girl first met the South African rapper who performed in Portland under the name of Young Merk. He had not been entirely well-behaved during his time in America and had previous felony convictions for burglary as well as for receiving stolen property. Katelyn, meanwhile, had graduated from the elite Waynflete private school in 2005 and had then dropped out of Boston College. Her parents had then forcibly enrolled her at George Washington University in Washington DC. By this time she had been seeing Johnson and they believed this was the way to break the young couple up. Katelyn and Reme were undaunted, however, and Johnson was often in Washington visiting Katelyn. Her parents' worst fears were confirmed a short while later when Reme was convicted of possessing a stolen weapon for which he was sentenced to six months' imprisonment.

Four days after her boyfriend had reported to the authorities to begin his sentence, Katelyn spoke to her parents on the phone. She told them about the pregnancy and they immediately asked her to come home.

## DESPERATE ACTIONS

When she arrived on the morning of the day after the phone call, Nicholas and Lola told her in no uncertain terms that she had to get an abortion. She refused and as a heated argument broke out, they tried to seize her. Her mother held her down and, Katelyn claims, spat on her in disgust. She struggled free and raced out into the yard of the house where, she said, her father 'tackled her like a football player', bringing her to the ground before tying her hands and feet together. He then picked her up and carried her out to the car, bundling her in and closing the door. They set out for New Hampshire.

In Salem, New Hampshire, about eighty-seven miles from North Yarmouth, Nicholas Kampf pulled over into the car park of a Kmart store. He needed to make a telephone call and Katelyn had managed during the journey to secrete his mobile phone on her person. He just thought he had left it at home. When they stopped, Katelyn begged her mother to be allowed to go to the toilet. Naturally, they had to untie her before she got out of the car.

In the shop, her father went into the men's room, leaving her waiting outside – he and his wife were obviously not the most proficient kidnappers. As she stood outside the men's room waiting for him to come out, she used his mobile phone to dial 911 and reported a kidnapping – her own! She then ran into another store where police arrived to find her hysterical, hiding in the back of the store. Her parents were found in the store's car park looking for their daughter. In the family Lexus officers found the Kampfs had been well prepared for the abduction. They found passports, a rope, a 22-calibre rifle, duct tape and ammunition. There were also a number of bags into which clothes appeared to have been thrown. The couple were charged with kidnapping as well as for the possession of marijuana that was discovered in the car. They provided statements but stopped short of confessing to kidnapping.

Katelyn, meanwhile, explained to police officers that she had been kidnapped because of her parents' attitude towards her boyfriend's race and colour. The girl was traumatised by the realisation of what they had done to her and what the ultimate objective of their action was – the abortion of her baby. They had opted to travel to an urban centre such as New York to have the abortion performed as the pregnancy was so far advanced it was likely that it would only be performed by an unscrupulous doctor.

## REGRETS AND RECRIMINATIONS

By the time the case came to trial the Kampfs had made a plea agreement with the district attorney's office – against Katelyn's wishes – by which they would plead guilty to misdemeanour charges of assault and disorderly conduct. The charges of kidnapping that could have brought lengthy jail sentences, were dropped. Nicholas and Lola had escaped going to jail and a chastened Nicholas was reported as saying, 'The whole experience has been a sad ordeal. We as a family have lost so much . . . I am sorry.' In a prepared statement Lola expressed a desire that time would heal the wounds that had been caused.

It seemed unlikely in court, however, where neither

of the parents cast a single glance in the direction of their daughter or their brand new grandson, D'Andre. Katelyn actually fled the courtroom in tears a short while after her parents entered the room. Returning a short while later, she broke down again and buried her face in her hands as her mother spoke.

For her part, Katelyn vowed that she would never forgive her parents for what they had done and for planning to abort her unborn baby. 'I want to tell them how much they hurt me,' she said, 'and how angry I am. I've never heard my mom say she was sorry, ever.' She said that the case was not over, in her opinion. She opposed the plea bargain and insisted they should face felony charges of kidnapping.

As part of their plea arrangement, the Kampfs have been ordered to undergo therapy that will involve sessions with Katelyn. She is insistent that these sessions will never take place. 'I can't do it. I can't face them,' she said.

Katelyn has been left to bring up her son D'Andre on her own. Reme Johnson was deported back to South Africa following his felony convictions.

# THE WEST NICKEL MINES AMISH SCHOOL SHOOTING

The Amish are an extraordinary group of people, renowned for their simple, clean living, their unassuming, plain clothing and their eschewal of the contrivances of modern life. They are most familiarly seen travelling in horse-drawn buggies and they speak Pennsylvania German, the language spoken by their forebears, the immigrants who arrived in Pennsylvania in the 17th and 18th centuries. There are around quarter of a million Amish living in the United States and Canada.

Amish life is generally quiet and uneventful, family and church being the hubs around which their existence primarily revolves. The impact that the taking hostage and shootings of young girls at an Amish school in the hamlet of West Nickel Mines in 2006 had on the local community can only be imagined.

A QUESTION OF INSANITY

## A TWISTED MIND

Charles Carl Roberts IV was born in 1973 in Lancaster County, Pennsylvania, but did not come from an Amish family. His father was a police officer and his mother had been employed by a Christian organisation to stage plays. On the morning of 2 October 2006, he walked his children to the bus stop where they would catch the bus to school. Roberts, a milk tanker driver employed by North West Foods, said goodbye to them and his wife, Marie – she was going into town – at around 8.45 and returned home where he wrote four suicide notes; one for his wife and one to each of their three children.

After ten, he drove to the tiny one-room school-house in West Nickel Mines where twenty-year-old teacher, Emma Mae Zook, was teaching a class. Also in the room were Zook's mother and several other family members, there to watch the lesson. Emma looked up to see the thirty-two-year-old Roberts standing in the doorway of the school holding a u-shaped piece of metal in his hand. When she went over to find out what he wanted, he told her that he had lost a similar piece of metal – he called it a clevis – somewhere on the road that ran past the school and wondered if any of the pupils might have seen it.

She immediately found his manner disturbing. He stood very close to her and seemed nervous, carefully avoiding making eye contact with her. Emma told him that no one had reported seeing the piece of metal but generously offered to interrupt the lesson – it was German and spelling – and send the children outside to help him look for the clevis.

Roberts turned round and walked back to his pickup truck, returning, to her horror, with a 9mm handgun in his hand. What had started as a normal day had, in that moment, changed into a horrific day by the end of which the name of the West Nickel Mines School would be known around the world.

## IT ALL TURNS NASTY

With the gun pointed at her, Roberts told Emma Zook that he wanted the boys in the class to help him carry stuff in from the truck. They stood up nervously from their desks and went out to the pickup, carrying back a number of items including a 12-gauge shotgun, a .30-06 bolt-action rifle, six hundred rounds of ammunition, several cans of black powder, a stun gun, two knives, a change of clothes, a board with hooks on it presumably to tie his victims to and a box containing a hammer, hacksaw, pliers, wire, screws, bolts and tape. He also had a tub of KY lubricating jelly. He brought in 2×6 and 2×4 boards to barricade the school doors before binding the arms and legs of his hostages, the little girls.

As he was preoccupied with this, Emma, her mother and the other family members, apart from Sarah, Emma's sister-in-law and a twenty-one-year-old pregnant woman, made a break for it, running out of the schoolhouse door to safety. Roberts jumped up and immediately ordered one of the boys, Peterli Fischer to go after them and tell them that if they did not come back he was going to start shooting. As the boy ran out the door, he was followed by his nine-year-old sister, Emma, who spoke only Pennsylvania German and had no idea what the gunman was saying as he shouted after her to stop or he would shoot. Emma probably saved her life by not understanding English; she carried on running. Sadly, however, her two older sisters were not so fortunate. Thirteen-year-old Marian was later shot dead while eleven-year-old Barbie was seriously wounded.

The women ran to a nearby farm where they dialled 911. Meanwhile, Roberts released the remaining adults as well as the fifteen boys in the class. He lined up the ten girl hostages in front of the class blackboard.

The police began to arrive around 10.42 and immediately tried to establish communications with the hostage-taker using their patrol cars' PA systems. Roberts was busy, however, nailing the boards he had brought across the schoolhouse doors and piling up desks in front of them. Thus secured, it is presumed that he had every intention of sexually assaulting the girls. He had brought the lubricating jelly for just that purpose.

Outside, a farmhand had crept up on the schoolhouse, approaching it from the rear accompanied by two large dogs. He quietly crept around to a side window beside which he flattened himself against the wall. It was a strategically useful position from which he might have gleaned information about what was happening inside, but as the first patrol car had arrived and looked as if it might drive past the schoolhouse, he chose, instead of remaining there, to run out into the road and stop it.

Roberts was still tying the girls' arms and legs using plastic ties. Looking out the window, however, he saw the police trying to get closer to the building. He jumped to the window and shouted to them to move back which they immediately did while ignoring his instruction to leave the area. Once again using their PAs they ordered him to throw his guns out the window and come out with his hands up. He refused again.

The girls were, naturally, very agitated, but two of them, Peterli Fischer's sisters, Barbie and Marian, began talking to him and, displaying extraordinary courage for such young girls, requested that he shot them first and spared their classmates.

The crowd of parents and neighbours who had, by this time, joined the waiting police officers were suddenly horrified by the sound of a child's screams from inside the schoolhouse. Some officers were now hiding behind a shed at the back of the building and on hearing the shout, requested permission to launch an assault. Senior officers denied them permission however, fearing that such an action would force the gunman to open fire on the girls.

They did not have to wait much longer, however. At 11.07, shots rang out from inside the classroom. It had started. Officers rushed the building from all sides but as they arrived at the door one last shot rang out before an eerie silence descended on the building. Roberts, it seemed, had reserved his last bullet for himself.

## A SICKENING SCENE

The scene inside was grim. He had shot several of the girls execution-style from point-blank range. Three were already dead or died at the scene – Naomi Rose Ebersol, aged seven, Marian Stoltzfus Fischer, aged thirteen, and Anna Mae Stoltzfus, aged twelve. Two others, Lena Zook Miller, aged seven and Mary Liz Miller, aged eight were rushed to hospital in a critical condition and died the following day. Five others were critically wounded.

## HIS EXPLANATION

The note that Roberts had left for his wife explained his motivation to some extent. He explained his disappointment with God for letting their daughter, Elise, die at birth nine years previously.

> *'I don't know how you put up with me all those years. I am not worthy of you, you are the perfect wife you deserve so much better. We had so many good memories together as well as the tragedy with Elise. It changed my life forever I haven't been the same since, it affected me in a way I never felt possible. I am filled with so much hate, hate toward myself, hate towards God and unimaginable emptiness it seems like everytime we do something fun I think about how Elise wasn't here to share it with us and I go right back to anger.'*

Puzzlingly, in a phone call to his wife during the siege he had explained how he had molested two young female relatives when he had been twelve years old and that he had recently been feeling the urge once again to molest young girls. Strangely, the two girls in question later denied that he had molested them.

The Amish community responded to the horror of the day with astonishing dignity and compassion.

One of the dead girls' grandfathers said, 'We must not think evil of this man.'

Dozens attended the funeral of Charles Roberts five days after the incident and an Amish neighbour had comforted Marie Roberts after her husband's suicide. In an astonishing act of kindness and forgiveness, they even established a charitable fund for her and her children.

As for the schoolhouse, it was torn down ten days after the shootings and the land on which it had stood was allowed to return to pasture. A brand new schoolhouse was opened nearby in April 2007.

# THE JOHNSON SPACE CENTER SHOOTING

The dangers associated with spaceflight are an accepted feature of an astronaut's life but for the humble men and women who work on the ground, such as those at NASA's Johnson Space Center, the hazards are considered quite minimal. However on a springtime Friday in 2007, it would be Houston's time to have a problem. After a supervisor's email called for an employee to change his ways, the recipient complied in a dramatic fashion boldly entering the space centre, shooting one colleague and taking another hostage.

## MISSION LAUNCH

Friday 20 April 2007 was just another ordinary end to the working week for the majority of the fifteen thousand personnel at the Johnson Space Center. Stretching over a vast 1,600 acres of south east Houston, Texas, the sprawling NASA development is home to Mission Control from where all human space travel in the United States is directed and monitored. With just over a hundred astronauts on site, the majority of the workforce is made up of humble civil servants and subcontractors, one of whom was about to skyrocket the Johnson Space Center to the front pages and television screens right across America.

His name was William Arthur Phillips Junior, a sixty-year-old employee of the Jacobs Engineering Group – a provider of technical services personnel – who had worked at the centre for over twelve years. On this springtime Friday morning, the sexagenarian entered through the main gate as he would any other day, flashing his ID badge, but this time he brought a handgun on to the premises. This breach of protocol went undetected by front-of-house guards despite a recent heightening of security. Institutions country-wide had been reassessing their safety measures after a lone gunman had gone on a rampage at Virginia Tech University killing thirty-two students and staff earlier in the week. Luckily for William Phillips, the NASA centre had concluded their security proce-dures needed no improvement.

### YOU'VE GOT MAIL

This moment had been building for the tech-support worker, his blood boiling for almost a month ever since he received a troubling email on 16 March from his supervisor. Its contents concerned his continual inability to attend meetings on time as well as highlighting a persistent failure to identify corrective actions at work. Fearing this poor performance review would lead to his dismissal, he decided to take drastic action. Two days later, he paid a visit to a local gun store and bought a .38 calibre snub-nosed revolver – believed to be a Smith & Wesson – along with twenty hollow point bullets. Such a severe reaction may be somewhat explained by the contractor's lifestyle and a past event in his career.

Originally from Tennessee, the introverted Phillips lived a simple existence with little in his life but his role at the Johnson Space Center. With no wife nor children to speak of, the position in technical support was his entire world and losing it filled him with dread. He had been fired fifteen years before when he worked at Westinghouse one thousand four hundred miles away in Washington DC. Despite giving twenty-three years to the electrical company, he was dismissed and from that moment on he lived in fear of losing his job.

Fearing the email echoed another redundancy, Phillips aimed to protect the one thing that gave his life meaning. In possession of a deadly weapon, it would however take several trips to work before the paranoid contractor chose to take violent action. It required something to tip the scales and force the issue, to bring the killer out in William Phillips. This trigger would come at lunch.

## BEEF AT LUNCH

The morning passed without incident inside Building 44; the workplace of the only armed engineer in the entire centre. One block west of Mission Control in a quiet area of the complex, this comparatively small, grey structure housed the offices and laboratories which handled the tracking of spacecraft such as the International Space Station and the shuttle. This would provide the location for William Phillips' sudden outburst of pent-up aggression.

At lunchtime, NASA employees witnessed Phillips seated with a fellow employee named David Beverly, a sixty-two-year-old electrical parts specialist and quality control engineer employed by NASA. A gregarious soul held in high regard by his colleagues, Beverly was the complete opposite of the Jacobs engineer. While Phillips had been brought to book over his unsatisfactory performance, the man across from him had recently been honoured for his twenty-five year service with the space agency.

As the pair ate their midday meals, they talked. What was discussed will forever remain a mystery for by the end of the day the two men would no longer be alive, taking their conversation to the grave. All that is known is that something was said to spark a sleeping ember within William, leading to a deadly encounter inside Building 44.

## FIGHT OR FLIGHT

A short time after one o'clock on this fateful Friday, still fuming from his lunchtime dispute and now with a focus for his frustration, William Phillips stormed into the second floor conference room brandishing his revolver. Interrupting a scheduled meeting, the gunman ordered everyone out; all except David Beverly. Pointing his weapon at the man from San Leon, he screamed, 'You're the one that is going to get me fired!'

As frightened employees scrambled out of Building 44, David Beverly attempted to calm his disgruntled colleague. At approximately twenty to two, filled with an unappeasable fury, Phillips opened fire on the man before him. Despite taking two bullets to the chest, the assaulted technician remained conscious enough to notice his attacker had left the room. While Phillips had gone to check on the growing media coverage on a nearby television, the injured Beverly endeavoured to barricade himself inside the conference room, manoeuvring a desk to block the doorway.

This attempt to escape further punishment proved

unsuccessful. When the gunman returned, he was able to push open the blocked door with ease and fire off two more shots at the hapless victim. At the second time of asking, William Phillips went from embittered employee to maniacal murderer.

## WATCH THIS SPACE

With his sole target of frustration lying dead on the conference room floor, Phillips pounced for further prey. Owing to her close proximity to David Beverly at the time of his attack, the gunman grabbed Francelia Crenshaw, a fifty-six-year-old contract worker employed by MRI Technologies, a local engineering and support services company.

He quickly bound his hostage with duct tape to an office chair, calling for her to remove her earrings so he could safely tape her mouth closed without causing unnecessary harm. Making an effort not to panic, Francelia Crenshaw showed enormous courage as she tried to calm the unstable NASA worker and, barricaded inside the room for the next three hours, she hoped to avoid the same fate as her colleague, David Beverly.

Meanwhile police were responding to the emergency call received at 13.45 reporting a man with a gun had entered the Johnson Space Center and that shots had been fired. In a short space of time, more than fifteen police cars along with bomb, canine and SWAT units were despatched to the scene and set up a perimeter around Building 44. The attending authorities ensured the office block was clear of extraneous NASA personnel and began shutting down access roads around the 1,600 acre complex.

While Mission Control, only a block away, was locked down as a precautionary measure, the remaining buildings, numbering over a hundred, were not evacuated. Instead, those inside were informed by email to remain where they were until further notice. These confined NASA employees waited, watching the standoff unfold on office TV sets, unable to think about work while the hostage crisis played out somewhere else on site.

## SPACE INVADERS

From two o'clock police negotiators endeavoured to open a line of communication with the hostage-taker inside. On the one occasion they managed to make contact, Phillips picked up the phone but refused to speak. With no demands nor deadlines imposed on the surrounding authorities, all they could do was stand their ground and hope that the situation did not escalate into further violence.

Meanwhile inside the makeshift bulwark on the second floor, William Phillips began to scribble names and numbers on a dry wipe board, contact information for the few relatives he would leave behind if his mission ended in tragedy. As he rambled to his captive audience of one that he was tired of being called stupid, it became alarmingly clear that Phillips was gearing himself towards a suicidal climax. Before his final move, he whispered to Crenshaw not to scream when the time came for his fatal exit.

At five o'clock, over three hours since the standoff began, police heard a single gunshot from within. Believing the gunman had taken his own life, the decision was made for the SWAT team to enter Building 44. As the special weapons unit invaded the block of labs and offices, the Houston police negotiators received a call from inside. It was Francelia Crenshaw, the hostage. She had managed to rip the duct tape from her mouth and get to the phone to report her captor was dead.

Moments later this information was confirmed by the tactical unit, discovering the two bodies of David Beverly and William Phillips, displaying a single gunshot to the head. Next to them, Crenshaw was still bound to the chair, the sole survivor of the three-hour standoff. She was quickly released and taken to St John Hospital where she was found to be physically unharmed by the ordeal. With the crisis finally over, a second email was sent out to staff throughout the centre, informing detained employees they were now free to leave at their own discretion.

## ONWARDS AND UPWARDS

Having had no dialogue with the gunman, police lacked any motive for the attack and quizzed Fran Crenshaw for an insight into William Phillips' brutal slaying of his fellow NASA colleague. All she could relay was that, for some reason, the vexed support technician blamed David Beverly for his bad performance review he had received a month earlier. When Jacobs Engineering – the killer's employers – were contacted, they informed both police and press that there had been no plans to fire Phillips. It appeared his fear of dismissal was misplaced making the deaths of both men even more tragic.

Despite the terrible loss of life, normal business was resumed as early as that evening. In central Houston, just a few miles from where the tragedy had taken place, NASA held its Annual Achievement Awards, where the efforts of the ordinary men on the ground were acknowledged. Employees then returned to the Johnson Space Center on Monday morning after a weekend of reflection and remembrance, to continue with their stellar work, still bewildered by the pointless savagery of that Friday afternoon.

# LISA NOWAK

You would find it hard to swallow if you read it in a novel. It was a case that had everything. Fit, good-looking people, heroes to the American public, involved in a love triangle that went terribly wrong and ended in an attempted kidnapping and possibly attempted murder. It sounds like a daytime soap opera but it was a real life drama that astonished the world in 2007. The participants of this drama were all members of a rarefied club – they were all NASA astronauts, involved in America's Space Shuttle programme.

## THE CHARACTERS

Lisa Nowak was married with three children but that had not stood in the way of a stellar career. Born in Rockville, Maryland in 1963, she had wanted to go into space since, at the age of six, she had watched Neil Armstrong take his first steps on the moon. She began to collect the requisite qualifications – degrees in aerospace, aeronautical and astronautical engineering and a Master of Science degree in aeronautical engineering. She had received a commission in the US Navy in 1985 and flew F/A-18 and EA-6B fighter jets. She has logged more than 1,500 hours flying time, gained in more than thirty different aircraft.

In August 1996, she achieved her ultimate ambition when she was selected for the NASA Astronaut Corps based at the Johnson Space Center. She became a mission specialist in robotics, first travelling into space on 4 July 2006 as a member of a crew assigned to the International Space Station. As mission flight engineer, she was given the job of operating the space shuttle's robotic arm during space walks. She was in space for thirteen days.

She had married Richard Nowak in 1988. He had been in her class at the Naval Academy and at Navy flight school and went on to work, like her, at the Johnson Space Center where he was a NASA contractor. In 1992 the couple had a son and then in 2002, twin daughters.

In 2004, Lisa Nowak became romantically involved with forty-one-year-old Navy Commander William Oefelein, a divorced fellow astronaut who piloted the space shuttle *Discovery* in December 2006. She had trained with Oefelein although the two had not gone into space together. He had learned to fly planes as a teenager in Alaska, had studied electrical engineering at Oregon State University and had gained a Master's degree at the University of Texas Space Institute. He arrived at NASA in 1998.

Nowak would later say that their relationship was 'more than a working relationship but less than a romantic relationship.' However, Oefelein gave her a mobile phone to be used solely to communicate with him and it was used a great deal. The day after his return from his mission on the space shuttle, she called him a dozen times and sent him seven text messages. Records show, however, that he failed to pick up her messages for two days. When he finally spoke to her on 24 December, they had a seven-minute conversation. During the remainder of December and through January, they spoke on the phone more than a hundred times, although it is not clear who initiated the calls. They also met once that month for lunch at Oefelein's apartment and continued to train together for a cycle race they had both entered.

The truth was that Oefelein's feelings for Nowak were cooling and he was gradually trying to extricate himself from their relationship. Furthermore, he had begun another relationship with US Air Force Captain Colleen Shipman, who worked as an engineer with the 45th Space Wing at Patrick Air Force Base, close to the Kennedy Space Center.

## A TOUCH OF JEALOUSY

Nowak discovered that Oefelein was seeing Shipman and started to follow her. For two months Shipman felt as if she was being stalked. When Nowak discovered that Shipman was taking a commercial flight on 5 February 2007 from Houston in Texas to Orlando in Florida, she decided to take action. She drove furiously the nine hundred miles to Orlando to meet her plane, reportedly wearing nappies all the way – just like astronauts do in space for launch and re-entry – so that she would not have to stop en route to go to the toilet. In her car were a number of items including latex gloves, a BB pistol, pepper spray, a brown trench coat with a hood, a two-pound hammer drill, black gloves, rubber tubing, plastic rubbish bags and a knife with an 8-inch blade. She was carrying $585 in cash and also had her computer with her. She had in her possession copies of emails between Oefelein and Shipman and a letter to Oefelein from her that told him how much she loved him.

Arriving at the airport, she parked her car before waiting for an hour near the baggage hall. She caught sight of Colleen Shipman and, wearing the trench coat and a wig, followed her to the car park. Shipman, immediately aware of someone following her, rushed to her car, jumped in and locked the doors. She heard footsteps running towards the car and was shocked to see Nowak, slapping the closed window and asking for a lift. When she burst into tears, Shipman lowered the driver's side window a little. Suddenly Nowak reached up and sprayed pepper spray into the car leaving Shipman temporarily blinded and having difficulty breathing. She had the presence of mind, nonetheless, to start the car and drive at speed to the exit booth where she told the attendants to call the police.

Police officers arrived shortly after and one reported seeing Nowak throw a bag into a litter bin. When retrieved it was found to contain the wig and the BB gun.

Lisa Nowak was arrested and charged with attempted kidnapping, battery, attempted vehicle theft with battery and destruction of evidence. Shipman made a request for a protection order against her rival, claiming that she had been stalking her for the two months prior to the incident at the airport. Although she told police that Nowak was an acquaintance of her boyfriend, she tried to keep him out of it by not mentioning his name. The police recommended that because she had shown signs of elaborate planning, had used disguises and was in possession of weapons, Nowak should not be granted bail.

## A HINT OF A SCANDAL

Meanwhile, as the media began to sense a sensational story in the making, two senior astronauts – Christopher Ferguson, the senior Naval Officer in the NASA Astronaut Corps and retired Air Force Colonel Steve Lindsay, senior astronaut at NASA, who had commanded Nowak's space shuttle mission, flew to Florida to try to limit the damage to NASA's image and to help where possible. They both appeared in front of a judge on 6 February as character witnesses for Nowak. The case made by the prosecution was that Nowak had devised a detailed plan to kidnap and possibly injure Captain Shipman. Nowak's lawyer, meanwhile, argued for bail for his client and the judge ordered her to pay $15,500 bail and to wear a tracking device on her ankle. She was also ordered to stay away from Shipman.

As Nowak was about to be released, however, she was shocked to learn that the Orlando police, unhappy that she was being freed on bail, were now also charging her with attempted first-degree murder. An attempted murder charge was one way of keeping her in custody. At her second hearing, however, the judge merely raised the bail by $10,000 and she was freed.

Lisa Nowak's arrest and previous conduct had huge implications for NASA which was engaged at the time in the selection and screening of astronauts for a planned mission to Mars, a voyage lasting thirty months in which personnel, men and women, presumably, would be in close contact with each other. People questioned how relationships might develop over such a prolonged period and whether jealousies and conflict might ensue. There was also criticism of NASA's treatment of astronauts as heroic special beings, placing huge social pressure on them as individuals. Others suggested that it was precisely because of this view of astronauts that Nowak seemed to be receiving lenient treatment by the judicial process.

Lisa Nowak pleaded not guilty to the charges of attempted murder and attempted kidnapping. The authorities ultimately did not pursue the attempted murder charge.

The case continues with Nowak undergoing psychiatric examinations. Although she was awarded the Space Flight Medal, awarded to any astronaut who takes part in a United States mission into space, her assignment to NASA as an astronaut was terminated by the space agency in March 2007.

# PART FOUR

# FOR
# FINANCIAL
# GAIN

# CHARLES ROSS

While kidnapping was not unheard of in early American history thanks to the Native Indians child-stealing practices, the first major publicised instance of a hostage for ransom in the United States came in the late 19th century and involved the kidnapping of a local merchant's son in the state of Pennsylvania. This debut abduction for money became a media event and to this day is still shrouded in mystery.

History was made on 1 July 1874 when four-year-old Charles Brewster Ross and his brother Walter, two years his senior, were snatched from the front garden of their large family home in the once Quaker Germantown. Two men in a horse-drawn carriage known as a buggy pulled up and enticed the two tykes to come and buy fireworks in nearby Philadelphia. After two hours driving around in the city's northern quarter it was not long before little Charley began to miss home and started to cry so the two men drew up next to a store and gave Walter twenty-five cents to buy fireworks. When Walter exited the store, firecrackers in hand, the carriage was gone and so was his younger brother.

When Christian K. Ross, the father of the two boys, stepped out of his mansion to look for his two boys he found an empty yard. Speaking with his neighbour he discovered they had been spotted boarding the buggy. Gripped with terror, the father began to search, keeping the news from their mother who was convalescing in Atlantic City. In a short space of time a relieved father was reunited with his eldest son who had been found by a concerned citizen and returned to Germantown but now the search for his youngest son became his sole focus.

## RANSOM REQUIRED

The following day Christian Ross received the news he had been dreading. Arriving in the mail a poorly-handwritten letter told him his youngest son was being held for ransom. The kidnappers demanded $20,000 for the safe return of the boy. This was a huge figure for 19th century America particularly as there had been a stock market crash the previous year. The country's financial slump had affected Christian Ross who was already in some debt and despite outward appearances paying such a price was not in his power.

With no money to pay Christian felt he had no

option but to contact the authorities despite being warned against this in the barely legible ransom note which stated, '... if any aproch is maid to his hidin place that is the signil for his instant annihilation. If yu regard his lif puts no one to search for him you money can fech him out alive...' A further twenty-two notes from his son's captors arrived through Christian's letterbox over the next few months all insisting the ransom be paid meanwhile the kidnap-ping had made front page news all across the nation. Concerned Philadelphians procured the services of the renowned Pinkerton Detective Agency who fashioned a poster campaign with flyers depicting little Charley Ross's round, dimpled face surrounded by ringlets of fair hair. Soon the lost boy's angelic features were famous throughout the land. Even a song – *Bring Back Our Darling* – was composed to appeal to the hearts of those who knew of his whereabouts. Finally a reward matching the ransom figure was posted to attract some good news.

The fervent desire to find Charley Ross took hold of America. While the detectives pursued every pos-sible lead searching criminal hideouts and interview-ing possible witnesses the ordinary men and women in the street endeavoured to find the stolen child with little regard for the law. Believed by many to be child thieves, many gypsies came under attack and one band of travellers was nearly lynched in Pennsylvania a month after the kidnapping because they had a child matching Ross's description.

The Ross mansion was flooded with countless crank letters purporting to know of Charley's location and every now and then another genuine ransom note would come through the door with them. The police urged Christian not to pay but adamant he would see his son again he liaised with the kidnappers. Despite the Ross family's keenness to acquiesce to their demands whenever a money drop was arranged his son's captors failed to show and soon the letters stopped arriving.

## A CRIMINAL'S CONFESSION

Charley had been missing for three weeks when the case caught its first real break. On 21 July 1874, New York police received a tip from a contact in the underworld naming two men responsible for the kidnapping. They were partners in crime: William Mosher and Joseph Douglas who between them had a criminal record reaching back twenty years. They were currently fugitives from justice having escaped from prison while awaiting trial for burglary. The illegible scrawl of the ransom note was compared with their handwriting and they found a match: it came from the hand of Mosher.

All concerned with the liberation of little Charley would have to wait several months before authorities caught up with those responsible and even then it was by accident. On 14 December, one hundred and fifty miles northeast of Germantown, Holmes Van Brunt witnessed two would-be thieves about to enter his brother's Long Island home next door. Acting swiftly, he assembled his household staff and gave them weapons to detain the burglars and surrounded the property belonging to Judge Charles Van Brunt. In the ensuing gunfight Holmes' men took down the two intruders; they were Mosher and Douglas. As Douglas lay dying he had some interesting last words for the police confessing to the kidnapping of Charley Ross. He claimed while he did not know where he was being held Mosher did know. Unfortunately Mosher would not be confessing anything. He had already succumbed to his mortal wounds.

Douglas' final words before his death gave hope to the Ross family being reunited with their lost son maintaining the boy would be returned to them within a few days. The eldest son, Walter, was asked to identify the bodies of the two dead robbers and confirmed they were the same men with whom he had driven to buy fireworks that fateful summer day noticing, in particular, Mosher's misshapen nose which he described as being like a monkey. For most the matter was settled but there was no happy family reunion. Charles Ross remained missing. Christian offered yet another reward for his son's safe return, this time for $5,000, but there were still no takers.

A third man was later picked up, charged and tried for his involvement in the kidnapping. A former Philly cop, William Westervelt was a known associate of the monkey-nosed Mosher and provided the Ross family with another sliver of hope when, while in jail awaiting his trial, he told Christian that his child was still alive at the time of the Long Island burglary. Westervelt was tried the following year but with a severe lack of evidence together with Walter Ross's own testimony that he was not one of the men who snatched them that July day a not guilty verdict was inevitable. He was convicted on three lesser counts of conspiracy to kidnap, extort money and defraud a child's liberty and received a seven year sentence. Even in jail, he continued to profess his innocence and swore he did not know where Charles Ross could be found.

## THE SEARCH CONTINUES

With the culprits of the crime either dead and buried or behind bars, the Ross family had some justice but were still no closer to finding their missing child. Christian Ross was not about to give up. In 1877 he published his account of the kidnapping case called *The Father's Story of Charley Ross: The Kidnapped Child* with all proceeds put towards funding the ongoing search. He even managed to get the famous circus impresario, P.T. Barnum, to offer a $10,000 reward for Charley's recovery during his company's coast to coast tour.

Over five hundred boys had been personally checked by Christian by 1878 and still no Charley. Every lead no matter how tenuous was followed by the father even travelling to England on a lead but to no avail. With every passing year hope dwindled as the Ross family went from interviewing angelic boys to teenagers and eventually adult males in their twenties. All were found to be hoaxes.

The search cost Christian Ross dearly. Expenses ran to three times the ransom over the twenty-three years before his death when in 1897 he died of a broken heart having never been reunited with his youngest son. His mother soon followed in 1912 and Walter passed away in 1943 never knowing whether he would be outlived by his younger brother who, if alive, would be seventy-three years of age.

With the brother gone it seemed all connections with Charley Ross were coming to an end. The family mansion had been demolished nearly twenty years earlier and the last fake claim to be the stolen child was now four years in the past. The kidnapped four year old boy from Germantown, Pennsylvania had been lost to the world and never to be seen again. And yet his name still lives on: a missing persons database in America – the Charley Project – was named after him to honour his memory. This fitting tribute marks the final entry in this tragic case. Yet this dreadful debut of profit-related child-purloining would not be the last of its kind, doing nothing to prevent hostage-taking for ransom from becoming many a criminal's sure-fire plan for easy money.

# EDWARD CUDAHY
## JUNIOR

The next major hostage situation to grab the nation's interest was that of Eddie Cudahy Junior, the sixteen-year-old son of a wealthy meatpacker in Omaha, Nebraska. This turn of the century hostage-taking caused a sensation with its nationwide manhunt and loopholes in the law which eventually saw the culprit become a celebrity.

The Cudahy family had achieved substantial success with their plant which had become one of the main five meatpacking companies in America making Edward Senior a millionaire well-known throughout Nebraska. His mansion stood proud atop the hill within the affluent Old Gold Coast neighbourhood and this open display of wealth placed him in the forefront of the minds of some nefarious villains out to make a fast buck.

Accompanied by his pet collie, Edward Aloysius Cudahy Junior, the tycoon's spoilt teenage son, left his high-value home to run an errand on the wintry evening of 18 December 1900. Returning some books the family had borrowed from Doctor Fred Rustin just a few doors down on Farnam Street, Eddie Junior had no idea he was being watched. On his way home a horse-drawn carriage pulled up beside him and, before he could run, a man jumped out and bundled him aboard. As the buggy made its getaway the driver tossed a large stick into the Cudahy front yard.

His well-heeled father found out about his missing son only after returning from a dinner engagement much later that night where his household servants were already concerned as the collie had come home alone. Edward Senior acted fast calling the police and two cops on cycles were dispatched but any news of the abduction would not arrive until the following day.

After a sleepless night Cudahy shut down his plant and called upon his two thousand-strong workforce to help look for his son. In a show of faith and solidarity his meatpacking competitors downed tools and joined them and soon they had over seven thousand people searching the streets of Omaha.

## GIVE UP THE COIN

The captors' silence was broken at nine o'clock that morning when Cudahy received an anonymous call suggesting he take a look in his front yard. There his coachman found a note written on brown wrapping paper tied to the stick thrown by the driver the previous evening. It made for terrible reading. The abductors required $25,000 in exchange for the boy giving strict instructions that the money must be in gold coins in only five, ten and twenty dollar denominations. The ransom note revealed in no uncertain terms to, '… give up the coin. Money we want and money we shall get.'

Along with directions for the money drop this snail mail stick-up came with graphic threats for non-compliance, warning him they would pour acid into the teenager's eyes if their demands were not met. They prayed on his fears reminding him of the fate of Little Charley Ross and how his father died never seeing his son after not paying the ransom. With this sword of Damocles hanging over his head Edward Senior chose to ignore Police Chief John Donahue's plea not to give in to the kidnappers and go ahead with the pay-off in what he saw as his only chance of getting his boy back.

## THE DROP

The ransom note ordered the drop to take place that evening on the country road to Fremont a full twenty-four hours after the abduction. Earlier in the day his coachman was sent to collect the money from Omaha National Bank and, packed in a twelve dollar suitcase, the $25,000 ransom was placed on board Cudahy's carriage destined for a drop deep in the dark hinterland several miles west of the city.

The millionaire meatpacker with only his head cattle buyer Paddy McGrath for protection, followed the instructions to the letter leaving the mansion around seven in the evening. They were told to look out for a lantern decorated with black and white ribbons near a bridge over Little Papio Creek. They soon spotted the dim glow of the marker and Cudahy duly left the money along with a note in reply to the kidnappers making clear he expected them to now keep their side of the bargain before returning home to await the fate of his actions.

Thankfully, the Cudahy household did not have to endure further agony. At one in the morning Eddie Junior surprised them all when he shuffled into the kitchen parlour with barely a hair out of place. The prodigal son had returned and was restored to the family fold. As far as the Cudahys were concerned it was money well spent but many disagreed with the pay-off condemning the action as a bad precedent and accused the magnate of having a blasé attitude when asked to comment on the decision to buy back his son.

## MANHUNT

Cudahy may have appeared nonchalant about paying

the ransom but he was by no means finished with the affair. The tycoon pledged a $25,000 reward for the capture of the now-flush kidnappers and the Pinkerton Detective Agency was called in once more to lead the manhunt.

Eddie Junior provided the authorities with a detailed account of his kidnapping. His statement told how he was driven around in circles for hours before being led blindfolded into a dilapidated house and held in a room containing only a chair and gas stove. Despite having his legs manacled and being given nothing but crackers, coffee and cigarettes he felt he had not been subjected to any undue cruelty. As for his kidnappers he gave the police adequate descriptions informing them that one possessed a strong accent and stank of drink. After the drop, he was driven around in the carriage once more before being released a short distance from home walking the rest of the way into the loving arms of his family.

The nation was gripped with the thrill of the chase. Armed with this information everyone from press men to the general public endeavoured to pick up the scent. It was two reporters – Eugene Mayfield and E.H. Henning of the *World Herald* – who struck gold first finding the hostage-takers' hideout: 3604 Grover Street in South Omaha. This shack was confirmed by Eddie Junior as the place where he had been held.

By this time the police had a firm favourite whom they suspected of having held Eddie hostage: a thirty-one-year-old career criminal by the name of Pat Crowe. A flashy, dashing, square-jawed scoundrel, Crowe was a lovable rogue who in his fine clothes robbed far and wide from Denver to Philadelphia. Photos were shown to witnesses near the rented hideout and all confirmed he was their man. They had further cause to suspect the well-travelled thief. Crowe had twice been undone by the Cudahy family after his small butchering business had been undercut by the meatpackers and was forced to close. Later, working at a Cudahy store, he was accused of stealing and fired by the company.

All fingers pointed to Crowe but with so many eager to claim the reward the fingers pointed in countless directions with sightings in such diverse places as Nantucket Island and even aboard a steamship in Honduras. Despite all the nationwide press attention Crowe could not be found. In March 1901 in a further bid to unearth the elusive villain, Omaha City Council matched Cudahy's reward and Chief Donahue resorted to calling upon the services of a hypnotist to make some progress.

Later that month it came. A shifty Irish drifter called James Callahan was arrested for public insobriety and fined, paying the charge with a shiny twenty dollar gold coin – exactly the same as those given as ransom. As he was also a known associate of the hard-to-catch Crowe the police closed in and observed the drunk stumbling from tavern to tavern along the Q Street in Omaha paying for booze with yet more gold coins.

On 21 March Callahan was arrested for robbing Edward Cudahy Senior and went to trial but there was a problem. Despite witnesses, including the hostage himself, testifying that Callahan was one of the kidnappers, Nebraska State had no kidnapping statute that applied to a boy of sixteen within the city limits. At that time kidnapping only related to those under ten who were taken across city lines. New laws correcting this loophole were quickly ratified but could not be retroactively applied to the lucky Irishman who was given a not guilty verdict on 28 April. The presiding Judge Baker was shocked at the jury's decision.

## AS THE CROWE FLIES

As for Crowe, he remained hidden. However, in October 1901, six months after the Callahan trial, Crowe wrote to both Cudahy and Chief Donahue offering to turn himself in along with the remainder of the ransom if the $50,000 bounty on his head was scrapped. They both agreed to his latest demands but Crowe failed to show and instead slid back into the shadows once more.

It was not until Spring 1905 that Crowe resurfaced, turning up like a bad gold coin in Omaha impudently giving an interview to a *World Herald* reporter. Quotes suggesting he was ready to reform hid the truth that he had blown all the ransom. Yet again he disappeared before police could lay hands on him. They came much closer later that year when he was spotted at a tavern on 16th and Hickory Street not far from downtown Omaha. Detectives rushed to the scene but after a lengthy shoot-out in which a policeman was shot Crowe managed to escape. Fortunately this would prove to be the dandy fugitive's final vanishing act.

On 2 October 1905 Crowe was finally captured by police in Butte, Montana. Held in his cell, he became a public curiosity. From hostage-taker to heartbreaker, visitors paraded past his cell to stare at the prize prisoner including many besotted women fluttering their eyelashes. The notorious outlaw drew huge crowds of supporters at every station on the train journey back to Omaha.

Crowe faced two trials covering his many misdemeanours. The first held on 28 November saw four days of testimony and less than two hours of deliberation for the jury to acquit, stunning many locals present. The second trial took place in February 1906 with nearly a hundred prosecution witnesses called to the stand. Crowe's defence called none hanging its case on the summation. Filled with hyperbole and endeavouring to portray the wealthy Cudahy as the villain despite a damning confession letter written by Crowe to a Catholic priest claiming full responsibility the jury declared him not guilty agreeing with the defence that the letter was a sufficient act of contrition. Such a travesty of justice proved, as one newspaper put it, Omaha was now, 'a happy hunting ground for savages and malefactors.'

## HERO TO ZERO

Crowe's notoriety garnered fame and considerable fortune as the exonerated offender toured the Vaudeville circuit telling tall tales of short cons across America. In August 1906, *New York World* paid a princely sum for the king of kidnappers' exclusive story. His exploits soon became common knowledge as he lectured his rehashed stories from town to town and soon the limelight began to fade. The gasps grew quieter and interest waned and soon the sideshow attraction turned backstreet bum hitting the bottle and moving from one drug and disorderly charge to the next. He became such a nuisance he was ordered to leave Omaha for good. Gone were the days he was the major catch, now they were letting him go.

Crowe returned to New York pitching ideas to

press offices but soon found himself living in the Bowery flophouses broke and alone. Even then he did not let Cudahy Junior forget. On hearing his young hostage had wed in 1919, Crowe sent the groom a telegram wishing him happiness in the hands of his new kidnapper. From hero to zero, Pat Crowe slipped once more into obscurity and on 29 October 1938 he died of a heart attack surrounded by news cuttings of his past exploits.

The Cudahy kidnapping had a profound effect on the community not only influencing future hostage-takers hell-bent on turning a profit, but also persuading Omaha businessmen to keep a closer eye on their offspring. Some took more drastic action. Gurdon W. Wattles, for example, escaped the rising Omahan tension for the bright lights of Hollywood becoming a major financier of the movie industry.

Former hostage Edward Junior followed suit moving away from his hometown taking his family to Chicago in 1910 and after serving in the Great War returned to lead his father's company into further prosperity making him a millionaire several times over. He retired to Arizona in 1961 and passed peacefully away five years later having led a long and successful life proving there was no substitute for hard graft in the search for great wealth.

# THE LINDBERGH
# BABY KIDNAPPING

The kidnapping of the Lindbergh baby was one of the most sensationalised crimes to come out of America in the 1930s. Stolen from his crib one wet and windy night, this child of a national hero remained missing for over two months while his famous father and an intermediary handled over a dozen notes from the kidnapper. This tragic tale helped change the law and became known as the crime of the century.

## LITTLE EAGLET LOST

The scandalous kidnapping shocked America as the Lindbergh name was renowned from coast to coast. An aviator, author and inventor, Charles Augustus Lindbergh had become a media celebrity and national hero after his record-breaking flight across the Atlantic in May 1927. Flying The Spirit of St Louis monoplane non-stop and solo the 3,600 miles from New York to Paris, he was awarded the Medal of Honour and was idolised countrywide as the Lone Eagle. Two years later the introverted idol married writer and poet Anne Morrow and on the 22 June 1930 the couple had their first child; a healthy baby boy with distinctive overlapping toes called Charles Augustus Lindbergh III.

Befitting his private sensibilities, Lindbergh had a house built on an isolated 390 acre site in an almost unreachable area of New Jersey. This hideaway home near the small town of Hopewell was their weekend residence away from their usual place in Englewood. On the last weekend of February 1932 the area was hit by severe gales and torrential downpours and with the twenty-month old baby suffering from a cold, the family decided to remain at their remote address.

The Lindberghs were still in rural Hopewell on the evening of Tuesday 1 March. As the wind howled outside, Anne Lindbergh and nursemaid Betty Gow put the sick child to bed in the second floor nursery. At ten to eight Betty looked in on the infant and found him sleeping soundly. Half an hour later Charles Lindbergh arrived home from a business engagement but did not visit his son. It was ten o'clock before anyone checked the child's bedroom. The nursemaid peered across the darkened room and to her horror found the cot empty.

## RANSOM NOTE

Lindbergh was known as the family joker and had previously hidden his son and pretended he had been kidnapped. Both Betty and his wife thought this was another of his pranks and questioned the flying ace. From his reaction it was evident this was no wind-up and Lindbergh ordered Ollie Whately, the butler, to call the police while he searched the grounds armed with his Springfield rifle.

Searching the bedroom they had found an envelope on the nursery's window-sill, but Lindbergh prevented anyone from touching what could prove to be crucial evidence. When Hopewell police chief Harry Wolf and fingerprint expert Frank Kelly arrived the letter was opened to reveal a single sheet of paper. Written in blue ink they found a ransom note littered with spelling mistakes and grammatical errors demanding fifty thousand dollars in various denominations to be handed over without police involvement in the next two to four days.

The ransom letter was not the only piece of evidence found at the house. Traces of yellow clay on the bedroom floor led to footprints outside below the window and in the nearby scrub a crude, homemade ladder with its top rung broken was discovered. Despite these two finds no fingerprints could be gleaned from the items nor anywhere in the nursery.

Whoever had snatched the Little Eaglet had managed to leave very little in the way of clues. The New Jersey police now on the scene were ready to take charge but, being the heroic star, Lindbergh was adamant he would head the investigation into the kidnapping of his only child.

## LINDBERGH LIAISON

Lindbergh's decision to do things his way proved to have a profound effect on the case. The lack of official procedure ensured communication with the kidnapper was both protracted and erratic. On 6 March a second ransom note with a Brooklyn postmark arrived informing them the ransom had been increased to seventy thousand dollars; a penalty for involving the police. The authorities including the Bureau of Investigation (later to become the FBI) wanted to stake out postal letterboxes in the Brooklyn area but fearing this would further anger the kidnapper, Lindbergh refused.

Day after day contact via classified sections of local newspapers continued but after he had denied Lindbergh's choice of liaison they reached an impasse. Enter seventy-two year old Dr John F. Condon who placed an advert in the Bronx Home News offering to act as the mediator. This eccentric self-promoter even added an extra one thousand dollars to the ransom which was duly accepted by the nameless kidnapper.

Keeping it a secret from the police, Lindbergh and Condon entered into payment negotiations with further newspaper ads and notes hidden beneath stones. On Saturday 12 March Condon met a stranger going by the name of John at Woodlawn Cemetery near 233rd Street and Jerome Avenue. The man who said he was a Scandinavian sailor spoke with a German accent and would not budge on reducing the ransom back to fifty thousand dollars. Condon believed the man was genuine but demanded proof that he did indeed have the Lindbergh's child.

As this hour-long secret meeting came to an end Cemetery John – as he quickly became known – promised to supply a token of the child's identity. On Wednesday 16 March the kidnapper's seventh note arrived along with a baby's one-piece sleeping suit identified as the same suit Charles Junior had been wearing when he was taken.

Into the third week of communication, the kidnapper had still to provide a time for payment despite Condon and Lindbergh confirming they had the money ready. On 1 April another note was delivered. Cemetery John was now ready to receive the ransom and told them to prepare for a hand over the following evening. They duly complied and on a

Saturday evening the pair drove to St Raymond's Cemetery in the Bronx for the pay-off.

Just as the last cemetery rendezvous, Condon met with John alone. He managed to reduce the ransom to the original fifty thousand but was told there would be no simple exchange; the baby could not be handed over for another few hours. Demanding to know the child's location, the mediating medic coerced the kidnapper to give him yet another note explaining that the child was okay and being looked after by two women aboard a twenty-eight-foot boat called *Nellie* near Martha's Vineyard.

## BABY FOUND

Fifty thousand dollars lighter and no baby, Lindbergh, along with the authorities, took to the skies to search the piers and bay areas of Massachusetts but no boat called *Nellie* could be found and, sadly, no Charles Lindbergh III. But it was not long before news of the missing son of the record-breaking aviator came to end the hunt.

On Thursday 12 May approximately four miles southeast of the Lindbergh home in Mercer County the Little Eaglet was discovered. William Allen, a truck driver, had pulled over on the highway to urinate when he saw the dismembered body of a young baby face down covered in leaves. The corpse was in an advanced stage of decomposition and was missing its left leg and both hands. The body was positively identified as being Charles Junior from the remaining right leg which possessed his distinctive overlapping toes. At the parent's request no autopsy was performed but the initial examination suggested the baby had been dead for around two months – around the time of the kidnapping.

Now a murder case, the Bureau stepped in to take over. Rewards totalling $75,000 (equivalent to $1.2 million today) were offered for information leading to the capture of Cemetery John. Despite being front page news across the globe bringing no end of tipsters, hoaxes and cons to the attention of the police, suspects were thin on the ground.

For a time Violet Sharpe, the twenty-eight-year-old English housemaid at the Englewood home was under suspicion. She soon cracked under the pressure of the intense scrutiny and committed suicide; only then did witnesses come forward proving her innocence. Doctor Condon then took over as the main suspect. His phone was tapped and the Bureau opened his mail and questioned him on several occasions but found nothing to incriminate the Lindbergh middle man. Weeks dragged into months and soon over a year had passed with no solid break in the case.

## DEAD CERTS

With no luck in locating the kidnapper the authorities focused on the ransom money. The majority of the payment had been made in gold certificates and all the serial numbers had been recorded. With the Government's decision to withdraw from circulation this form of payment by 1 May 1933, the authorities hoped this would force the kidnapper to reveal himself when handing them over at a Federal reserve bank. Some of the ransom certificates did resurface during the exchange from as far as Chicago and Minneapolis but no suspect was ever found.

Still the Bureau searched for answers to this unsolved case. Over a year later on 20 August 1934 sixteen gold certificates were located in the Yorkville and Harlem areas. Detectives James Finn and Thomas Sisk who had been working the case for nearly thirty months marked each find on a map realising they were being used in corner shops by a man fitting the description of Cemetery John. The net was slowly closing in.

## KIDNAPPER CAUGHT

After months of dead-ends and deceptions the authorities picked up the scent of the elusive kidnapper thanks to an alert gas attendant on Lexington Avenue. On 15 September 1934, Walter

Lyle took a ten dollar gold certificate from a man with a German accent and had the presence of mind to note down the licence plate of the man's 1930 dark blue Dodge sedan.

The car was issued to a Bruno Richard Hauptmann who lived on 222nd Street in the Bronx. Police surveilled his home and on the 19 September the suspect left his house and was swiftly apprehended. On his person they found a ransom gold certificate in his billfold and searching his house they found more stashed in the garage totalling $14,000. The police had their man.

Bruno Hauptmann had a shady past. A native of Saxony in Germany he had fought in the Great War as a machine gunner where he had been exposed to poison gas. Discharged from service, he was unable to find work as a carpenter so turned to robbery. He managed to escape from prison and made his first of three attempts to get to America in July 1923 stowing away aboard SS *Hanover* where he was found and deported back to Germany. On board the *George Washington* in November it was third time lucky. Two years later he married Anna Schoeffler, a fellow German immigrant, and had a son, Mannfried. Bad investments in 1931 saw him return inevitably to crime to end his financial worries.

## SNATCHER SENTENCED

On 8 October 1934 Bruno Hauptmann was indicted for the murder of Charles Lindbergh III and sent to Hunterdon County Jail to await trial. This media event began on 3 January 1935 and ran for five weeks with the prosecution basing their case on circumstantial evidence. Wood from the ladder matched the wood in Hauptmann's attic and writing experts attested the ransom notes came from his hand. Together with the testimonies of Lindbergh and Condon this was enough for a jury to find him guilty and on 13 February after twenty-nine court sessions Hauptmann was sentenced to death. Two subsequent appeals were both denied and after one successful reprieve the German expatriate was sent to the electric chair at Trenton state prison, New Jersey on Friday 3 April 1936.

Meanwhile the Lindberghs had flown to England the previous winter to escape the media attention where they remained until 1939. Returning to America, the Lone Eagle campaigned against involvement in the war against Hitler. His pro-Nazi stance had come to the fore the previous year when he accepted the Commander Cross of the Order of the German Eagle from Hermann Goering which somewhat tainted his heroic status back home. Despite his pro-Nazi leanings the attack on Pearl

Harbor in December 1941 changed his mind and he flew fifty combat missions for the Allied forces before the end of the war.

Over thirty years later and after the death of Lindbergh in August 1974, Anna Hauptmann was still fighting for her husband's innocence. With claims of contaminated crime scenes, ineffectual representation and doctored evidence she campaigned until her death in 1994. Books were written and conspiracy theories created all suggesting Hauptmann was not the kidnapper and killer of the Lindbergh baby. Nobody knows for sure.

One concrete fact to come out of this high-profile baby's death was what became known as the Lindbergh Law. On 17 June 1932 Congress made kidnapping across state lines a federal offence in a bid to curb the rising number of snatchings across the nation. From now on kidnappers and hostage-takers faced lengthy prison spells and even capital punishment if caught. As we shall see this failed to prevent such crimes in America.

# FRANK SINATRA JUNIOR

1963 was not a very good year for Frank Sinatra. Having taken the world by storm with his smooth swing sound, the legendary crooner would – in deadly quid pro quo fashion – have something taken from him that year: his only son. On Sunday 8 December a gang of misfits snatched the teen Sinatra in an audacious kidnap for ransom forcing his famous father to part with nearly a quarter of a million dollars.

Franklin Wayne Emmanuel Sinatra was born on 10 January 1944 to the singer's first wife, Nancy Barbato in New Jersey. Living with his mother and two sisters, young Frankie found it hard to compete with the high life for his distant father's affections and perhaps in an attempt to feel closer to him he turned to music. Discovering it was in the blood, the neglected son became a gifted pianist and composer enrolling at UCLA. Before he graduated he was invited to sing with the Tommy Dorsey Orchestra; something his father had done at the start of his career. This was an opportunity too good to miss so little Frankie dropped out of college to sign on for a thirty-six-week tour of various hotels in a bid to emulate his father's success.

## THE HOSTAGE-TAKERS

Barry Keenan was also no stranger to fame and fortune. Attending University High School whose alumni consisted of Elizabeth Taylor, Judy Garland and Ryan O'Neal, he was surrounded by wealthy children and unsurprisingly became obsessed with money. With his parents divorced and his father a failed stockbroker, young Keenan wanted to be like the rich kids and set out on his plan to become a millionaire by the age of thirty. He started well becoming the youngest member of the LA Stock Exchange in 1959 while still at college, however, soon things started to take a turn for the worst.

By the summer of 1963 the young stockbroker was in dire straits. A failed marriage and subsequent protracted divorce was followed by a car crash in Westwood, LA, leaving him with a persistent back problem which led to an addiction to the drug, Percodan. To add to the pain, the stockmarket crashed in 1962 and he lost much of his hard-earned money. Down but not out, Keenan set about regaining his swiftly-accrued wealth realising an even quicker buck could be made through illegal means. Discounting drug dealing and straight robbery as invalid ventures he settled on kidnapping for ransom.

Keenan still needed money so he approached his high school friend, Dean Torrence, himself a pop singer, for financial assistance. Far from hiding his intentions, he outlined his business proposal in full explaining away the moral irregularities by stating he intended to invest the takings and pay back the victim's family with interest. Not thinking he would ever go through with the harebrained scheme Torrence gave his pal $500.

The next phase of the plan was recruitment. Keenan needed business associates for his project and hired Joe Amsler another ex-schoolmate formally with the US Navy and built like an ox to act as the muscle. The other employee was a house painter named Joe Irwin, a forty-two-year-old, gruff-voiced man who had once dated Keenan's mother. He would provide the threatening voice to issue the demands when the time came. With his misfits recruited at $100 apiece Keenan had all but one part cast.

Initially Keenan's target was to have been Bob Hope's adopted son, Tony, but this was soon scrapped in favour of Little Frankie Junior. With links to the Mafia, Sinatra was a risky choice but Keenan saw the crooning sensation as someone strong enough to handle the temporary bout of grief that would be inflicted.

The first attempt to snatch the apple of Ol' Blue Eyes took place in October of 1963 during an appearance of the Dorsey Orchestra at the Arizona State Fair in Phoenix but it fell through. Take two came soon after. Everything was set. They had their location, renting a room at the luxurious Ambassador Hotel on Wilshire Boulevard from where they would seize their target soon after his show. The time was, with hindsight, a poorly chosen one, 22 November 1963. A date firmly etched on all minds throughout the civilised world: JFK's assassination. With the death of the President affecting the nation, the show was cancelled and so was their kidnap attempt. Time was running out for the luckless trio. Keenan and co. discovered they had one last chance to nab the nineteen-year-old before he left for the European leg of his tour.

## THIRD TIME LUCKY

The last chance was a gig a little over a week later at the Harrah's Casino in Lake Tahoe on the Nevada border. Putting the last of the seed money into the gas tank, they made for the Silver State in their rented Chevy Impala. By the time they pulled up at the casino's lodge they had only six cents between them. The ransom was top priority.

At nine o'clock that Sunday evening an hour before Sinatra was due on stage, Keenan knocked on the door of Room 417 with a special delivery for the singer. Dressed in his undershirt and halfway through a room service dinner with his trumpet player, John Foss, Frank Junior beckoned the man inside. From a wine box stuffed with pine cones, Keenan pulled a gun and summoned an armed Amsler to join him in tying up the trumpeter. Moments later the pair bundled a blindfolded Sinatra out to the Chevy where they made the eight hour drive through a severe blizzard to their hideout in the LA suburb of Canoga Park having to call upon their hostage to pay for petrol to get them there!

Meanwhile John Foss had managed to break his bonds within ten minutes of the abduction and raise the alarm. In the middle of filming *Robin and the Seven Hoods*, Frank Senior rushed to Nevada. From movie scene to crime scene a press conference was called where the anxious father offered a million dollars for the safe return of his boy. While police and the FBI frantically searched for the young Sinatra, Old Frank sat staring at the phone waiting for it to ring.

## THE PHONE CALL

Twenty-two hours after the abduction the phone rang and in a low, gruff tone Irwin read out the scripted ransom demand. Despite Sinatra's million dollar offer, Keenan stuck to his business plan and asked for a mere $240,000. For the prosperous performer it was a no-brainer. He would pay. The money was collected from City National Bank in Beverly Hills but before it went anywhere all 12,400 bills were photographed by the FBI and then packaged for delivery. A further six calls were made allowing father to speak to son and to rehearse the drop before the real thing took place. Sinatra followed the convoluted instructions called through to him at various pay phones. He was told to leave the loot between two school buses at a Sunset Boulevard gas station and just before eleven on a winter Wednesday evening FBI agent Jerome Crowe made the drop.

Keenan and Amsler retrieved the money without a hitch and were soon on their way back to the hideout to celebrate their successful extortion racket. All that remained now was to return their hostage to complete the business transaction but when the pair entered their LA Canoga lair they discovered Irwin and Sinatra Junior were nowhere to be seen.

Nerves had got the better of the most uneasy member of the gang who had panicked releasing the hostage prematurely on the Mulholland Drive overpass of the Interstate 405. The now free Frankie was left to walk along the freeway where he managed to flag down security guard George Jones who drove him to his mother's home where both his parents were waiting. The first words to his father were, 'I'm sorry, Dad'.

## SINGING LIKE A CANARY

While the Sinatras rejoiced in Bel-Air, the hostage-taking trio celebrated in their secret den laying out their ill-gotten gains and rolling around in the bills even using them to light cigarettes. They were ecstatic but the fun was about to end. Nervy John Irwin left the hideout with his cut of $40,000 planning to disappear to New Orleans. If only he had. Instead he chose to visit his brother in San Diego where he was unable to hold his tongue bragging he was behind the big news crime. Blood was clearly not as thick as Irwin believed for his brother's reaction was to call the police. Arrested and subjected to interrogation, it did not take long for Irwin to start ratting out his accomplices and Keenan and Amsler were soon picked up having only managed to spend $6,114 of the ransom.

Two months later the kidnappers stood trial. Flamboyant celebrity lawyer Gladys Towers Root was hired to defend them and believing attack was the best form of defence her strategy was to blame the victim. Suggesting Frankie Junior was complicit in his own kidnapping she focused on the apology he gave his father hinting that this was an admission of guilt, proposing that the son wished to raise his own profile and grab the attention of his famous father. This cheap trick fell on deaf ears and all three of the Sinatra stick-up team were convicted however, thanks to a liberal parole system existing at the time, Amsler and Irwin were free men after three years. Keenan the instigator and businessman was out within five.

## THE AFTERMATH

After the federal court conviction Frank Junior's singing career stalled. The insinuation that he was involved in the affair was enough for many – including an unsympathetic press – to label him guilty. Despite this he continued to follow in his father's footsteps with lesser singing and acting roles and even became his father's musical director and conductor for his later shows.

As for Keenan he stuck to legitimate business ventures and managed to make his first million in real estate. He waited until 1998 to tell his story giving *LA Weekly* the exclusive and five years later the tale was adapted for the screen in Columbia Pictures' *Stealing Sinatra* starring David Arquette as the money-grabbing mastermind. Keenan nearly hit the jackpot once more earning $1.5 million from the production until Sinatra Junior filed a lawsuit preventing him from profiting from the movie.

Despite also having a brief stint in the movie business as Ryan O'Neal's stand-in, Joe Amsler was less publicity hungry and, riddled with guilt, later retired to a white house in Salem, Virginia where on 6 May 2008 aged sixty-five he died of liver failure. He left a son, Christian Amsler, who ironically became a musician.

# BARBARA MACKLE

On 17 December 1968 Barbara Mackle, the young co-ed daughter of a real estate magnate, was snatched from a motel in Decatur, Georgia, by two masked criminals, and buried in a makeshift coffin for three days. From botched ransom drop to boat-chase this ordeal saw a master criminal's perfect plan foiled by the vigilance of a few Floridian citizens and the long arm of the law.

## KRIST THE CRIMINAL

Barbara Mackle's captor was one Gary Steven Krist, a twenty-three-year-old kleptomaniac originally from Pelican, Alaska. Living in this small port town miles from anywhere with unsupportive parents, he found solace in theft, stealing candy, coins and later cars, which became a self-destructive obsession. During this life of crime Krist managed to graduate from high school, revealing himself to be a bright student with aspirations to enter the medical profession. However, before he could pursue his dream of becoming a doctor he fell foul of the law once more and found himself incarcerated rather than in university.

It was while in juvenile detention that Krist began to plan what he believed was the perfect crime: a kidnapping. He was prepared to bide his time. It would be another four years before he would make his move. Other crimes saw his first stay in prison, but after eight months inside he escaped, taking his Californian wife and son across country to Boston, where Krist assumed the name George Deacon. Under this false name the fugitive took well paid roles at universities in the North East until, believing his true identity would be discovered, he moved the family down to Florida, where he got a job at the University of Miami's Institute for Marine Research.

In September 1968 Krist met his kidnapping colleague. While working as a deckhand on a two week research trip to Bermuda he began an affair with Ruth Eisemann-Schier, a pretty, twenty-six-year-old student from Honduras who was keen to inject some much-desired heat into his now stone-cold love life. As Christmas approached Krist came clean to his wife, who promptly took the children back to the West Coast, leaving him to plot the finer details of the kidnapping with his new lover.

## THE CHOSEN ONE

Krist scoured the social registers at various libraries to find his ideal target, finally whittling his list down to one: Barbara Jane Mackle – a twenty-year-old student at Atlanta's Emory University. Barbara was the daughter of Robert Mackle, who, along with his two brothers, ran Deltona Corp, one of the biggest land developing companies in America, worth a purported $65 million (£32.5 million).

With Christmas less than a fortnight away and end of term exams to sit before the break, Barbara had her head buried in books. She was also sick with Hong Kong flu, which had spread across the country and had reached epidemic proportions at the university.

Concerned for her daughter's wellbeing, Barbara's mother decided to travel up from the Mackle home in the affluent Coral Gables district of Florida to take care of her while she studied. On 13 December, Barbara's mother checked in to the Rodeway Inn, not far from the college campus, in order to play nurse to her sick student daughter. Mrs Mackle planned to take her daughter back home for the holidays in a few days time. Unfortunately Krist had other ideas.

The crook and his lover had also made the twelve hour journey to Georgia, and Krist quickly gleaned Barbara's whereabouts, staking out the motel to discover what room she and her mother were in. On the evening of Monday 16 December, the pair watched as a young man in a white Ford pulled up outside Room 137 and went inside. This was Stewart

Woodward, Barbara's close friend. Stewart spent the evening with the two women, before leaving around midnight. Mother and daughter continued to talk well into the night and were still awake at 4 am, when there came a knock at the door.

### UNDER THE WEATHER TO UNDER THE GROUND

On the other side of that motel room door stood Gary Krist, claiming to be the police investigating a traffic accident involving a man in a white Ford. Thinking Stewart had been hurt, they opened the door only for two masked people to barge their way in to the room. Krist, accompanied by a disguised Ruth Eisemann-Schier, quickly got to work. They knocked-out Barbara's mother using chloroform and tied her up, before bundling her sick daughter into the back of the waiting station wagon.

They travelled twenty miles north, to a remote pine forest near Duluth. At some point in the journey Krist made Barbara hold a sign saying, 'Kidnapped' and took a couple of Polaroids, as well as an opal ring from her finger. Soon they were at their destination. Guided through dense undergrowth, Barbara Mackle was brought face-to-face with the true horror of what lay in store.

The capsule – as Krist called it – was made of plywood and fibreglass and, measuring 90 cm x 2.10 cm

(3 ft x 7 ft) and only 90 cm (3 ft) deep, was more like a coffin. However, it was equipped with a battery-powered lamp, air pump to remove excess rainwater and two plastic pipes linked to the surface, this was a coffin with a crucial difference.

Barbara begged not to buried in the capsule, but became more acquiescent when plied with chloroform. The pair lowered her into the capsule, fastening the lid with over a dozen screws. Barbara began to panic as she heard her kidnappers drive away, leaving her all alone. Using the lamp she studied the inside of the box, finding food, water and extra clothing together with a note that read: 'Do not be alarmed. You are safe. You'll be home for Christmas one way or another.' After just three hours, the lamp's battery died, plunging her into complete darkness.

## MONEY DROPPED

By the time Barbara found herself 'encapsulated' the alarm had already been raised. Still tightly bound, her mother had managed to break out of the room and into her car, where she sounded the horn with her head. Lawmen from state police to the FBI were now on the case of the missing Mackle.

At 9.30 am, the Mackle family received a phone call at their high-end home directing them to a note left under a rock in the garden. It described their daughter's terrifying predicament and demanded $500,000 (£250,000) in old $20 bills for her release, instructing them to place an advert in the Miami Herald if they were prepared to stump up the cash.

The advert confirming their agreement ran the next day and later, if proof were needed, a delivery came in the post: a Polaroid of Barbara holding the sign along with her opal ring. It was all going to plan for the clever con.

In the small hours of Thursday morning Krist called the Mackles with details for the drop. Robert was to leave immediately for Biscayne Bay and drop a suitcase full of dollar bills on a seawall along Fair Isles Causeway. Krist watched his orders being followed from a boat out at sea and as soon as the compliant father was clear he made for the shore to pick up the booty. It was at this point that the foolproof plan started to fall apart. At 5 am a local resident was stirred from his sleep by the sound of the approaching boat and, believing it to be linked to a recent spate of beachfront burglaries, called the police. Unaware that a federal crime had been committed, two officers responded to the call and spotted two figures at the scene. On seeing the cops the pair ran, dropping the suitcase containing the ransom.

Not only did Krist and his accomplice leave the money but they had also abandoned the blue Volvo containing evidence linking them to the kidnapping. Along with a host of steamy Polaroids of the couple, police found another picture of Barbara.

## TAKE TWO

With their plan in tatters, Krist and Ruth decided to separate, agreeing to meet again in Austin, Texas before jetting off to Europe. While Ruth headed West, Krist – eager to be rewarded for all his hard work – called the Mackle magnate yet again to arrange a second delivery of the ransom. The frantic father consented to the drop and at the end of a dirt road nine miles west of Miami the suitcase was delivered.

With no conscientious observer to scupper the pick-up Krist got his hands on the loot, but by now the FBI had issued warrants for his arrest and were closing in. He had to use all his smarts to remain out of sight. At a West Palm Beach marine supply store his brains deserted him, paying for a sixteen-foot motorboat with bundles of the stolen $20 bills. This alerted the owner, who had been following the big news story and after Krist departed with his new purchase a call was made to the police.

It was now Friday 20 December and poor Barbara Mackle had been buried alive for three whole days. Her grief-stricken parents waited for a call to end the nightmare and twelve hours after the successful drop the FBI received vague directions to her hiding place. Over one hundred agents combed the wooded area north east of Atlanta for the missing student finding her only after hearing her knocking weakly on the capsule walls. They tunnelled through the 45 cm (18 in) of earth that lay on top of the capsule and pried open the lid to find the hostage relatively healthy and enormously relieved. She had kept her spirits up by singing happy songs, recalling positive memories and even conversing with God.

Though she had lost 4.5 kg (10 lb) in weight Barbara Mackle had gained her freedom and was flown by private jet to be reunited with her parents in Coral Gables. Yet while the ordeal was over for the Mackles the authorities had a criminal to hunt.

## THE CAPTURE

While the Mackles rejoiced, Krist was speeding west by moonlight across the Sunshine State, navigating his boat along its many canals and waterways. The runaway felon moved from lock to lock telling each keeper he had lost his registration documents. One doubted his veracity and reported the hurrying boat-man, bringing lawmen to the scene and in next to no time they were on his tail. Krist beached the motorboat on Hog Island near Fort Myers and disappeared into the thick jungle. The authorities caught up with Krist sneaking along the shoreline nearly twelve hours later. Ruth Eisemann-Schier, his partner in crime, fared little better. She was placed on the FBI's Most Wanted list – the first female ever to make the roll of dishonour – and was arrested seventy-nine days later in Norman, Oklahoma.

The pair stood trial and both were found guilty of kidnapping charges. Ruth served four years in prison before being deported to her native Honduras while Krist was paroled after a paltry ten years for his leading part in the crime, but it could have been much worse. Thanks to a merciful testimony from Barbara Mackle the hostage-taker sidestepped the death sentence.

## A RETURN TO CRIME

Released from jail on 14 May 1979 having been a pillar of the prison community, the now thirty-three-year-old Krist vowed to spread the word of God. This idea was soon rejected in favour of another calling: his dream to become a doctor and, pulling some strings, received a pardon to allow him to attend medical school. He practised in Chrisney, Indiana for a short time until his employers discovered his past misdeeds. Krist's attempts to go straight – whether sincere or not – were summarily blocked. His criminal history haunted him wherever he went and he soon returned to what he knew best: crime.

On 6 March 2006, Krist, along with his stepson Henry Gleeson, docked his twenty-seven-foot sailboat at Mobile Bay, Alabama, only to be surprised by a horde of FBI agents. On board they discovered over 17 kg (38 lb) of cocaine paste stashed in the cooler and four illegal immigrants from South America who had each paid Krist $6,000 (£3000) to bring them back to the United States. Four days later agents searched his house in Barrow County, Georgia, and discovered old habits die hard. Krist had stuck with his penchant for underground hideouts. Through a concealed trapdoor beneath a shed they found a subterranean drug lab fully equipped to turn the narcotic paste into powder. His newfound career as drug smuggler had been laid to rest and on 19 January 2007 Gary Steven Krist – now sixty-one years old – was sentenced to over five years in prison. Now Krist spends his time languishing behind bars with a drug addiction, whilst Barbara Mackle enjoys her freedom at her home in Florida with her husband, the close friend from her student days, Stewart Woodward, having put the horrors of that winter behind her.

# THE D. B. COOPER
# HIJACKING

On Wednesday 24 November 1971, the day before Thanksgiving, a swarthy-looking man wearing a black raincoat over a smart dark suit and tie buys a ticket at the Northwest Orient counter at Portland International Airport. Paying in cash for a one-way ticket to Seattle he gives his name as Dan Cooper and is assigned his economy seat: 18C. Carrying his unchecked briefcase the nondescript man will step onto the plane as just one more travelling businessman but only a few hours later will make a daredevil jump out of his hijacked aircraft and into the history books.

## DAYFLIGHT ROBBERY

With all thirty-seven passengers on board the Northwest Orient Flight 305 to Seattle safely in their seats air stewardess Florence Schaffner took her position for takeoff. The Boeing 727 was under half full on this Thanksgiving Eve and she surely must have expected an uneventful journey.

As the plane reached its cruising height and passengers were free to vacate their seats Dan Cooper approached the twenty-three-year-old flight attendant and handed her a note. Believing it to be his phone number in a poor yet routine pick-up attempt she placed the note in her pocket without reading it. At this point the man leaned across to her and urged her to read the handwritten note. She quickly discovered her fears of a flirtatious traveller were pure fantasy; the man was there not to steal her heart but to hold the passengers to ransom.

Cooper required $200,000 in unmarked non-sequential $20 bills together with two sets of parachutes which were to be delivered to the plane when they landed. Failure to comply would result in the detonation of the bomb hidden inside his briefcase.

The skyjacker permitted the frightened stewardess to inform the cockpit and on hearing the bad news Captain William Scott asked her to ascertain whether the threat was real. She returned to Cooper who agreed to open the briefcase. Inside the sight of two red cylinders and a large battery linked with coloured wires was enough to convince Florence Schaffner that the bomb was genuine.

Seattle's Air Traffic Control was quickly notified and in turn state police and FBI were assigned to the case. Not wanting any loss of life Donald Nyrop, the president of the airline, made it clear the crew was to cooperate fully with the hijacker. This was music to the ears of Cooper who sat back with a bourbon and soda, the plane circling in a holding pattern above Puget Sound, waiting for word that his demands had been met.

## MEETING THE DEMANDS

The FBI got to work assembling the money. Ignoring Cooper's demands for non-sequential bills, the agents chose notes with serial numbers starting with 'L' issued by the Federal Reserve Bank in San Francisco. They also took a microfilm image of every single one of the ten thousand $20 bills in order to trace them if Cooper ever managed to pull off this audacious air raid.

The acquisition of the parachutes was more problematic. Agents were planning on giving Cooper military issue versions from McChord Air Force Base but the hijacker made it clear he wanted civilian chutes as they possessed manually-operated ripcords. After some searching, and with time running out on an imposed thirty minute deadline, the FBI finally found the type at a local skydiving school and rushed them to the airport.

At 17.24 hours Captain Scott received word that the cash and chutes were ready for delivery. Cooper then gave permission for the plane to land and fifteen minutes later Flight 305 touched down at Seattle-

Tacoma International Airport. The hijacker directed the pilot to move to a remote section of the runway and ordered for the cabin lights to be dimmed to impede any sniper attack.

A lone Northwest Orient employee made the journey to the plane with Cooper's requests and handed everything over to flight attendant, Tina Mucklow, via the aft stairs. Keeping his end of the bargain Cooper promptly released all thirty-six passengers along with Florence Schaffner. Their ordeal was over. For Captain Scott, Tina Mucklow, First Officer Bob Rataczak and flight engineer H. E. Anderson, who remained with their captor, they would have to wait a little longer.

## COOPER CHUTES OFF

After a slow refuelling of the plane due to a vapour lock which tested Cooper's patience the Boeing 727 took to the skies once more. He had given the flight crew instructions to head for Mexico City at a steady speed of 200 mph and at an altitude no higher than 10,000 feet, well below the normal cruising height.

Unfortunately First Officer Rataczak had calculated that, at those flight conditions, the tank only had enough fuel to travel another thousand miles. As the Mexican capital was over two thousand miles away a new destination was needed. Cooper decided on Reno, Nevada where they would land to refuel.

Following a federal, low altitude flight path called Vector 23 that avoided the perilous peaks of the Cascade mountain range, Cooper ordered the cabin to be depressurised. This was the next clue to his plan of escape. Having the plane pressurised ran the risk of a sudden rush of escaping air if any exit was opened.

Mucklow was then told to join her flight crew in the cockpit. As she obeyed her captor she spotted him tying a rope around his waist; Cooper was preparing to make his move. At around eight o'clock Captain Scott noticed a light flash on the instrument panel informing him a door had been opened at the rear of the aircraft. Using the intercom, he asked if Cooper needed any help to which he replied with a curt 'No'. This would be the last word heard from the hijacker.

At exactly 8.24 pm the flight crew felt a sharp drop in air pressure as their ears popped and shortly after noticed the plane's nose dip slightly suggesting the aft stairs had been lowered. Scott called to Cooper over the intercom once more but there was no response. As the Boeing 727 passed over the southwest corner of Washington State they all felt a bump as if some-one was now walking down the stairway to nowhere.

With the twenty-one pound pack of bills bound to his chest by the nylon cords from the spare chute, Cooper jumped into the eighty knot ice-winds. This perilous leap into a rainstorm with no light source from the ground to guide him would be mulled over for decades. Did Cooper succeed or did he perish?

## THE SEARCH

At a quarter past ten in the evening, despite having a set of lowered stairs hanging from the rear, Flight 305 managed to land safely at Reno Airport. The FBI swept through the entire plane finding only a selection of unrecognised prints along with the hijacker's black tie, mother of pearl tie pin and one of the parachutes. Cooper, his briefcase and the bundle of cash were nowhere to be seen.

The four hostages were individually interrogated and all gave near-identical descriptions of their hijacker. This allowed the FBI to create a composite sketch which would feature on wanted posters throughout the country beginning one of the most extensive manhunts in US history.

An exhaustive aerial and ground search for both man and money took place throughout the following months but came up empty. This was largely down to the fact that Cooper's drop zone could not be accurately deduced. The horrendous weather conditions and cloud cover masked his descent from the F-106 jet fighters that were tracking Flight 305 so the terrifying leap went unseen.

It was first thought that Cooper's landing zone was southeast of Ariel, Washington near Lake Merwin. However, the pilot of a Continental Airlines flight travelling four minutes behind the hijacked aircraft soon testified the landing was twenty miles east of this location. Such diverse reports without definitive answers severely handicapped the hunt for D. B. Cooper.

Even the search for the microfilmed money fell short of success. Despite banks all over the world being notified of the serial numbers and over $30,000 in reward money being offered for one Cooper-stolen bill not a single one resurfaced. With no hijacker in custody and no cash turning up a federal court was forced to charge Dan Cooper in absentia. The charges of air piracy still stand to this day if he is ever caught.

## CLUES AND CHANGES

This audacious crime is now approaching its fortieth anniversary and over the four passing decades various clues have surfaced. In 1978 instructions on how to lower the rear steps of a Boeing 727 were found by a hunter a few miles north of the projected drop zone. Two years later eight year old Brian Ingram found $5,880 in $20 bills on the banks of Columbia River whilst on a family picnic. The serial numbers were a match but a search of the riverbed revealed no sign of Cooper.

The arrival of DNA testing allowed the FBI to obtain a partial DNA profile from Cooper's tie abandoned on the Boeing and a few months later in December 2007 further details from the case were released online to trigger memories from the past. Despite this revival no major developments were made.

Thankfully there were changes made to air travel after the hijacking of Flight 305. Metal detectors were installed at major airports bringing an end to the unhampered hijacker simply walking unchecked onto his target. There were also modifications made to the planes themselves. All Boeing 727 aircraft were fitted with an aerodynamic wedge which stopped the aft stairs from being lowered during flight. With a nod to the elusive hijacker it was named the Cooper Vane.

With over one thousand two hundred suspects in the case including a convicted mass murderer from New Jersey and a copycat hijacker four months later not a single DNA match has been found. It seems destined to reside in the annals of unsolved crimes waiting for a case-breaking lead. Questions still remain over the death-defying denouement of Cooper's hijacking. Maybe somewhere in the world there still lives an old man in his eighties with all the answers.

# THE CHOWCHILLA
# BUS HIJACKING

Originally the home of a brutal, war-like tribe of Yokut Indians called the Chau Chili meaning 'murderers', the small town of Chowchilla in Madera County, California, revisited this violent, darker past in the summer of 1976. On a sultry-hot July afternoon a busload of children from the town's sole high school were kidnapped and held hostage for thirty-six hours while their money-motivated captors focused on obtaining a five million dollar ransom.

## UNSCHEDULED BUS STOP

On Thursday 15 July 1976, Frank Edward Ray, a local farmer and part-time driver of the Dairyland Elementary School bus was taking twenty-six children home on a balmy afternoon. With three stops made, he was on the country road of Avenue 21 when he saw a white van at the side of the road seemingly broken down. Ray decided to make an unscheduled stop and see if he could help. This move was to prove disastrous for all those aboard the school bus.

All of a sudden a man in a mask boarded the bus and ordered Ray to the backseats. The children aged between five and fourteen didn't know what to make of this intrusion. A mix of giggles and sobs filled the next few minutes as two more masked men appeared and forced the bus to pull into a drainage slough a few minutes down the road.

With the engine cut and the bus out of sight, the white van backed up to the bus doors and the masked men ordered half of the passengers to enter its dark interior. The giggles had vanished as they were packed inside the white van, its windows covered with old newspaper. The door was locked and the van drove away. Soon after a second white van arrived and the remaining passengers were forced inside. Packed like sardines inside these vans and suffering from the suffocating summer heat the panicked children lost all track of time. Their captors drove the two vans around for approximately eleven hours during which time some of the children dozed. All the hostages were getting hungry and some even soiled themselves. However, this was just the start of the terror they would endure over the coming hours.

## BURIED ALIVE
Eventually the vans came to a halt at a rock quarry in Livermore about one hundred miles northwest of

Chowchilla. Ray, the driver, was let out first. He was ordered to give his name and forced to remove his trousers and boots before being directed to a ladder which was sticking ominously out of the ground. One by one the children followed their bus driver down into the cavernous hole where they soon discovered their underground chamber was in fact an old removals van buried beneath the surface.

With just a few dirty mattresses to sit on and some crude holes in the corner for toilets the children and their charge longed for home. Some of the older children tried to while away the hours by conducting a sing-along to calm the younger ones but the fear of being buried alive soon took over. Twelve hours into the ordeal Ray and two of the older boys began looking for a means of escape. They piled the collection of mattresses high enough to allow them to reach the roof of the van.

Bob Barklay was one of these boys. He led the way managing to lift the metal lid and wedge it open with a wooden beam. He dug his way through the earth tunnelling to the top until he reached the surface. Bob squeezed through the tight space and gave the all-clear. The twenty-seven incarcerated captives climbed out of their burial chamber having spent a total of sixteen hours underground. Weak and disorientated they staggered towards the light in the distance. It came from a nearby guard shack at the quarry entrance where two employees were working. Shocked to see the ex-hostages walking like zombies towards them, they called the police.

Having been given food and water by the quarry workers, the victims were taken to Santa Rita Rehab Centre. This involved another bus journey which unnerved them all. They were swiftly examined by the centre's staff and deemed fit for questioning. At four in the morning of 17 July the schoolchildren and bus driver arrived back in Chowchilla; Ray reunited with his wife and children and the boys and girls with their parents.

## SEARCH FOR THE KIDS

A day and a half earlier, the parents of the kidnapped schoolchildren had been worried sick ever since their boys and girls had failed to arrive home after school. As dusk fell mothers and fathers called the school and officials traced the bus route. With no sign of the bus, police and the county sheriff were notified; the hunt was on for the missing children of Chowchilla.

The authorities deduced that the bus had made three successful stops and that something had happened before the fourth drop-off point. At around eight o'clock that evening a sheriff officer discovered the school bus beneath a covering of bamboo and bush nine miles west of the town. Unfortunately there was no sign of the children or the driver.

Before a thorough search of the area could be made a freak storm hit the small town. By the time the severe weather had passed the rains had washed away all potential clues. The quiet town then braced itself for the inevitable media storm as reporters descended on them from far and wide.

As parents prayed and police puzzled over what little evidence they had gleaned, the call came in from the quarry workers. The children had been found. The authorities had the buried removals van pulled from the ground and examined unearthing some key clues. The van had been bought by one Fred Woods whose father was the owner of the Livermore quarry. When police contacted Fred's parents, they were told that he was missing along with his friend, Jim Schoenfeld. In his bedroom they found a handwritten note detailing the crime's plan. The police knew their perpetrators, now for the hunt to bring them to justice.

## THE KIDNAPPERS

Police were indeed on the right path. Fred Woods and Jim Schoenfeld along with his younger brother, Rick, were three high school graduates with privileged backgrounds who together had concocted a plan to bring them instant wealth. The three twentysomethings lived with their families in their rich suburban homes and all felt they were disappointments to their parents. Their minds turned to hostage-taking as a means to money-making and the three friends would talk endlessly about the perfect kidnapping plan until its was tightly honed and ready for execution.

Now, on Friday 16 July 1976 their plan was in motion. The driver and his charges were buried in a disused removal van deep in a rock quarry and now they were ready to move to stage two: the ransom. Settling on the substantial figure of $5 million, the young hostage-takers made their planned call to the police to demand the money, however this was when their get rich quick scheme began to unravel.

Thanks to the huge public interest in the missing children of Chowchilla, the police phone lines were jammed with the many reporters, tipsters and crank callers that were bombarding the switchboard. The hostage-takers were unable to get through to demand their money! After hours of trying to get through, Fred and the two brothers gave up. With no alternative arrangement in place the young kidnappers chose to split up and sleep on the problem. They awoke on Saturday morning to the news that the hostages had escaped their makeshift subterranean dungeon.

## ON THE RUN

The removal van buried in the quarry was never meant to be found. Because of this the trio had not taken any steps to disassociate themselves from it allowing the police to identify them without trouble. There was only one thing left to do for the three rich kids; they decided to escape the town and flee to Canada. Rick chose to return home and keep quiet while his brother Jim packed up a car with provisions to take him to the border. Meanwhile Fred Woods caught a flight from Reno to Vancouver and checked into a hotel. Once there they agreed he would visit the Vancouver post office twice a day to rendezvous with Jim.

While Fred had no problems getting to Canada, Jim found it impossible to cross the border. On the Sunday evening he approached the crossing and told the guard he was meeting a friend in Edmonton before heading off to Montreal to see some of the Olympics. With a car full of provisions and little money the border guard did not believe him and refused him entry.

The following day Jim pawned some of the car's contents in Spokane, Washington, in a bid to get more money so as to add credence to his story. However his next attempt at crossing the border saw the guards search his car whereupon they found a gun belonging to Fred. Luckily, Jim was not charged

476

but was turned away a second time. On Tuesday 20 July, Jim Schoenfeld decided to pawn the remainder of the provisions and abandon the car in Coeur d'Alene, Idaho. With the money he bought a dilapidated truck and headed for Washington state once more.

## CAPTURED

Three days later on Friday 23 July the two fugitives heard the breaking news that Rick had confessed to his involvement in the kidnapping and was being held on bail. This news broke Jim's resolve and he decided to turn the truck towards home arriving in the Bay Area on Sunday. Too afraid to go to the police or to his parents, Jim drove the truck to the ocean and camped out on the beach for a few days.

Meanwhile Fred was still in Vancouver waiting for Jim. Realising his partner in crime was not coming, he broke his silence writing to an old friend he thought he could trust back in California. He told his friend not to tell anyone he had written but to write back using his alias at the Vancouver post office. The trustworthy friend passed the letter to the FBI on receiving it and a police watch was put on the Canadian post office. On 29 July a postal clerk had a man using Fred's alias inquire about some incoming mail and Fred was quickly apprehended.

Fred was the last to be caught as Jim had already been picked up earlier that day. He had been recognised driving the truck near his family home and the police were quick to track him down and make the arrest. Now all three hostage-takers were in custody.

## EMOTIONAL SCARS

The three perpetrators of the Chowchilla bus hijacking were reunited in a courtroom on the 4 August where they pleaded to over forty felony charges. The trial dragged on through endless arduous months as various motions and appeals were made. Not until 25 July 1977, one year and ten days after the multiple kidnapping occurred, was there anything like a conclusion to the case. The three finally pleaded guilty to twenty-seven counts of kidnapping for ransom without inflicting injury.

Still dissatisfied, the prosecution insisted injury had been imposed on the twenty-six children and their school bus driver. After testimonies from three of the children persuaded the judge harm had come to the victims, the three prisoners were sentenced to life without parole on 15 December 1977.

According to local psychiatrist, Leonore Terr, who was asked to assess the emotional states of the children by their concerned parents, there certainly had been considerable injury caused to the victims of the

Chowchilla bus hijacking. Almost all of the twenty-six children who had been held hostage exhibited similar problems such as stomach aches, bladder control issues, obesity and an overwhelming pessimism towards their future. One young teenage girl had not managed to grow an inch since the incident.

Even Bob Barklay, the heroic teenager who helped lead the rest to freedom, was affected by the hostage-taking. While he managed to avoid sharing the physical problems of the others, the kidnapping nightmare manifested itself in an altogether different way. Eighteen months after the ordeal, the Barklay family noticed a strange car parked outside their home. Bob went to investigate and, pulling out his BB gun, shot a Japanese tourist who had simply broken down. The memories of the white van at the side of the road had clearly triggered a reactive violent reaction in him.

Despite behaving like model prisoners throughout their time behind bars and showing remorse for their actions that fateful summer in 1976, the three under-achievers have, to this day, been regularly denied parole time after time.

# THE MIRACLE OF COKEVILLE

In a small backwater town deep within the desolate Wyoming countryside, an elementary school was seized in the grip of a crazed couple hell-bent on ransom and revenge. This deadly afternoon in the middle of May rocked a Mormon community. Sightings of angels preceded an explosive climax, leaving all present believing they had witnessed a bona fide miracle.

## SMALL TOWN

Cokeville is a small ranch town set in the sparsely-populated south west corner of the rural Wyoming prairie. During pre-war years it was the sheep capital of the world, and by the mid 1980s its human population numbered a mere six hundred and fifty. Our story begins in 1979, when this sheep-farming dot on the landscape was policed by just one man. He was thirty-five year old David Young, the town marshal. Originally from Iowa, Young developed a love for guns which continued into adulthood. Wielding his six shooter like Wyatt Earp, Young saw himself as a hero with a badge, however only six months into his detail he was fired for misconduct. In typical Western fashion the gun-toting ex-Sheriff was ran out of town. He headed south, settling in Tucson, Arizona with vengeance on his mind.

Young had seven years to stew on his dismissal before returning to the small town to settle his score. On Friday 16 May 1986 at one o'clock in the afternoon the fired lawman, together with his wife, Doris, arrived at Cokeville Elementary School. Young marched into the head's office and presented the principal Max Excell with a typewritten document filled with the words of Socrates and Shakespeare. This was his manifesto, entitled *Zero Infinity*. He was there to start a revolution.

Meanwhile his co-revolutionary wife was gathering children and staff from all the classrooms, misleading them with suggestions of an emergency and even a surprise birthday party. Many of the youngsters had just returned from a picnic lunch in the park when, sitting in their reading groups, she beckoned them away from their books. A total of one hundred and sixty-seven confused schoolchildren and oblivious teachers were brought to a first grade classroom, where they were confronted by a scruffy man standing in the centre of the room surrounded by guns, with a strange contraption by his side.

The smell of gasoline in the air hinted at what was to come. Tied to his wrist with a shoelace was a crude trigger device, itself linked to a homemade bomb large enough to level the entire building. As police and parents assembled outside the school gates, the mentally unstable activist submitted his demands. He wanted two million dollars for every child he held captive. As if $300 million was not enough, he also required an audience with the President of the United States, Ronald Reagan, to whom he would put his vague political message.

## BIG BANG

While attempts were made to contact the White House, tension in the small classroom was mounting. The youngest children, who had been given colouring books and crayons as well as a TV to take their minds off the situation, were growing restless, often bursting into tears and even vomiting in the classroom washbasin. Many of the hostages also took to praying,

At a quarter to four, over two and a half hours into the hostage situation, one mistimed action brought an answer to their prayers. Heeding the call of nature,

David Young handed the trigger to his wife and made his way to the toilet several doors down the hall. The hostages saw Doris make a sudden move, causing her hand to slip from the device, triggering the bomb, which exploded, filling the room with black smoke. Windows were smashed and hostages' clothes and hair caught fire. Quick-thinking teachers put out the flames and, taking advantage of the confusion, started to scramble the children out of a blown-out window. Seeing their sons and daughters emerging from the smoke-filled room parents broke through the police barricades to rescue them.

On hearing the blast, David Young rushed back to the classroom to find his wife fatally wounded. Some remaining hostages witnessed Young say goodbye to Doris with a bullet to her head, before leaving the room for the last time. His revolution at an end, a suicidal Young took a gun back to the bathroom from whence another smaller explosion came; this one wholly intentional.

## MIRACLE OR MISTAKE

With the hostages released through slip-up and suicide, the crisis was now over. The seventy-six injured were taken to hospital to be treated for flash burns, while fire fighters inspected the damage inside the school. The lack of destruction confused investigators, because the size of the bomb meant the blast should have obliterated the building and all those within it. Further study showed the device had malfunctioned. Only one of its five blasting caps had been activated when Doris pulled the trigger.

Many of those involved in the ordeal at Cokeville had other answers for their lucky escape. Rather than a defective device, it was divine intervention they held responsible for the diminished death toll. After the incident, the Cokeville Miracle Foundation created a 500-page book entitled *Witness to Miracles*. It contains many witness accounts claiming that angels were present at the school that day. Its pages are full of descriptions of celestial figures in white informing the hostages to go to the window, and assertions of angels appearing over the heads of each captive child. Others describe hearing ethereal voices predicting the disaster but saying their lives would be spared.

The religious slant to the accounts is not surprising. Cokeville is a close-knit community overseen by the Church of Jesus Christ of Latter Day Saints. Whether heavenly help or hiccup, the town continues to remember the explosive event, acknowledging how blessed they were that afternoon in May.

# GLADBECK
# HOSTAGE CRISIS

It began as a failed bank robbery in a small West German town yet after countless acts of flawed policing and an over-eager press hell-bent on reporting on the exclusive it ended as one of the most notorious cases of kidnapping in German history. Clocking up over four hundred miles and three dead bodies in fifty-four hours, the televised road trip brought fame to the fugitives and disgrace to law enforcement.

## BANK RAID

It was around eight o'clock in the morning on Tuesday 16 August 1988 when the staff inside the branch of Deutsche Bank in the small coal-mining town of Gladbeck were preparing to open for another day's business. All of a sudden two armed men barged their way inside and began to demand money from the vaults. While the cash was being collected hopes for a swift exit were soon dashed as their forced entry had not gone unnoticed.

485

From his first floor practice a doctor had witnessed the break-in and at 8.04 am he made the emergency call to the police. A unit car was despatched to the scene whereupon it was spotted by the thieves. Realising they had been discovered the two men disappeared back into the building where they held a cashier and a customer advisor hostage.

The two armed men holed up inside the Deutsche Bank were Dieter Degowski and Hans-Jürgen Rösner two career criminals in their early thirties. While the rat-faced Degowski was the elder of the two, it was Rösner, with his heavily tattooed arms and an unkempt beard, who was clearly the man in charge. He had been convicted at the tender age of fourteen and had spent eleven of a thirteen-year sentence in jail and was currently wanted for violating his parole back in 1986.

The first of countless interviews was conducted while they were inside the bank. The pair contacted a radio station who managed to glean their textbook demands: 300,000 Deutsch Mark and a getaway car. Despite shooting out of the windows to show they were serious and threatening the lives of the two frightened bank clerks the surrounding police took several hours to grant their wishes finally delivering the money and a white Audi 100 to the front door.

At a quarter to ten that evening the hostage situation went mobile. After more than twelve hours inside the bank, Rösner and Degowski, along with the two hostages, made their getaway. Closely followed by the police, the vehicle made its way into the inner city to make its first stop: to pick up Rösner's thirty-four year old girlfriend, Marion Löblich. The pursuing police were rendered useless unable to make a move without risking the lives of the two clerks and as night turned into day the white Audi made its unrestricted journey heading north east out of Gladbeck.

## BUS HIJACK

It was now Wednesday 17 August and the white get-away car had hit the autobahn on course for the port city of Bremen and thus crossing district lines. As police from three different counties fought for control of the situation, the kidnappers meanwhile were the epitome of calm taking time to do a spot of shopping in a local boutique. However it was their next stop that would dramatically alter the nature of the situation.

Believing that they needed more collateral than just the two clerks with which to ensure their safe passage, the two felons pulled up next to the number 53 bus in the district of Huckelriede just outside of Bremen and at seven o'clock that evening hijacked the red single-decker along with its thirty-two passengers.

As the police looked on from a safe distance unable to hatch a plan to effect a successful siege and rescue, a growing number of journalists moved in for a closer look. They found Rösner and Degowski willing inter-viewees, happy to answer their questions and pose for photographs outside the bus. As he explained his criminal past to the press, Rösner illustrated to what desperate lengths he was prepared to go by sticking his Colt handgun into his own mouth.

With this impromptu press conference over, the dangerous duo were ready to move on. With far more lives at stake the authorities had no choice but to let the hijacked bus leave Huckelriede. Back on to the autobahn the bus travelled eighteen miles east and between junctions 50 and 51 decided to stop at the Grundbergsee service area where the police finally made their first move.

## ARREST MADE

As night set in, the bus pulled into the service station where the hostage-takers gave further interviews to the shadowing reporters. Meanwhile Rösner's girlfriend left the bus venturing inside the service station to answer a call of nature. Seeing an opportunity to capture one of the perpetrators two police officers seized Marion Löblich and pinned her to the floor. The tension at its peak, the hostage-takers were angry at this act of defiance and threatened to kill one of the passengers every five minutes until their accomplice was returned.

Inside the bus fifteen-year-old Emanuele de Georgi held onto Tatiana, his nine-year-old sister, praying for an end to the madness. The police refused to surrender their captive and at shortly before eleven a single gunshot was heard emanating from inside the bus.

At 11.06 pm the body of Emanuele de Georgi was dragged out by two journalists; a gunshot to the head. Rather than trying to save his life the horde of paparazzi manhandled the young teen to get their own shots in. With no ambulance in attendance it took twenty minutes for help to arrive but the paramedics were unable to save him. Löblich was then given back to the bus-stealing brigands one dead child too late.

## BORDERING ON BRAINLESS

In the small hours of Thursday 18 August the bus moved on making a bee line west towards the Netherlands. At around half past two in the morning they were surrounded by Dutch police near Oldenzaal where a tense standoff took place. The Netherlands authorities were a little more steadfast in their discussions with the pair of hostage-takers informing them that no negotiations would be entered into while they held children hostage. Rösner and Degowski relented releasing two mothers and their three children and with dawn fast approaching they called for a new getaway car.

At half past six Dutch police granted the kidnappers' request delivering a silver grey BMW 735i saloon. In exchange the border-crossing bandits released all but two of the hostages – Silke Bischoff and Ines Voitle – who were forced to accompany the three criminals in the German sports car. Friends since the age of seven, the two teenage girls were forced at gunpoint into the backseat with Degowski while Rösner and his girlfriend sat in the front as they made the decision to leave Holland and return to West Germany.

Thanks to some clever thinking the getaway car had some hidden features. As well as a tracking device the vehicle had been modified so that police could stall the engine by remote control when they saw fit. Unfortunately wisdom was in short supply. When the rigged car made its way back across the border the police discovered they had left the remote control behind!

## FOE DE COLOGNE

In their third getaway vehicle in as many days the felonious trio made for Cologne prompted by Rösner's desire to see the famous cathedral. At eleven that morning the press tracked down the saloon parked in a pedestrian zone next to a food stand in the heart of the city centre. Far from being an object of terror the car was soon surrounded by both media and shoppers all eager to catch a glimpse of the murderous men and their captives. Microphones and TV cameras were shoved into the faces of the passengers as they answered reporters' questions while drinking coffee and smoking cigarettes. With no thought given to the welfare of the hostages, the press appeared more concerned with their story. One morbid scene involved a tabloid photographer asking Degowski to hold the gun to Bischoff's temple for that killer picture.

The embarrassing effrontery of the press continued. As well as buying them coffee the reporters provided the kidnappers with photographs of policemen so they could avoid being tricked and, in the most impudent move, one journalist agreed to act as their guide. Udo Robel, the deputy editor of the *Cologne Daily Express* boldly got into the back of the BMW moments before the crowds parted and navigated them to safety before being dropped off at a nearby rest area several miles along the autobahn.

## RAIDERS RAMMED

Their three day tour took them back onto the high-speed highway towards Frankfurt over a hundred miles down the A3. According to Ines Voitle, their kidnappers were growing weary of the chase and were planning to release them beyond the district borders later that night. However as the convoy of police cars and camera trucks pursued the sports car past the turning for the West German capital of Bonn the authorities had other ideas.

Less than thirty miles down the A3 a short distance from the state border between North Rhine-Westphalia and Rhineland-Palatinate a tactical unit from the GSG-9 was waiting to engage the runaway bank robbers. An elite counter-terrorism division of the German Federal Police – the GSG-9 – meant business.

As the BMW sped down the autobahn several armoured vehicles suddenly appeared forcing the car off the road. Flash bombs and stun grenades were thrown to disorientate the hostage-takers as a full-on gunfight developed. Silke screamed for Ines to jump from the car which she managed to do, hiding from the bullets in a roadside ditch. However her friend was not as fortunate taking a bullet from Rösner's gun to the heart killing her instantly. While they sustained serious injuries from the gun battle, Degowski, Rösner and Löblich survived the ordeal ending a two and a half day span of chaos and murder.

## PUBLIC OUTRAGE

With the criminals behind bars all eyes focused on the behaviour of the press and the police during the incident. In the autumn of 1988 the Minister of the Interior for Bremen, Bernd Meyer, was forced to resign due to the catalogue of errors amassed by his police force. There followed public outrage at the behaviour of the press who were savagely criticised for their interference and attempts to aid and abet the fugitive criminals all in the name of a story. The German Press Council subsequently banned them from interviewing any of the hostages after the event and later the press code was altered to prevent repeat intrusions in the future.

On 22 March 1991 Rösner and Degowski were found guilty and given life sentences. Marion Löblich received a nine year prison term of which she served six and now resides in Magdeburg. Thanks to strict judgement from the Higher Court of Hamm, Degowski had his jail time increased in 2002 and Rösner has since been hit with a preventive detention order which will ensure he remains incarcerated even after his sentence is complete.

As for the surviving victim of the final ambush, Ines Voitle married three years after the incident but after a resultant bout of depression she is now divorced and lives with her sixteen-year-old daughter Svenja in Bremen. She owes her life to her friend Silke Bischoff whose memorial – a simple dark wood cross on the A3 – is the last remaining symbol of the deadly ordeal that August.

# HOLLY SHELDON –
# EXPRESS KIDNAPPING

In the summer of 2006 a British mother and daughter became victims of a crime which has become increasingly prevalent throughout many impoverished South American countries. Called 'express kidnapping' this growing menace involves opportunist thieves kidnapping unsuspecting victims and holding them hostage while their credit cards are used to empty their bank accounts.

Inheriting her mother's passion for backpacking Holly Sheldon, a well-travelled thirty-three-year-old teacher from London, was nearing the end of her South American adventure. She had experienced the magnificent sights of Peru, Ecuador and Colombia and decided to ask her sixty-seven-year-old mother to join her for the finale in Bolivia. The pair were in a dream state as they soaked up the sun at Lake Titicaca but a decision to take an independent bus to La Paz would turn their holiday into a living nightmare.

## CATCH A BUS

It was Thursday 15 June 2006 and the mother and daughter team of travellers were marvelling at the splendour of Lake Titicaca. The expanse of blue water which made up the highest lake in the world was truly spectacular but the pair had more to see. Deciding to leave this patch of heaven to experience La Paz, the Bolivian capital, they made for the nearest town to catch a bus that would take them on a one-stop journey to hell.

They found themselves in Copacabana, its main street lined with market stalls selling souvenirs. Amidst the crowds of the main plaza, the pair found a small white minibus and a Bolivian lady with a big smile and asked how much for the three hour journey to La Paz. The price – a mere ten Bolivianos – was a steal. Soon Holly and Jenny Sheldon would be too.

Eager to move on and see more sights they boarded the minibus and were soon on their way. Along with the driver and his wife, they shared the trip with one other passenger; a local with a heavy cold who tried to engage Holly in conversation between the coughs and sneezes. Both mother and daughter were happy sitting in silence taking in the last remnants of daylight as the night quickly enveloped them.

The first sign that all was not what it seemed came at various points on the journey when the minibus driver failed to stop for waiting passengers. This was unusual. Holly had been on countless bus trips during her Latin American tour and was accustomed to minibuses full to bursting point with paying customers. Why was this driver turning down bona fide fares?

## BACKPACK HIJACK

Holly was right to be concerned. Two hours into their bus ride to the capital their minibus made an abrupt turn off the main road and onto a dirt track. As the rough road narrowed Holly noticed they were following a red car. All of a sudden the car braked hard forcing the minibus driver to make an emergency stop to avoid a rear-end collision.

Before the two women knew what had happened four men burst from the four doors of the red car and set upon the minibus. The side door was thrown open and guns were aimed at their heads. In next to no time they were forced on to their fronts and their hands were bound by parcel tape behind their backs. As more tape wrapped around her mouth to stifle the screams Holly wondered why there had been no response from the driver, why his wife had not cried out in alarm. As the hijacked minibus was driven away with them inside she quickly realised they were all in on the act. Holly and Jenny Sheldon were victims of a planned kidnapping.

At around ten o'clock in the evening the bound and gagged bodies were dragged out of the vehicle and into one of the many shabby buildings of a town in the middle of nowhere. They were bundled into a makeshift cell, thrown onto a grubby mattress on the floor and searched. It was swift and violent. The kidnappers raided their pockets and, after some manhandling, quickly found Holly's money belt secreted under her clothes. A knife was pulled out and without ceremony the belt was cut from her.

## THOSE ALL-IMPORTANT DIGITS

Once their attackers had availed themselves of all their valuables they approached Holly. Placing a gun to her head the chief kidnapper showed the petrified backpacker her credit card and said one simple word: 'Pin'. The shock of the incident made it almost impossible for her to recall the four simple digits. Her mind was a complete blank. As she tried to compose herself and recall the numbers she looked up and hanging on the wall in front of her was a picture of Jesus. Gazing up at this image of peace gave her the moment she needed to gather her thoughts and she reeled off the code to her cash. As the muggers moved onto her mother, Holly instinctively put on her blindfold. She was aware the less she saw the more chance she would have of getting out of this alive.

In possession of their pin numbers the kidnappers left them squirming on the mattresses while a smaller team drove into town to the nearest cash machine. With a sarong wrapped around her eyes as a make-shift blindfold, Holly was able to make out five guards through the thin material. This nearby threat made it impossible for her to relax, adrenalin still coursing through her veins. Holly decided to put this nervous energy to good use. Concerned for her mother's wellbeing, she wriggled her way across to where she was lying and, despite her restrictions, managed to stretch out a solitary finger.

The moment she made contact she heard her mother let out a long sigh. She was still alive. They lay there connected by one small digit, the healing power of touch going some way to alleviating the profound tension. However, the relief was short-lived as they heard the minibus pulling to a stop outside. The hostage-takers had returned.

## MONEY PROBLEMS

As the kidnappers got busy counting the money – a healthy return of $3,000 – the head hostage-taker approached Holly once more. There was a problem; one of her cards didn't work. The wild eyed robber explained they had only managed to take out a paltry twenty-five dollars and wanted as much as $50,000 before they would let them go. Holly could not understand why they were having difficulty withdrawing more money and endeavoured to help but informed her kidnappers neither of their accounts held the full bounty they desired. Fixing her with a villainous stare the leader enquired after her father. To deny them the chance to involve him and in turn prolong the kidnapping process she told them he was dead.

The rest of that day mother and daughter remained confined to their cell in some backwater Bolivian settlement. The trouble with the card had created an uneasy atmosphere and, unable to move or see, Holly used her ears to pick up important clues that might help with their survival. As the daylight began to fade she was confronted with an ominous sound. She could hear the sharp ripping of parcel tape in the next room. Her imagination ran wild trying to glean what they were doing. Fear helped form the answers. Maybe they were building a makeshift coffin for their bodies or creating a crude silencer for the gun that would be used to kill them. Into the night the tearing of the tape continued and became their nightmare lullaby. The truth was banal. They were in fact making a lampshade.

The darkness came for the second time. As the kidnapped pair tried to sleep through the snores of their captors they resigned themselves to losing their lives.

Holly was too afraid to sleep. Her mind was too busy picturing a painful end as visible as their breath during a long and freezing cold night in their unheated cell.

## NO MORE PRIVACY

After the darkest hours of their lives came the morning and with the new dawn came a renewed hope. They had survived the night, maybe they would survive the entire ordeal.

Holly summoned up enough courage to ask her captors if she could use the toilet. They consented and led her to a filthy cubicle inside the building. To her chagrin, she was forced to go while her captor stood guard. To fight back the humiliation she decided to make conversation with her leering sentinel asking him if they planned to kill them. Fearing the answer she was relieved to see him shake his head. He told her that all they had to do was cooperate.

With this concern put to rest another took its place. Holly was concerned her mother was getting ill. Nearby La Paz was the highest capital city in the entire continent and for those unconditioned to the environment, high altitude sickness was a major risk. Jenny Sheldon was exhibiting the symptoms of this sickness and her daughter wanted to alert the kidnappers to this. Their response was to make some cocoa tea to assuage her condition. When offered,

Holly decided to err on the side of caution and refuse the medicinal brew in case it was laced with something untoward. Besides she was not feeling ill. As for her mother, Holly insisted she drink the potion. To her utter disgust, Jenny Sheldon found herself thanking her kidnappers after drinking the healing hot drink.

Later in the day their quiet solitude was broken when two of the kidnappers barged into their cell and proceeded to roll them onto their fronts. Filled with fear of rape or worse, the two travellers braced themselves for what was to come. The men began to rummage in their back pockets and only after they left did Holly realise what had occurred. They had been given their passports back. Did this spell the end to their enslaved state? Would they soon be set free?

An hour or two later these questions were answered. Their kidnappers stormed the room and without warning dragged their bound bodies away. Optimism faded as they found they were taken not to freedom but to an adjacent room in the house. Using her limited senses once more, Holly heard foreign voices from their old holding area. Not the Spanish of their captors but Dutch. Through the diaphanous fabric of her blindfold she managed to make out two new bound and gagged forms on the dirty mattresses. The men had been busy taking another two backpackers hostage.

## NEXT STOP: FREEDOM

Holly and Jenny Sheldon were no longer alone. They were clearly victims of a hostage-taking industry; a production line of prisoners kidnapped for cash. Before they had time to wonder whether this made it more or less likely they would live the mother and daughter pair were on the move.

Befitting the entire episode they were both lifted roughly to their feet and swiftly hauled outside to the waiting minibus. Jenny was the first to be bundled out followed by Holly whose guard decided he wanted more than just money. As the minibus engine revved outside, Holly's captor began to thrust his hand down the front of her jeans. She resisted long enough for a call from one of his conspirators to interrupt the proceedings and she was dragged away to join her mother.

The minibus pulled away from their Bolivian prison and drove into the dark night. The journey into the unknown was a blur for poor Holly who had not seen the last of her lustful guard. He persisted with such carnal intent to pursue his desires that, thinking he would never give up, she decided to surrender. Closing her mind to the brutality she chose to let it happen hoping freedom would be right around the corner.

Thankfully it was. Just after midnight the white minibus reached its destination screeching to a halt at the side of the dusty road. The passengers were forced out, pushed to the ground and handed their less valuable possessions before the van disappeared into the darkness. They paused before daring to remove their blindfolds, uncertain the nightmare was over. It was then the Sheldons discovered they had been released along with the Dutch backpackers.

Introductions were made and hugs bestowed. Yet relief was fleeting. Holly had taken a look at her surroundings and knew they were still in considerable danger. The hostages had been dropped off in the centre of gang territory. The four vulnerable visitors were still susceptible to attack despite their freedom. Spotting lights on the horizon, they all linked arms and made for civilisation and, hopefully, rescue.

The terrorised tourists finally arrived at a town store which appeared open. Frantic banging on the doors and windows brought a bemused shopkeeper who, after listening to their story, quickly called the police. After a short while a unit car pulled up outside to take them to the nearby police station in El Alto.

## EMBASSY EMBARRASSMENT

On arrival at the station Holly made her first call to the British Embassy. Hoping to hear a friendly voice, she was shocked to meet with indifference and disdain. The woman at the embassy berated her for not taking greater care on her travels and informed her there was nothing that could be done until Monday morning. It was now Friday night.

Unable to believe what she was hearing Holly pushed for assistance. The unhelpful woman told her if she wished the embassy to open out of hours she would have to pay seventy pounds for the privilege. Having just spent over twenty-four hours at the hands of Bolivian thieves she was now being swindled by her own countrywoman. Thankfully Eva and Johannes, their Dutch companions, had had more luck with their consul who kindly put them all up in a hotel to recover from their ordeal.

Fully rested Holly quickly spread the word to warn other travellers of the dangers they had faced, posting messages on internet travel sites and sticking notices up in tourist areas. After five days of constant phone calls to airlines, banks and insurance companies, Holly and Jenny made the decision not to fly home straightaway. Not wanting their kidnapping to be the last memory of their trip they chose to stay on in Bolivia for ten more days taking in the sites they had travelled six thousand miles to see before taking their original flights home.

# SHANNON
# MATTHEWS

Karen Matthews had seven children by five different fathers. Living on a sink estate in Dewsbury, North Yorkshire, she was claimed by one British newspaper to have had her children simply to gain benefit money – £286 a week, it was suggested in some quarters – from the state. This was not enough, however, and she devised a scheme by which she would snare a great deal more money. The idea came from the television show, *Shameless*, in which members of a family living on a similarly rundown fictional estate, hid their daughter with a friend in order to collect reward money. She would make it look as if her daughter, Shannon, had been abducted and would share the reward money with the man who would in the meantime be looking after Shannon, the uncle of her partner, Craig Meehan. Chillingly, she chose Shannon of all her children because she was a girl and was more photogenic than her other children. She wanted to maximise the publicity surrounding the disappearance and, by so doing, maximise the amount of money to be made.

## LACKING IN TLC

According to later reports, thirty-three-year-old Karen Matthews had never been much of a mother. Her day was said to revolve around day-time television, beer, pizzas, video games and cigarettes. Her children were of little consequence to her as notes shown by Shannon to her older brother show. In them, she asks him if he thinks they will get any tea that night and warns him not to talk too loud or he might receive a beating. Karen Matthews reportedly refused to buy nappies for her children when they were babies, preferring instead to tape plastic bags to their bottoms. She demonstrated just how little she seemed to care for her children by not even remembering how many she actually had. When Shannon first disappeared she was asked how many children she had, replying that she had six. It took her days to remember that she actually had seven.

Life was harsh for these children but for Shannon, on 19 February 2008, it was just about to get a lot harder.

Karen Matthews enlisted the help of forty-year-old Michael Donovan to put her plan into operation. Donovan was himself no model parent, his two daughters having been taken into care after he allegedly made them watch him have sex with prostitutes. Social workers also discovered love letters from him to one of his daughters in her lunchbox. He had been born Paul Drake, but had always fantasised about being someone else. Aged nineteen, he realised his ambition when he changed his name by deed poll to Mike Donovan, a name taken from the hero of a 1980s television science fiction series, *V. Donovan*. Like Karen Matthews, he lived on benefits, after receiving serious head injuries in a crash involving the delivery van he was driving. He suffered from learning difficulties and had been in trouble with the police since the age of eleven. Karen Matthews met him at a family funeral in 2007 and realised he was exactly the right kind of person to help her carry out her plan.

## THE KIDNAP

On the afternoon of 19 February, Shannon left school. A video released later shows her putting her coat on as she leaves Westmoor Junior School in Church Lane, Dewsbury Moor, at 3.10, a little girl at the end of the school day, looking forward to going home. She had been dropped off there after a visit to the swimming pool at the local sports centre. The school was only half a mile from her home, but somewhere on that road she disappeared.

What had actually happened was that she had been met by Michael Donovan in his Peugeot 406. He told her that he had been asked by her mother to take her to a local fair and Shannon was happy to jump into the car with that prospect ahead of her. Instead of going to the fair, however, Donovan drove her to his flat in Lidgate Gardens in Dewsbury. She would remain there for twenty-four days before being found.

## MASSIVE MANHUNT

Shannon's disappearance instigated the biggest manhunt since the Yorkshire Ripper had created terror in the north of England in the 1970s. Involving in excess of three hundred police officers and more than half of the country's specially trained victim recovery dogs. The search would end up costing a staggering £3.2 million. More than one thousand eight hundred premises were searched, and extensive house-to-house enquiries were conducted; more than eight hundred CCTV tapes and computer hard drives were examined. The search spread beyond the immediate area into Cumbria and Nottinghamshire.

The Matthews family were closely scrutinised. A family tree, complicated by the large number of relationships Karen Matthews had enjoyed, was constructed that included three hundred names. The complexity and size of the family tree was one of the principal reasons that it took investigating officers so long to track down Michael Donovan who, if he had been looked at early in the investigation, would undoubtedly have become a suspect.

While the police search was going on, Shannon was settling into a difficult existence at Lidgate Gardens. Donovan provided her with a list of rules amongst which he listed: 'You must not go near the windows; you must not make any noise or bang your feet; you must not do anything without me being there, keep the TV volume low – up to volume eight.' She was told that she was allowed to play some games on the television and music CDs and the list ended with the letters 'IPU' – 'I Promise You.'

When Shannon was found, she was medically examined and a test on her urine revealed rather more sinister ways of keeping her out of sight. She had been dosed with the tranquiliser, Temazepam, as well as travel sickness pills called Traveleeze.

Her movement was also restricted by a long strap by which she was tethered to a roof-beam in the loft of the flat. It permitted her to roam freely within the flat but she was not able to get as far as the front door. It is likely that the strap was used when Donovan went out.

Publicity became intense although there was a great deal of debate in the media about the attitude to the disappearance of this girl from an impoverished background compared to that of Madeleine McCann, daughter of two doctors who had disappeared from an upmarket Portuguese holiday resort the previous summer. According to some commentators, the Shannon Matthews case exposed the class rift in British society. One newspaper suggested that even the most minor developments in the Madeleine McCann case garnered more news coverage than the Shannon Matthews case. The disadvantages of Shannon's background were displayed, another newspaper said, in the way that the articulate and media-savvy parents of an abducted middle class child could mobilise an effective and ongoing media campaign while an abductee from a lower class, less well-educated background had a great disadvantage.

Karen Matthews and her boyfriend of four years, Craig Meehan, were vigorously interviewed on BBC Radio 4's *Today* programme. Allegations were put to them that Meehan had been violent towards Shannon, but Karen Matthews always denied them.

Meanwhile, West Yorkshire police created a website to help in the search. It was called 'Missing Shannon Matthews Appeal'. Rewards were offered for information leading to the discovery of Shannon, *The Sun* newspaper initially putting up £20,000 but increasing the amount to £50,000 on 10 March. Significantly, that was the amount that Karen Matthews and Mike Donovan had been waiting for. The plan was then to release Shannon in Dewsbury market and for Donovan to find her and claim the money.

Shannon was eventually found following a police decision to extend their house-to-house search to a one mile radius around the Matthews' house from the previous half-mile radius. Donovan's house was now in the search area but when it was visited there was no reply to the knocks at his door. Neighbours insisted, however, that he was indeed at home. One woman who lived below Donovan's flat, said that she had heard him inside that morning. Interestingly, she added that she was certain she had also heard the footsteps of a child up above.

Police forced their way into the flat to initially believe it to be empty. As one officer searched a bedroom, however, he heard the voice of a little girl say from inside the base of a double bed, 'Stop it! You're frightening me!' The officer pulled open the base and there was Shannon, crying. On the other side of the bed base they discovered Michael Donovan. He was immediately arrested.

Donovan was charged with kidnapping and false imprisonment while Karen Matthews was arrested on 6 April and charged with perverting the course of justice, child neglect, kidnapping and false imprisonment. Police also looked into approaches that had been made to the Madeleine McCann fund, soliciting money to help the search.

Others had become embroiled in the scheme. Karen Matthews' sister, Amanda Hyett, was arrested on suspicion of perverting the course of justice, as was Craig Meehan's mother, Alice Meehan. Meehan himself was sentenced to twenty weeks' imprisonment for possessing child pornography on a computer that police had seized from the house he shared with Matthews and her children.

At her trial, Karen Matthews denied any involvement in her daughter's kidnapping, blaming Craig Meehan. Michael Donovan, meanwhile, said that he had become involved only after Karen had threatened violence towards him if he refused. Nonetheless, they were both convicted and sentenced to eight years in prison on 23 January 2009.

After her discovery, Shannon was made the subject of an emergency Police Protection Order and taken into the care of Social Services where she has remained ever since.